STRATEGIC MANAGEMENT

MANAGING WITH SAVI™

Graham Fane
Capilano College

McGraw-Hill Ryerson

Toronto Montréal Boston Burr Ridge, IL Dubuque, IA Madison, WI New York
San Francisco St. Louis Bangkok Bogotá Caracas Kuala Lumpur Lisbon London
Madrid Mexico City Milan New Delhi Santiago Seoul Singapore Sydney Taipei

The McGraw-Hill Companies

McGraw-Hill Ryerson

Strategic Management
Managing With SAVI
First Edition

ISBN: 0-07-0926743

1 2 3 4 5 6 7 8 9 10 MP 0 9 8 7 6 5 4

Printed and bound in Canada

Care has been taken to trace ownership of copyright material contained in this text; however, the publisher will welcome any information that enables them to rectify any reference or credit for subsequent editions.

Vice President, Editorial and Media Technology: Patrick Ferrier
Executive Sponsoring Editor: Nicole Lukach
Developmental Editor: Tracey Haggert
Marketing Manager: Kelly Smyth
Copy Editor: Gillian Scobie
Production Coordinator: Kathy Ko
Cover Design: Greg Devitt
Interior Design: Greg Devitt
Printer: Maracle Press

National Library of Canada Cataloguing in Publication

Fane, Graham
Strategic management : managing with SAVI / Graham Fane.

Includes index.
ISBN 0-07-092674-3

1. Strategic planning. I. Title.

HD30.28.F35 2003 658.4'012 C2003-906831-5

About the Author

Graham S. Fane

Graham's credentials, diploma of technology in administrative management, bachelor of science in administration, masters in business administration and certified management accountant, come from the province of British Columbia and from Washington State.

Graham's real education came from 25 years of teaching about and working with practical management principles in real management situations. Graham has self-published writings on budgeting, strategic planning, decision making and performance management. These writings have been the reading materials for management workshops devoted to improving the business acumen of managers. Over 7,000 middle and senior managers from public and private organizations have attended Graham's workshops from across Canada, from the major electric utility in Russia, and from government ministries in Colombia, South America.

Graham is a professor in the school of business at Capilano College in North Vancouver where he teaches strategic planning, cost accounting, performance management, decision making and business simulation.

Graham is a member of the board of directors of the CMA society in British Columbia.

Table of Contents

Preface

It is generally understood that strategic planning is a critical activity for organizations that want to succeed. It is also understood that strategic planning alone isn't enough. Organizations must follow a good plan with good decision making and good performance management.

— Graham Fane

I wrote this book to fill a specific need: it is written for people who are having their **first encounter** with strategic planning.

I hope it does one thing: that it makes people realize the importance of planning, decision making and performance measurement so they will do whatever is necessary to ensure the success of their organization.

The adage that a failure to plan is planning for failure is true. All successful organizations plan for the future by constantly monitoring their world and matching their skills to meet their changing world. Success should be celebrated, but it should not be a signal to stop striving for even better results. At the very core of strategic planning is the idea that we must constantly move forward, trying to reach a moving target.

Strategic planning can be a very complex subject. The issues keep changing, the environment in which we do business is fast-paced, and new challenges present themselves every day. Strategic planning is also an essential subject, because planning is essential to success. Everyone needs to plan, everyone needs to act on the plan, everyone needs to measure the effectiveness of the plan...therefore, everyone needs to understand strategic planning.

It is the job of a college or university to develop the skills that enable business students to contribute to planning efforts, to help implement solutions to problems and to be a part of the success of an organization. A student's study of business begins with tools and tactics and continues with marketing, accounting, data processing, human resources, math and economics. Thinking and applying tools take place at the end of the study of business. My experience, in 25 years of teaching strategic management, is that the concept of **thinking strategically and applying business tools that deliver results on strategies** is a new, and sometimes foreign, concept to most business students; it is a challenging and complicated concept, and most of the texts currently available introduce so many alternative ways to approach strategic planning that students are confused.

This book is thus designed to introduce basic strategic planning practices to make the framework of planning, decision making and performance measurement clearly understood. It systematically uses a small number of tools in a framework and establishes some groundwork in the study of strategic planning so that, later on, students can more easily examine the broad range of tools available in the marketplace to deal with each element of the framework.

In a nutshell, to use a car analogy, this book is about how the engine works. And once people understand the engine, they can begin to look for more horsepower or new ways to improve fuel economy.

THE RANGE OF COVERAGE

The range of alternative methods and models used here is not broad. In fact, some might say this is not an academic text at all, but more closely resembles a document prepared by a business consultant to show the business what it should do to succeed. Consultants review alternative methods of achieving results, find the method most suitable to the business and then work towards seeing that the method is used effectively.

I have used the same tactic here: this book is about taking specific tools and making them work. It is more about applying certain tools than it is about studying the whole range of tools available to solve a problem or to take advantage of an opportunity. Studying the range of available tools is best done by students in the upper levels of a business program, or, better still, by those with experience in a business. I believe that you can only truly discover the best process to use for a business when you merge practical experience with a basic understanding of how the system works.

What will this book do for its readers? It will show them how applying the tools takes place; make them aware of the benefits of planning, implementation and measurement; and create a mental framework that will improve their ability to search for, evaluate and choose solutions to problems in the future.

THE THREE SECTIONS OF THE BOOK

The SAVI model contains three distinct tools that are designed to be simple to use, easy to understand and effective. They are represented in the following diagram, which forms the foundation of the book.

Figure 1 The Management Cycle

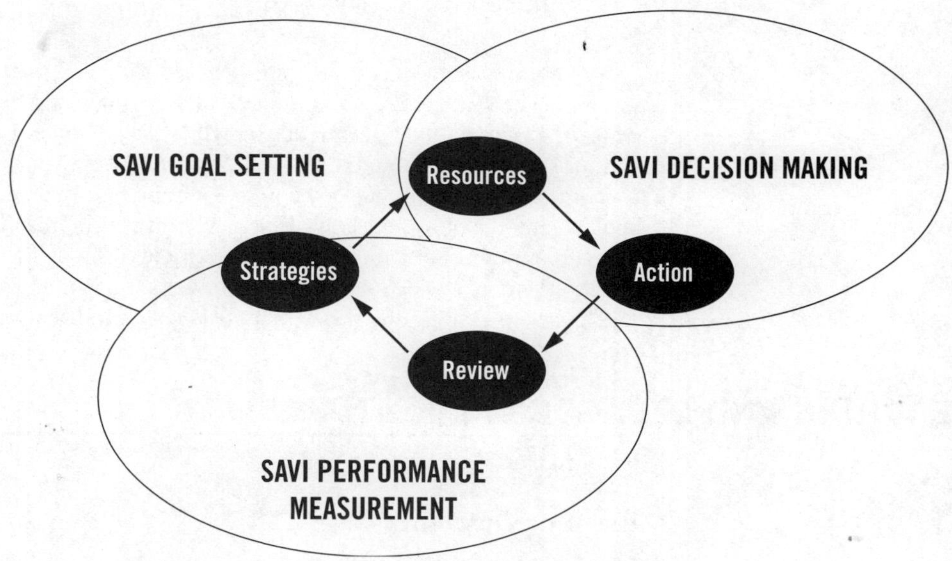

SECTION 1: GOAL SETTING

The **GOAL SETTING** tool helps managers carefully match what is possible with what is desired by preparing a set of strategic goals to meet stakeholders' needs. The tool is essential to the management cycle because:

Stakeholders need Added Value from their Investment.

A wide variety of stakeholder interest groups make investments in organizations which enable the organization to function, and these interest groups have expectations about investment returns: financial investors, creditors and owners have expectations about profitability and risk; customers have expectations about quality and value; "social investors," the general public, employees and governments have expectations about complying with environmental and safety laws.

The **GOAL SETTING** tool prepares a set of action-oriented strategic goals that govern the activities of the operational level of the organization to realize corporate strategic goals.

These goals deal with the top-level view of the organization, where shareholder, customer, management, employee and the general public's needs are satisfied.

Section 2: Decision-Making and Control

The **DECISION MAKING AND CONTROL** tool includes both resource and action planning. It is a framework for preparing and evaluating proposals for new projects and programs, or for evaluating existing projects and programs that will maximize strategic returns. The decision-making aspect uses a systematic and logical decision-making tool. The control aspect uses a budgeting tool. These tools are used for:

Screening **A**dded **V**alue **I**nitiatives.

Section 3: Performance Measurement/Management

The **PERFORMANCE MEASUREMENT/MANAGEMENT** tool enables results and outcomes as well as activities in financial and non-financial terms to be measured. This tool captures a host of measures from the view of stakeholders, senior management, middle management and people on the line. It measures:

Speed, **A**ccuracy, **V**olume and **I**nvestment.

The bottom line is that if customers are served when they want to be served (Speed), with something of value to them (Accuracy), in the right quantity to meet all customers (Volume), and at the right price (Investment), we will satisfy them and earn the right to stay in business and prosper in the future.

The models for planning, decision making and performance measurement discussed in this book are not the only models available. They have been proven to work in a wide range of business applications but many other models work just as well. I am presenting these models because my experience in a wide variety of organizations shows me that these models work well.

The key to making any business model work is to use it, enthusiastically and constantly.

LEARNING AND PEDAGOGICAL FEATURES

Each chapter contains the following:

Learning Outcomes

Key "Learning Outcomes" are identified for each chapter. These will be useful in setting student expectations. In addition, instructors will find the learning outcomes useful when creating course outlines.

Your Responsibility

Learning is a partnership between faculty and students. Each chapter begins with an expression of what the students need to do to fulfill their part of the deal.

Chapter Introduction

The chapter introduction provides a brief description of what is to come and it highlights the transition from the previous chapter. The introduction also puts the chapter in the context of the overall SAVI model for strategic planning

On This Topic: A Real-World Example

Each chapter has several real-world anecdotes that validate concepts by showing how those concepts apply in the real world. Where appropriate, Web sites to the organizations mentioned have been provided.

Chapter Summary

The chapter summary revisits the learning outcomes and summarizes what has been discussed.

Closing Remarks

Closing remarks provide a high-level view of what happened in the chapter, link to the model for strategic planning and provide a segue into the next chapter.

Terms Introduced in the Chapter

Terminology is defined using a layperson's vocabulary to achieve a higher level of understanding.

Questions for Class Discussion

The highlights of the chapter are presented in a number of thought-provoking questions. These questions are a vehicle by which students will be able to participate in applying the concepts.

A Case For Strategic Management: Malcolm and Ruby's Next Step

This running case, introduced in Chapter 1, follows the systematic steps of the strategic planning, decision-making and performance management processes.

Chapter Ending Case (new in each chapter)

Each chapter also features a stand-alone case designed to reinforce chapter content and concepts.

SUPPLEMENTS THAT ACCOMPANY THIS TEXT

INSTRUCTOR SUPPLEMENTS

Strategic Management: Managing With SAVI™ includes a variety of supplemental materials to help instructors prepare and present the material in the textbook. Please contact your local McGraw-Hill Ryerson *i*-Learning Specialist for details concerning policies, prices and availability.

i-Learning Sales Specialist

i-Learning ADVANTAGE
McGraw-Hill Ryerson

Your Integrated Learning Sales Specialist is a McGraw-Hill Ryerson representative who has the experience, product knowledge, training, and support to help you assess and integrate any of the below-noted products, technology, and services into your course for optimum teaching and learning performance. Whether it's how to use our test bank software, helping your students improve their grades, or how to put your entire course online, your *i*-Learning Sales Specialist is there to help. Contact your local *i*-Learning Sales Specialist today to learn how to maximize all McGraw-Hill Ryerson resources!

Instructor's Manual

The Instructor's Manual includes a wealth of information to assist instructors in presenting this text and their course to its best advantage. Available as a downloadable Word document on the Instructors' Centre of the OLC (see below), this robust teaching aid contains lecture suggestions, answers to end of chapter questions, sample exams and other tips and tricks to help instructors achieve more with SAVI.

Microsoft® PowerPoint® Presentation Slides

This downloadable supplement found in the Instructors Centre of the OLC, offers instructors a complete set of Microsoft® PowerPoint® slides corresponding to each chapter of the text.

Instructor Online Learning Centre – www.mcgrawhill.ca/college/fane

Along with the Student OLC (see below), *Strategic Management: Managing With SAVI™* includes a password-protected Web site for instructors. The site offers downloadable supplements to enhance the classroom experience. Supplements include the Instructor's Manual — featuring lecture notes, answers to end-of-chapter questions, and sample exam questions — and a series of Microsoft® PowerPoint® Presentations for each chapter.

PageOut

McGraw-Hill's unique point-and-click course Web site tool enables users to create a full-featured, professional quality course Web site without knowing HTML coding. PageOut is free for instructors, and lets you post your syllabus online, assign McGraw-Hill OLC content, add Web links, and maintain an online grade book. (And if you're short on time, we even have a team ready to help you create your site.)

Primis Online

You can customize this text and save your students money off bookstore prices by using McGraw-Hill's Primis Online digital database, the largest online collection of texts, readings and cases. Contact your McGraw-Hill *i*-Learning Sales Specialist for more information.

WebCT/BlackBoard

This text is available in two of the most popular course-delivery platforms — WebCT and BlackBoard — for more user-friendly and enhanced features. Contact your McGraw-Hill *i*-Learning Sales Specialist for more information.

i-Learning Services Program

McGraw-Hill Ryerson offers a unique *i*Services package designed for Canadian faculty. Our mission is to equip providers of higher education with superior tools and resources required for excellence in teaching. For additional information visit www.mcgrawhill.ca/highereducation/eservices/

Student Supplements

TOTAL IMPACT ANALYZER™

The author has designed this decision-making software to help students with the often complex financial side of strategic planning and management. An appendix to Chapters 8 and 9, the TOTAL IMPACT ANALYZER™ is an Excel spreadsheet that does a complete financial evaluation and social impact evaluation of alternative solutions to problems. In addition, the spreadsheet provides an evaluation matrix that helps rank alternatives in a logical order. This downloadable supplement, as well as the Users' Guide, can be found on the Student Centre of the Online Learning Centre (see below).

Student Online Learning Centre – www.mcgrawhill.ca/college/fane

The *Strategic Management: Managing With SAVI™* Online Learning Centre (OLC) is a Web site that follows the text chapter-by-chapter. Students can review concepts, prepare for exams and also have access to the downloadable decision-making software, the Total Impact Analyzer.™

ACKNOWLEDGEMENTS

I would like to express my deeply felt thanks to those who assisted in many tangible and intangible ways.

The following individuals who reviewed the manuscript and whose comments and suggestions helped make this text stronger:

Richard Appleby, Okanagan University College
Beverly Linnell, Southern Alberta Institute of Technology
Chuck Minken, Sheridan Institute of Technology and Advanced Learning
Bob Nichols, British Columbia Institute of Technology
Maureen Nummelin, Conestoga College

My faculty colleagues at Capilano College who have patiently listened to and willingly commented on my theories.
And finally, to Sylvia, my partner and friend, without whom nothing about me would be possible.

Graham Fane, Dipl. Tech., BSA, MBA, CMA

Part 1

THE BASICS OF STRATEGIC PLANNING

AN OVERVIEW OF CHAPTERS 1 to 5

This book is presented in three sections, Strategic Planning, Decision Making and Performance Management. In each section, we will be using the acronym "SAVI" to present a broad picture of what that section of the book is about. In the first section, strategic planning, the acronym refers to Stakeholders need Added Value from their Investment. In the second section, decision making, SAVI refers to Screening Added Value Initiatives, and in the third section, performance management, SAVI refers to the four dimensions of measurement: Speed, Accuracy, Volume and Investment. The SAVI tool in its three forms is a systematic model for managing three very important elements of any organization, how to plan, how to make decisions and how to improve performance.

Managing with SAVI is about being concerned with **everything** that is important about running a business, ensuring that all the critical elements of success are managed effectively and efficiently. Today's manager is expected to have a thorough grasp of all elements of the business (seeing the big picture) including marketing, human resources, production and accounting/finance, and to spend each day making sure that that balance is maintained so that no single factor gets out of control to the extent that it harms short-term or long-term performance. It is important to manage the factors congruently, always keeping in mind that the whole set of factors is important.

In the first section, Chapters 1 to 5, we will focus on Strategic Planning.

Let's begin with a definition of Strategic Planning. Thinking strategically is thinking at a high level, i.e. having a broad, all-encompassing perspective and making sure that all the issues inside and outside of the organization are factored into the thinking process. Planning focuses on the future, trying to make the best out of what is to come. SAVI, as explored in Section 1, is a tool that helps to bring strategic thinking and planning together to formulate a strategic plan.

Today and in the future, stakeholders will be putting pressure on management to improve performance so that returns can be protected and enhanced.

The term "stakeholders" refers to the various interest groups that lay claims on how the business functions. Traditionally we thought of stakeholders as the group of financial "shareholders" that expect long-term financial returns from a business. Recently our concept of stakeholders has expanded to include customers, the general public, employees, government, competitors, suppliers and creditors, to name a few. All these groups have claims ranging from fair and legal business practices to effective environmental practices in business operations. We will deal with the nature of stakeholders' claims in more detail later in this book. For now, suffice it to say that there are multiple interest groups who exercise their claims on a business in such a way that the business operations must reflect the needs of a broad range of interest groups.

Surviving and excelling in the future will be nothing like what it was in the past. We need to realign priorities, find out what is important to all levels of stakeholder claims, develop new skills and change management practices so that all aspects of a business will maximize the returns expected by everyone. Competitive forces and the rapid rate of change in our global business environment are making this task increasingly complex and difficult to control.

To help organizations be successful, we need to carefully examine successful organizations. Tom Peters, in his book *In Search Of Excellence* set the mark for excellence practices by finding the top performers and seeing what made them tick. He discovered excellence practices in a wide variety of dimensions such as financial controls, marketing strategies, customer service strategies and production processes. Other organizations emulated the practices of the "Best of the Best" in the hope that some of this success would rub off on them. What is most interesting is that in a sequel, Tom Peters revisited those top performers a few years later to find that most had lost the performance edge and many had gone bankrupt! It seems that excellence needs to be nurtured and supported for years to come. Like professional athletes, one good season does not make a career.

The search for excellence has resulted in a myriad of "new and improved" management models, all directed at changing an organization so that results can be optimized. Boards of directors and senior management have invested massive resources in change management strategies they hope will cause the organization to embrace change and make the future organization more efficient and effective. Some of these "change strategies" have worked; most have not. The most frequently cited cause of failure to change with the times is peoples' lack of willingness to make the necessary change happen. The responsibility for making change possible rests with top management, who must create an environment that makes change logical and safe. The responsibility for making change happen rests with everyone in the organization. Leaders need to show the way but followers also need to spend some energy making sure that they are making an effective contribution to following the lead.

Recent success stories tell us that old paradigms are being successfully challenged with new excellence practices. Nothing is permanent in the successful organization. In the most dynamic organizations, people at all levels of the organization embrace change and look forward to the rewards it will bring.

> ***Those who resist change are those who have prospered in the past.***
> ***Those who embrace change are those who might prosper in the future.***
>
> Theodore Roosevelt

People who resist change by being "naysayers" or by putting obstacles in the way of progress have a strong commitment to seeing that change does not happen in an organization, because they have something to lose. They are at risk of losing whatever success has come to them in the past. Resistors are very committed to their cause. On the other hand, people who are willing to change are less committed because what they have to gain is uncertain. Even though they are willing to change, they embrace change with scepticism and caution, waiting patiently. This is most unfortunate because the result is that more resources are spent trying to control the behaviour of negative people and fewer resources are spent trying to encourage positive people. To verify this, ask any manager how much time he or she spends trying to deal with negative people versus how much time is spent nurturing and assisting positive people. They will say the vast majority of time is invested in the negative people.

The same holds for organizational systems. More time is spent trying to maintain a system that doesn't work properly than is spent designing a new system that will work properly.

> ***I put out fires.***
> ***I wish I had time to figure out where they got the fuel.***
>
> Anon.

If people spent less time fixing problems and more time creating opportunities, performance would improve.

CHAPTER 1

GOALS: THE REASON FOR PLANNING

Stakeholders need **A**dded **V**alue from their **I**nvestments

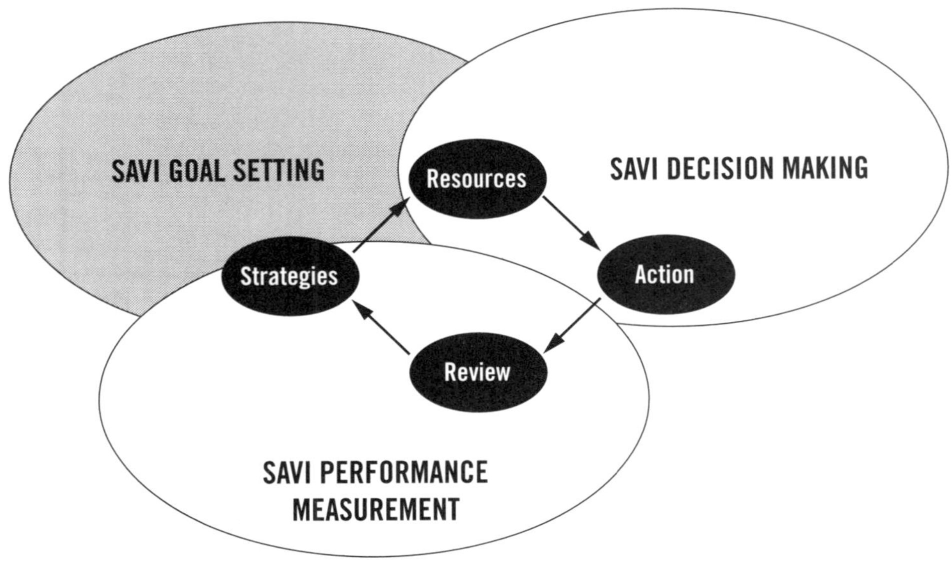

LEARNING OBJECTIVES

After reading this chapter, engaging in class discussion and doing the exercises, you will be able to:

1. Understand the need for an effective planning and goal setting system.
2. Understand the four dimensions that make up the SAVI model.
3. Understand the different and integrated roles that Goal setting, Decision making and Performance measurement play in successful organizations.

YOUR RESPONSIBILITY

To improve the likelihood and level of achievement of these outcomes, it is your responsibility to read, listen, consider, challenge and share your ideas. You have an opportunity to learn from everyone around you, not just the person at the front.

INTRODUCTION TO CHAPTER 1

Most books on strategic planning begin with a study of Vision and Mission, trying to get a long-term picture of success. Then they use a systematic process to create goals by linking vision and mission to organizational strengths, weaknesses, opportunities and threats.

This book will do the same, beginning in Chapter 2.

This book is different in that the first chapter introduces theories of corporate and operational goals, then in later chapters moves to how those goals are developed.

Why this different approach? Because goals are the most important outcome of the strategic planning process. Goals cause actions; actions cause results. Therefore, results don't happen until the process has been given a framework for improvement, a reason to change, a target to look for. Goals come from a dynamic process, a world that is constantly changing, expectations that are always being revised.

As we move through our study of how to achieve goals, we will find that the goal itself will be challenged and revised as new discoveries are made. Keep an open and inquisitive mind.

This chapter will put the whole strategic planning process in context, based on the idea that the most important thing we can strive for is the realization of our goals.

AN OVERVIEW OF THE CYCLE OF ACHIEVING GOALS

Achieving goals, as represented by the following diagram, is a systematic approach, flowing from one step to another. The cycle ensures that everyone involved in the process of realizing goals understands the flow of efforts and the results that will come from successful efforts.

The cycle of achieving goals, and the management of change are simple and logical processes. Planned accomplishments, (strategies) require **resources**, **action** and **review**.

FIGURE 1.1 The Cycle of Achieving Goals

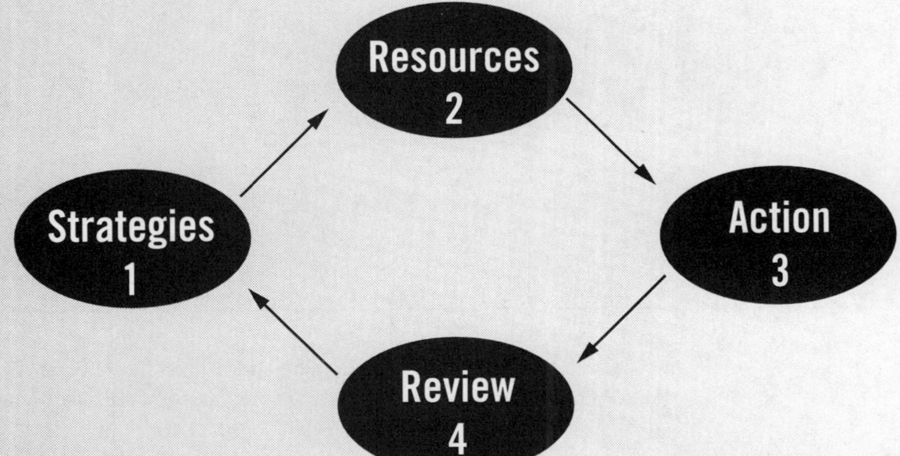

Resources include capital and operating dollars as well as organizational commitment. **Action** requires a project management approach and the use of controls. The **review** process provides information about success and failure, identifying opportunities for celebrating success and correcting failures.

The first step in the cycle is to develop a set of strategic goals. These goals are developed in order to meet the needs of stakeholders. Some of the principal areas of concern in setting strategic goals are to maximize:

- financial returns,
- sustainability of the business in the future,

- safety of the public and employees, (including the motivation and retention of employees),
- stewardship of the natural environment and
- satisfaction of customers.

These strategic goals are not presented in order or priority. They simply represent the full set of goals. Organizations, depending on their sense of urgency around the goals, will change the order to match their situation.

The strategic goals then feed into the cycle which prompts various levels of activities such as budgeting, project management and performance measurement.

Well-stated strategic goals will then provide the framework to determine the capital and operating resources needed to get the job done (Figure 1.2).

FIGURE 1.2 Strategies to Resources

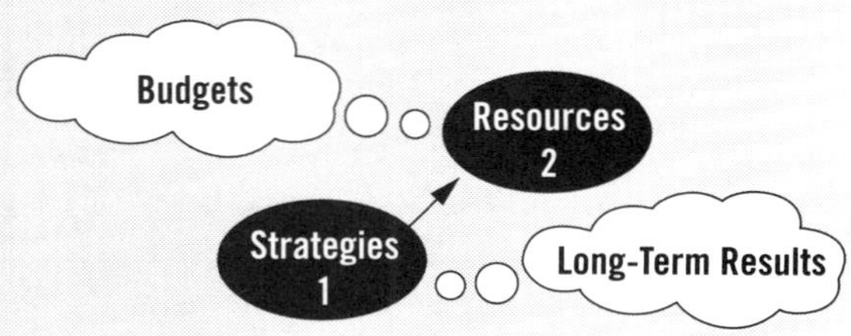

The resource plan (capital and operating budgets) causes the development of the action plan (project management), which identifies the individual activities necessary to undertake the projects, programs, and initiatives that help achieve strategic goals (Figure 1.3).

FIGURE 1.3 Resources to Action

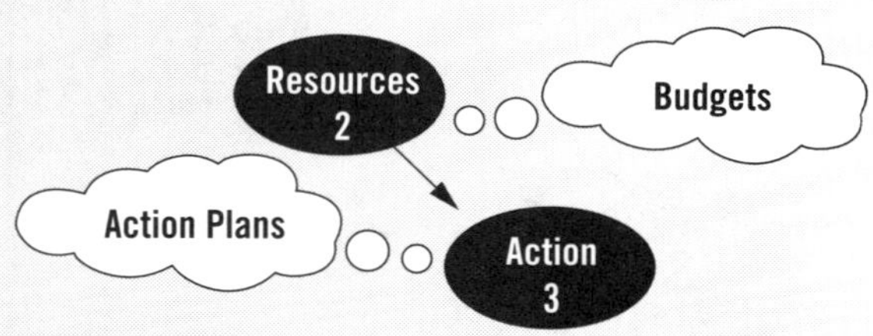

Once the action plan is complete and projects have been identified, there must be a performance management system that tracks progress towards achieving strategic goals (Figure 1.4).

FIGURE 1.4 Action to Review

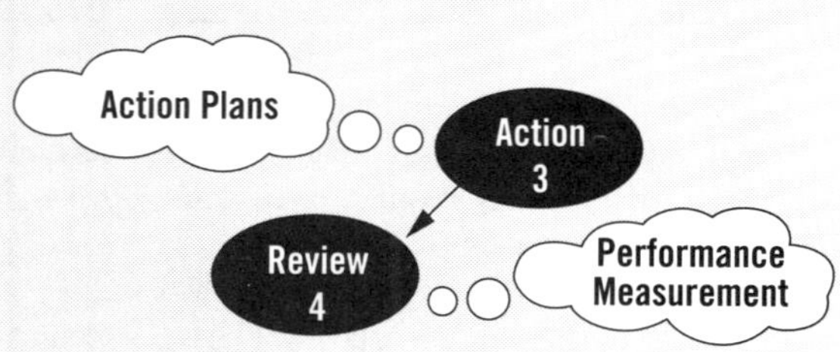

The performance management system feeds measured results into the strategic plan to see if goals are being met, to resolve problem areas and to enhance success areas (Figure 1.5).

FIGURE 1.5 Review to Strategies

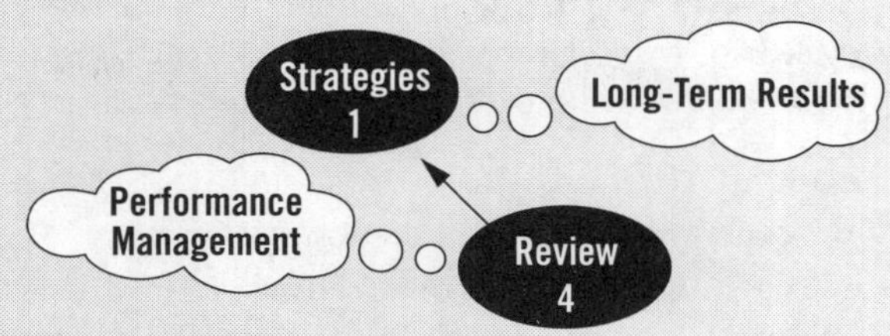

When the cycle is complete, measured results will have been linked to strategic goals. We begin by asking, "Where am I going?" We end by answering, "Did I get there?"

THE TRADITIONAL VIEW OF STRATEGIC PLANNING

We are not building on good experience!

One legacy of our last century is our incredible appetite for strategic planning, with its mission and vision, values and principles, goals and objectives. Organizations have invested vast resources in developing comprehensive strategic plans to "take us to the new millennium!" Many plans were visionary in the long run but they lacked sufficient detail and resolve in the short run to pinpoint the actions necessary to get the results they were looking for.

Another legacy is our lack of willingness to do anything with the plans. Great documents, hollow words, no commitment, no results. If we had invested even a fraction of the "planning resources" we have consumed in writing visionary plans into **doing something with the plans**, we would be much farther ahead.

The traditional view of strategic planning, in its simplest form, is defined as:

The act of matching what is desired with what is possible.

We determine **what is desired** by reviewing the competencies of the organization, now and in the future, and creating vision, mission, values and goals that will carry the organization into the future.

We determine **what is possible** by carefully assessing the environment, the economy, the industry and our organization in the industry to determine the options and opportunities we face.

From this activity we develop strategic goals for all levels of the organization. Then we wait for results to happen. A framework for a traditional strategic planning model follows in Figure 1.6.

FIGURE 1.6 The Beginning of the Model

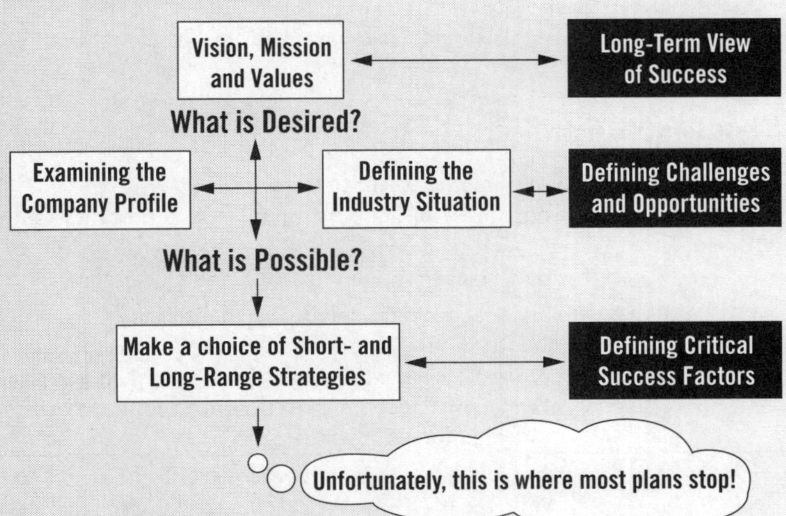

This traditional strategic planning process has been improved upon with the introduction of the SAVI model. The SAVI model takes the process and links it to the full management cycle by providing tools that will enable each step of the cycle to be managed effectively.

As mentioned previously, the complete cycle of achieving goals goes through four distinct phases:

PHASE 1: DEVELOPING STRATEGIC GOALS

- The Strategy phase involves setting vision, mission, values and strategic objectives to reflect long-term targeted goals to maximize the returns for all stakeholders.
- By documenting our strategic goals we are then able to prioritize the projects and initiatives that are most important to the organization's future success.

PHASE 2: GETTING THE RESOURCES NEEDED TO ACHIEVE STRATEGIC GOALS

- In the Resources phase, managers identify, through the capital and operating budget process, the financial resources that will be necessary to achieve strategic goals. Resources are not just money. Managers must also budget for the commitment and enthusiasm of people and the alignment of all financial and non-financial resources needed to get the job done.

PHASE 3: IMPLEMENTING THE ACTIONS NEEDED TO ACHIEVE STRATEGIC GOALS

- The Implementation/Action phase is one of the most important parts of the management cycle. Change does not happen by thinking about it, change happens by doing something about the problems or opportunities we face.
- Implementation involves efficiently managing the development of the project to ensure that it becomes operational, and it involves budgeting and control tools while operations are underway.
- It is critical to consider human resource management as change cannot take place without properly preparing the people working in the system. Do the knowledge, skills and attitudes exist to ensure success of change?

PHASE 4: MEASURING THE RESULTS OF THE ACTIONS TAKEN TO ACHIEVE STRATEGIC GOALS

- Performance measurement, in the Analysis & Measurement phase, involves quantifying actual results, comparing them to expected results and suggesting remedial action to eliminate performance "gaps." Performance information feeds into the strategy phase to enhance the long-range planning process of the organization by tracking results and reporting progress frequently.

These four phases represent the complete SAVI model. The model is illustrated in Figure 1.7 on page 9.

If the SAVI model is followed effectively and efficiently, the following benefits accrue:

Benefits Of Using The Model

1. **It forces management to think.**
   - Sometimes the act of planning is as important as the plan itself. Having a scheduled goal-setting activity will, at least, begin the process of thinking about the opportunities and challenges an organization will face in the future.
2. **It enhances problem-solving capabilities.**
   - The worst condition for decision making is urgency. The best is planning. A decision becomes urgent when we have failed to plan and the asset is broken or the product is not meeting customers' needs. If decisions are well planned we will have the benefit of available time for effective analysis.
3. **It improves the quality of decisions with the group approach.**
   - While the motivation for strategic goal setting comes from top management, the process involves all levels of the organization. Sometimes the best solutions to problems come from those closest to the problem, at the operating or functional level.

FIGURE 1.7 The SAVI Model

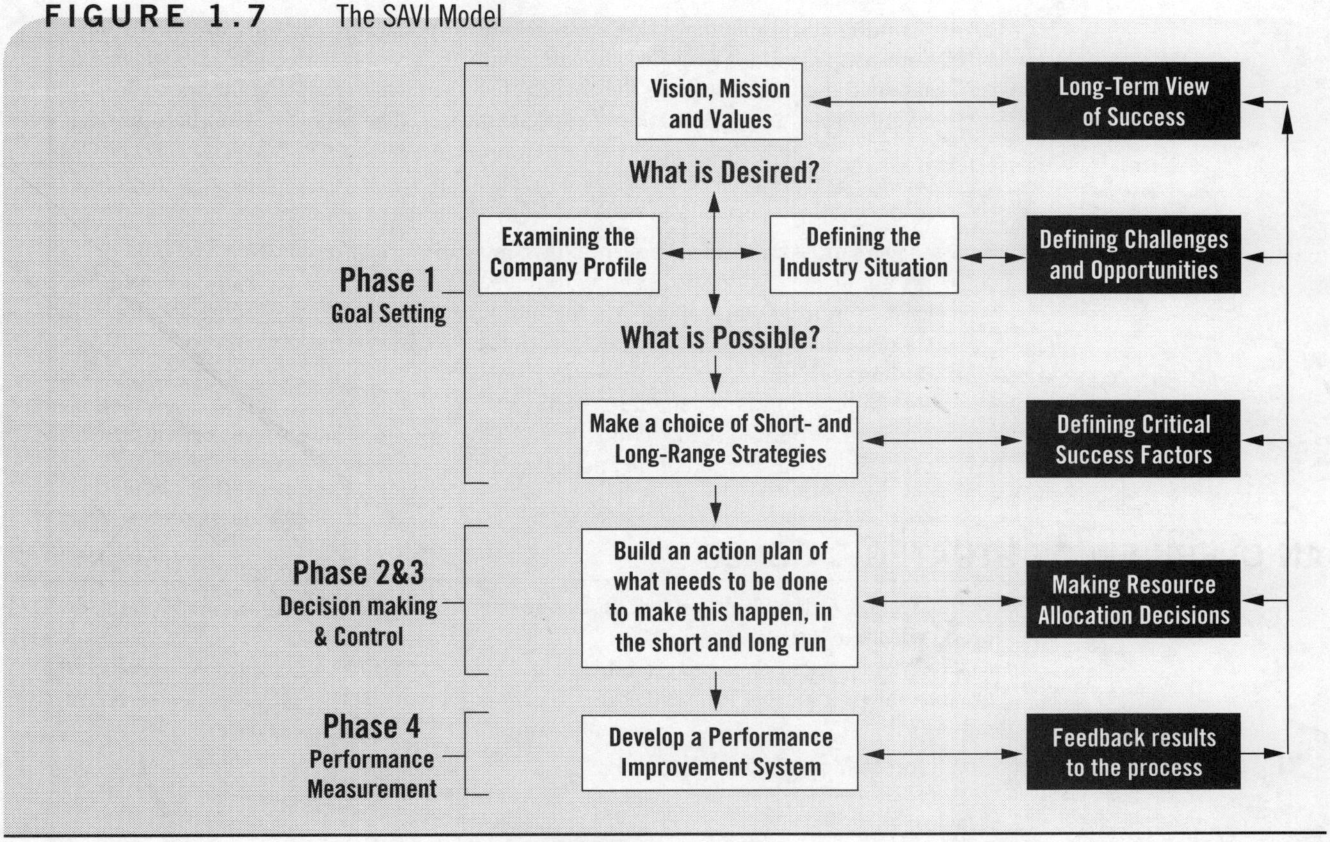

4. **It identifies resource shortfalls.**
   - Resource allocation decisions involve identifying what you have and comparing it to what you need. The foresight given to resource allocation decisions in the planning process enables the discovery of shortfalls before they occur.
5. **It reduces resistance to change.**
   - Change is resisted because of the uncertainty of the outcome. Uncertainty often comes from feeling that change is out of control. Effective and co-operative strategic goal setting provides a sense of control of the process and enhances the "buy-in" at all levels of the organization.
6. **It builds a framework for performance improvement.**
   - Performance improvement should be proactive, not reactive. In a reactive system, you discover that performance was bad in the past and now you are taking action to improve performance. In a proactive system, one sets expectations for the future and uses measurement to reinforce positive outcomes.

Risks Of Using the Model

While the value of the benefits exceeds the value of the risks, it is necessary to review potential risks so that their existence can be recognized and their impact reduced.

Some of the potential risks are:

1. **The process is time consuming.**
   - SAVI activities take time away from other management tasks. Managers complain when their important routine is interrupted if they regard SAVI activities as unimportant. If they are done well, managers will realize their importance and they will willingly allow the time to be taken up. This is why senior management must support the process with words and action.

2. **If planning and implementation are separate, responsibility is shirked.**
   - Some organizations develop "strategic teams" of cross-functional members who are assigned the task of writing the goals. When the task is complete, the teams are disbanded and other "implementation teams" are created. The problem with this approach is that blame can be fixed on others when implementation fails. We must be careful to include as many goal setters as we can in the implementation process so that ownership of the goals is effectively transferred from one team to another.
3. **Managers must be trained to respond when results are different than expected.**
   - We are most comfortable reacting to the past because of the certainty involved. We are least comfortable managing into the future because of the uncertainty. We are well trained and experienced in dealing with the past, but we need to improve skills in dealing with the future. "Not meeting the plan," either with failure or too much success should prompt management to examine the planning process and to examine the environmental conditions that contributed to the situation. This is a continuous learning process, learning from failure and learning from success.

AN OVERVIEW OF STRATEGIC GOALS

In this section of the book, we will focus our attention on Phase 1 of the SAVI model, **developing strategic goals**.

The Management Cycle diagram below in Figure 1.8 defines where strategic goal setting fits into the process.

FIGURE 1.8 Goals in the Management Model

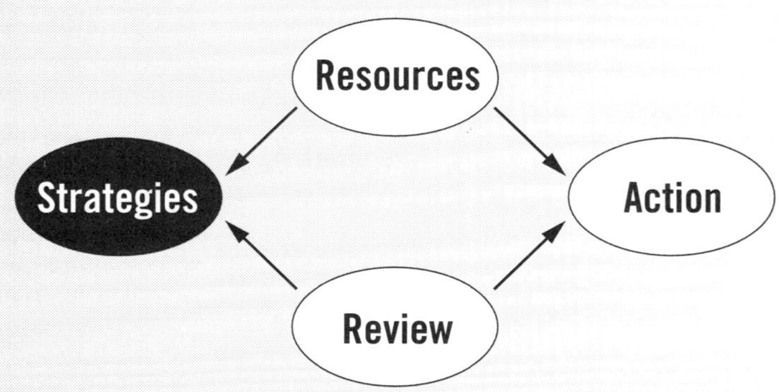

Strategic goal setting is an interactive and dynamic process involving constant review and assessment of:

- external environmental factors, now and in the future,
- internal business profile factors, now and in the future,
- performance tracking to measure results.

PREPARING FOR EFFECTIVE STRATEGIC GOAL SETTING

Effective strategic goal setting does not happen naturally. What is natural is for us to manage from the past, deal with things that make us comfortable, make the least risky choices and spend time controlling what we are presently doing.

Good strategic thinkers will deal with things that are uncertain and uncomfortable, take calculated risks and challenge what they are presently doing. If an organization is to make effective use of strategic goal setting, it must have the correct organizational culture, from top to bottom. That culture cannot be stated simply as policy, nor can it be purchased as a single event with training or consulting. Culture is developed gradually by training and coaching, leading and showing and sharing in successful results. An effective culture will come from the whole process of strategic goal setting, decision making and performance measurement to report results and outcomes.

The two most important issues of effective strategic goal setting are:

1. **Don't wait for the culture to be in place before you begin.**
   - Make changing the organization and changing the people in the organization concurrent activities, otherwise you will never begin the strategic planning process. Far too often we defer planning because we want to be sure that the people are completely ready for what will happen in the planning process. The process itself is an important cultural development activity.
2. **Make the necessary investment to keep the process alive.**
   - Setting goals can be painful. There will be some "muddling through" the process, frequent changes and frequent challenges as to whether or not this is worthwhile.

     Keeping the process alive will involve constant investment in motivating people to stay tuned in, making sure every opinion is heard and respected and making sure everyone trusts the process.

Other important issues of effective strategic goal setting are:

3. **Remove the fear.**
   - Fear comes most frequently from uncertain consequences. To help remove the fear, senior management should communicate very clearly the consequences for success (celebration and rewards), and the consequence for failure (correction and revision). This communication, along with a strong endorsement of the planning process and a commitment to using the results of the planning exercise will go a long way towards reducing the fear.
4. **Keep an open mind and be honest with yourself.**
   - It is easy to minimize our weaknesses, overstate our strengths and underestimate the competence of our competition. This is very dangerous. An effective plan must be based on the realities of **what you can do** and **what you are facing,** not **what you would like to be able to do** based on **what you would like to be facing**.
5. **Be willing to challenge current practices.**
   - There are many excellent strategic gains waiting in present practices. We tend to think that the best initiatives come from doing something new. The truth is that a host of potential gains can come from doing something old in a new way. Defending current practices by saying we have "always done it this way," or rejecting an old idea that has been raised for consideration again by saying "it didn't work before, so it won't work now" are two frequently used and completely illogical arguments. If those arguments won all the time, we would never change and never do anything new! People who say this can be huge obstacles to success. If they cannot buy into the change process, they may have to leave the organization.
6. **Look outside for best available practices.**
   - Learn from the best, not just the best in your industry. Being the best shoemaker of all shoemakers used to be a significant achievement, but the evolution of technology, robotics, e-commerce and the globalization of competition has moved the shoemaker into a new realm. We can no longer confine the search for best practices to our competition; we must look into other industries to see how they function. For example, shoemakers might learn something about exporting from toaster makers, and the computerized inventory system used in a retail store might be the best fit for a boat manufacturer. To maximize success we should be looking for best practices in Marketing, Finance, Resource Management and HR Practices.
7. **Complete the full cycle of the model.**
   - The planning model is a cycle, and as such the cycle must be completed before the strategic gains can be realized. In many ways, if an organization is not committed to completing the cycle, it would be better off not to begin. The negative impact on morale and commitment among employees when "another plan hits the paper shredder" is too great.

8. **Use success as an opportunity to share rewards.**
   - To achieve long-term success we must encounter a series of short-term successes. Some senior managers think that long-term gains should yield long-term rewards for employees, speaking about the "great future that is in store if we work hard and act as a team." The problem is that if the reward is too far away from the action, it is not motivating. It's like telling a two-year-old child that if he or she learns to live without a diaper, you will buy the child a car at 16. You are out of the child's realm; he or she doesn't place a value on "car" and has no idea when 16 happens! Success occurs in small, current pieces; therefore rewards should match the significance and timing of the success. (See the performance measurement chapter in this book, Chapter 10).
9. **Use failure as an opportunity to correct and improve.**
   - Analyzing a failure is not about assigning blame and delivering punishment. If it was, people would be motivated to hide information about failures or at least lie about the significance of the failure because of a fear of the consequences.

     We should try to make it "safe to fail." We don't advocate failure; we advocate trying something new. Should we fail, we will use that failure to learn how to avoid that situation in the future. If we can do this, we have found a way to tap the intelligence and creativity of all employees. This will result in better decisions, more creativity and better results.

ON THIS TOPIC

A Real-World Example

A number of years ago Chevron Canada had a very centralized organizational climate where the personal consequences of having an idea fail were very negative to the management team. The consequences of failure were so negative, the team avoided anything new or anything that had even the slightest risk of failure.

This highly centralized management style, which still exists in many organizations today, collected decision making and creativity from among a small group of senior managers.

In the late 1980s, a newly appointed CEO (Jerry Franciscovitch) realized that many good ideas were being lost, and that the management team lacked motivation to try something new. To promote experimentation and to make trying something new "safe" for employees, he introduced a "freedom to fail" program. He said, **if we as a group approve an experiment**, and if it fails, **we as a group will recover together**. No individual, especially the originator of the idea, will suffer a personal negative consequence.

Yes, this made the approval of initiatives more rigorous, but it also opened the floodgates to new and innovative ideas.

www.chevron.ca

The issues of effective strategic goal setting are meant to improve the likelihood and extend the value of a success. Like strategic goal setting itself, the issues are not set in concrete. They will change with the environment and with the organization itself. The nine mentioned above are a starting point.

The Situation At Present

Most organizations have recently completed a strategic planning exercise that is the beginning of an ongoing process of developing strategic plans and following the plans through implementation to performance measurement. The process has defined key areas where results are necessary from a corporate and departmental view. Unfortunately, currently there are many organizations that have set high-level goals who now sit and wait for some miracle to happen. They think that talking about or writing about success will make it happen. They will be waiting for a long time! Strategic goals can only be accomplished if expectations are translated into meaningful implementation plans.

ON THIS TOPIC

A Real-World Example

The BC Ferry Corporation, a Crown corporation responsible for the operation of ferry services to the islands off the coast of British Columbia has developed strategic and operational plans for years. It's not an easy process to balance fiscal constraints against meeting growing customer demand. The corporation enjoyed 30 years of stable, although not profitable operations. Its primary strategy was to provide safe, reliable and cost effective transportation (a highway on the water).

In the late 1990s, the corporation, on the direction of politicians in the provincial government, departed from its traditional business practices and developed a new and innovative way to build vessels. It became a strategic research and development company, trying brand-new technologies. It departed from the plan to try something new.

The idea behind this was to stimulate the economy by creating a new industry in aluminum boat manufacturing, to create jobs, to improve service to customers and to become state of the art in this new technology. Thus, "Fast Ferries" were born.

The design and construction of three aluminum high-speed catamarans was budgeted at $180 million.

Because the crown corporation had never been in the strategic research and development business, the vessels wound up costing $540 million, they proved to be unreliable, they couldn't achieve the speeds they promised and they were expensive to operate.

They were eventually sold for $17 million, the party in power was virtually destroyed in the next election and the crown corporation was privatized!

www.bcferries.bc.ca

Critics of public sector organizations are quick to say that because these organizations are government funded and because they lack accountability for performance, the planning process is not powerful as a management tool. This is because the consequences for not realizing plans are not significant. These critics also say that this condition would not occur in the private sector because accountability is much greater, and the consequences of failure are much greater there.

It is true that accountability and consequences are greater in the private sector, but it is not true that the failure to implement plans does not exist in the private sector. Many private organizations have adopted high-level corporate strategies and have failed to follow through with implementation strategies and so their investments in strategic planning have been lost. If you think about major corporate failures, Eatons, Woodwards, airlines and high-tech companies in the recent and distant past, they all have something in common: good vision, but a bad business model for implementation.

To reduce the likelihood of this happening, we need to examine the various levels of strategic goal setting and the action plans that evolve from each level.

There are two basic levels of strategic goal setting: the corporate level, which identifies long-range goals, and the operating or functional level, which achieves long-range goals by realizing short-range goals.

The Strategic Goal-Setting Tool

In its simplest form, strategic goal setting is the process of matching the competencies and strengths of an organization to the environmental opportunities that exist outside of the organization. A strategic goal is a reflection of what is desired and what is possible. As the following diagram (Figure 1.9) indicates, we go through a sequence of steps, from vision to goals.

Defining "what is desired" and "what is possible" is not a sequential process; it is a dynamic process. In other words, while strategic goal setting appears to be a systematic process where we go through a sequence of steps, we must keep in mind that each step will enable new discoveries about the realities of an organization that may well change the perceptions of previous steps in the process.

FIGURE 1.9 Goal-Setting Tool

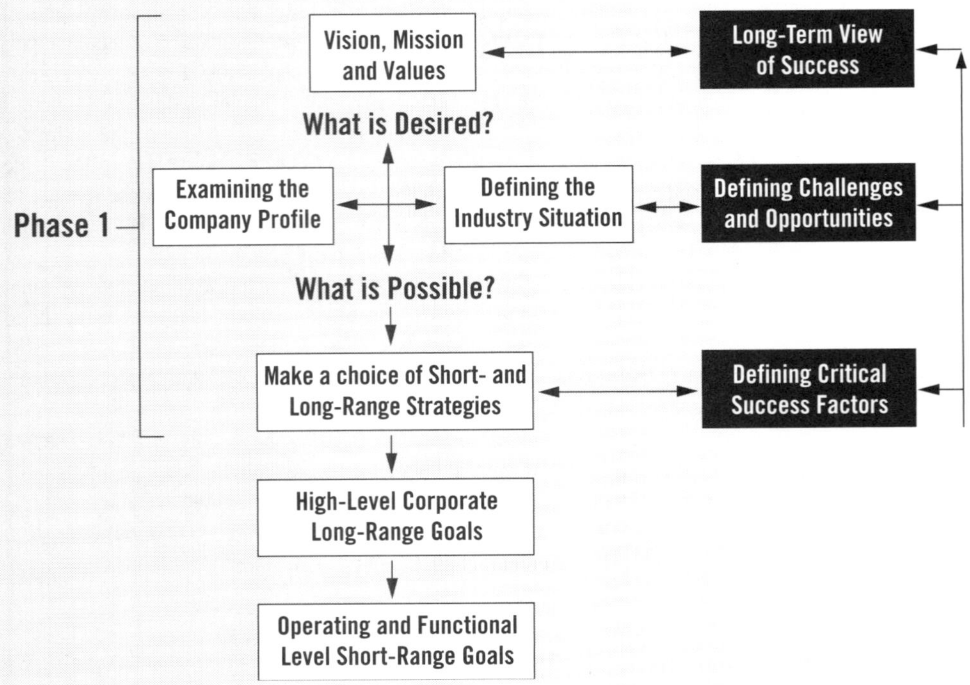

A good strategic goal is set in gelatin, not concrete. As new discoveries are made, the manager goes back to previous elements of the model to see if the new discovery has had an impact on the assumptions and facts used in previous steps. We are always willing to alter components of the model as we learn more about the organization from the process of strategic goal setting.

THE CORPORATE VIEW OF STRATEGIC GOALS

Boards of directors adopt high-level goals which senior managers use to govern the planning process, middle managers use to develop operating plans and policies, and operating and "functional level" employees use to control the daily activities of an organization. In theory, the people on the line, assembling part "A" with part "B," should recognize the contribution they are making to the overall strategic goals of the organization. The **most successful** organizations are the ones in which each and every employee understands the contribution he or she is making to the success of the organization.

From a corporate view, high-level strategic issues may include (not presented in priority order):

- maximizing the financial efficiency and effectiveness of the organization,
- sustaining the organization in the economic system,
- operating safely for the employees and the public,
- minimizing the impact of operations on the natural environment, and
- maximizing the satisfaction of customers at all levels.

These high-level issues are expressed as long-term goals where the organization has stated that change is both desirable and possible over long-range planning horizons. Senior management then empowers middle management to develop strategic implementation plans that reflect the high-level view of the organization. Some organizations refer to this process as "cascading goals," where operating level goals have a clear relationship to the realization of high-level goals.

In most cases, it is difficult to act on high-level goals directly because they are not clearly defined in terms of what is to be done and how success is to be measured. High-level goals define what is to be accomplished at the end of the long-range planning horizon, which may be from 5 to 20 years long, and operating or intermediate goals define what is to be accomplished in more specific terms and over shorter planning horizons such as 1 to 2 years.

Several organizations have adopted a framework for developing strategic goals, which encourage the organization to examine long-range goals from a broader perspective. Traditionally, the most important long-range goal has been to maximize profits, or long-term financial value of the organization. Recently, the pressure brought on by a variety of stakeholders' groups who expect non-financial returns has caused senior management to focus some attention on different kinds of strategic goals.

Where the former long-range strategy used to be "to maximize profits," the new strategic focus has profits pluralized with four S's (see Figure 1.10). This reflects the fact that there is more to profit than money. Profit is measured in financial terms while the four S's are measured in non-financial terms as strategic gains. In other words:

FIGURE 1.10 Five Dimensions of Goals

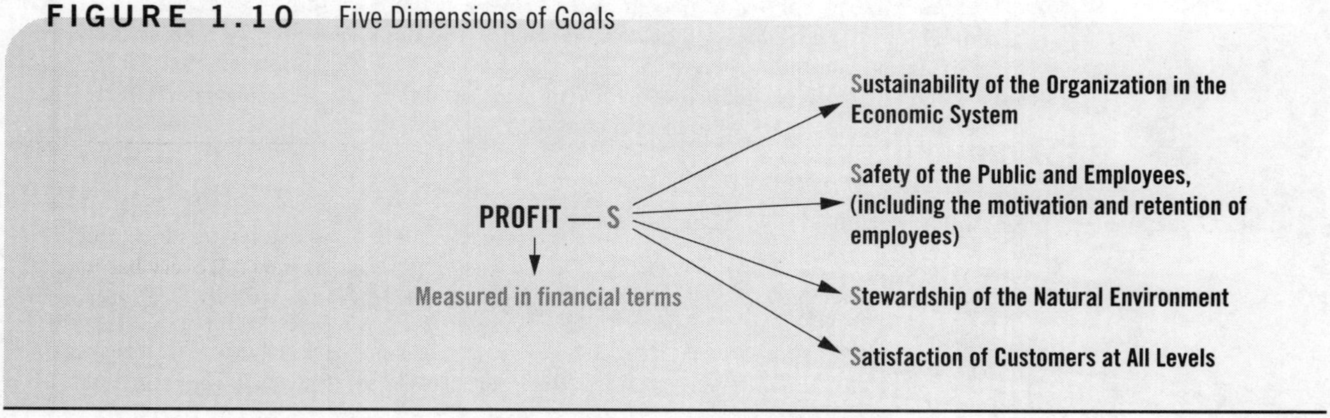

This system for high-level goal setting suggests that the most effective initiatives in an organization will have maximum profits, be sustainable, be safe, minimize the impact on the environment and maximize customer satisfaction. This system prompts managers to expand their analytical horizons so that initiatives are valued for the benefits they will bring to the organization in more than just financial terms.

Expanding the dimensions of goal setting to reflect multiple issues is consistent with the organization's aim to please a wide variety of stakeholders. When stakeholders review the objectives they should be able to see that their interests are being addressed by the organization and that the organization is committed to improving results in the areas where stakeholders have an interest.

Examples Of Long-Range Corporate Strategic Goals

Goals create a framework for measurement. It would be a waste of time to set a goal without some reference as to how that goal will be measured so that achievements towards reaching the goal can be reported and reviewed by decision makers. A common failing of goals is that they are so nebulous that measurement is not possible. Where measurement is not possible, the motivation to act on the goal disappears.

ON THIS TOPIC

A Real-World Example

It is very common for senior management to say:

"Our employees are our most valuable asset."

To make the commitment to employees more enthusiastically, some have included reference to the value of employees and the willingness to invest in their development as key strategic issues in their corporate plans and annual reports:

"We strive to be more proactive in valuing the contribution made by our employees."
"We are committed to employee development and promotion from within."

In most cases, the organization has not followed up with a measurement system or an action plan which reinforces the statements made in the plan and measures the improvement in morale or productivity among employees, the "most valuable asset."

When employees see that there is no plan that works towards improving the situation for the most valuable asset, they become disenchanted. They might say, "These are just words, they don't really mean it because they are not doing anything about it."

The fact is that senior management has done more harm than good. Their intended outcome was to improve morale and productivity. The real outcome was to damage it!

Sometimes a goal that can't be measured might be more appropriately stated as a vision or a value. Vision and values will be analyzed later in this book. For now we need to assume that goals are measurable.

Using the template defined above, a complete set of long-range strategic goals, including measures, might appear as follows (Figure 1.11):

FIGURE 1.11 Corporate Long-Range Strategic Goals

Strategic Issues	Objective	Goal
Financial	Maximize financial returns to stockholders	To maintain an average return on investment of a minimum of 15% for the next five years
Sustainability of the Organization in the Economic System	Maximize the impact of the organization on the regional economy	To create and maintain 50 new jobs per year for the next five years
Safety of the Public and Employees, (including the motivation and retention of employees)	Minimize the probability and severity of employee and public injury	To maintain an injury rate less than the national average for the next five years
	Maximize the motivation and retention of employees	To maintain a 90% satisfaction level of employees and to have a retention rate higher than the industry average within two years
Stewardship of the Natural Environment	Minimize the impact of operations on the natural environment	To reduce the level of solid particulate emissions to the landfill to 3 parts per million by June 2005
Satisfaction of Customers at All Levels	Maximize the satisfaction of customers at all levels	To achieve and maintain a 90% customer satisfaction level regarding service, product quality and perceived value for the next five years

This is a very simplified presentation. In reality there might be several objectives and then several more goals under each of the "Strategic Issues" headings. Later in this book we will be examining this model and introducing new complexities. For now, we need to focus on two things. First, as we move from strategic issues to goals, the dimensions become more precisely measured. Second, notice that there are five goals, not just one!

Measurement is essential to show the progress the organization is making, and multiple goals are important to show the organization that success comes from a mix of factors. Sometimes tradeoffs among factors have to be made. For example, it is difficult to minimize the impact of operations on the natural environment and to be financially efficient at the same time because environmental strategies cost money and virtually no revenues are generated. Therefore, the decision to proceed with an environmental management plan will be based on issues of corporate citizenship, public perception and/or regulatory compliance.

Many senior managers regard "satisfaction of customers at all levels" as the ultimate outcome that is being sought. Other goals, such as safety, efficiency and environmental stewardship are simply a means to achieve customer satisfaction. Other managers might say that financial returns drive everything. Others might say our primary goal is to protect the environment at all costs.

The five strategic issues have been presented as a model that would be tailored and modified, depending on the organization, its priorities, its mandate and its overall plan. Not all five strategic issues would be relevant, and the order might change, but experience has taught me that these five issues are the core of virtually every strategic plan I have seen, public organization or private, whether in Canada, the U.S.A., Russia or Colombia.

These high-level strategic goals are then translated into operating level action oriented goals and objectives.

THE OPERATING VIEW OF STRATEGIC GOALS

At the operating level, strategic goals:

- become more precise,
- focus on short-term planning horizons, and
- deal with measurable gains coming from daily operating activities.

The process of "cascading" goals is to take the corporate long-range strategic goal and send it to the operating and functional departments so the goal becomes the focal point for the development of operating short-term strategic goals.

For example, the long-range goal to "maximize financial returns" will be embraced by operating departments who pinpoint the contribution they can make to the long-range goal and develop short-range goals to feed into the long-range goal. The following figure (Figure 1.12) illustrates this point.

Departmental goals and implementation plans are a reflection of high-level strategic goals. Every goal at the departmental level should have a clear path to a corporate-level goal. You can see that if something is missed at the corporate level, something will be missed at the operating level.

Given that the results and outcomes of operating level and departmental goals are feeding into strategic goals, it follows that realizing goals at the operating level will inevitably result in realizing corporate-level strategic goals.

We will examine the relationship between corporate strategic goals and operating strategic goals in more detail later in this book. At this point it is important to realize that the "full cycle" of managing change for strategic gains involves a diligent and effective management of both levels, and a commitment to completing the cycle throughout all levels of the organization, including performance measurement, and feeding the results back to the corporate-level planners and decision-makers.

FIGURE 1.12 Corporate Goals To Operating Goals

Corporate Long-Range Goal	Measurement Concept
Maximize financial returns to stockholders	To maintain an average return on investment of a minimum of 15% for the next five years

↓

Operating Short-Range Goals by Department		Measurement Concept
Sales Department	Maximize revenues	Increase total sales by 5% this year
	Minimize selling costs	Reduce selling cost per customer by 5% this year
	Etc.	
Production Department	Minimize production costs	Reduce materials, labour and overhead production costs per unit by 5% this year
	Minimize production cycle times	Reduce the duration of time from initiating the production order to inspecting the finished good by 10% this year
	Etc.	

Regardless of the level or focus of strategic goals, the same basic model is followed. The model is a systematic approach to goal setting that ensures that the cycle is complete, all relevant issues are raised and dealt with and an honest and informed assessment of the organization and its capabilities is done.

At the end of this process we wish to have a set of clearly defined high-level goals and a set of clearly defined operating or functional level goals. The Strategic Goal Setting tool (Figure 1.13), however, introduces an interesting problem, much like the chicken and the egg parable.

From the top of the "Goal-Setting Tool," (Figure 1.9) defining a vision and a mission is very difficult if you have not first examined the industry and the company profile. Similarly, examining the industry is difficult if you have not first defined the vision and mission, which will indicate the industry you are in! It is also likely that discoveries at the operating level when goals are finally set might cause you to revisit the corporate long-range strategic goals.

Again, the tool is sequential only on the first iteration. After that, the tool becomes dynamic in that each section of the process might facilitate new discoveries that change the nature of all of the elements in the process.

Our study of strategic goal setting is therefore divided into four sections:

FIGURE 1.13 Four Sections of Goal Setting

Section 1	**VISION**
	Defining the long-term picture of success
	MISSION
	Defining the organization in terms of what is done, who it is done for, where it is done and how it is done
	VALUES
	Defining how the people in the organization will treat customers, stakeholders and employees
Section 2	**CHALLENGES AND OPPORTUNITIES**
	Defining the opportunities that exist for the organization through an assessment of the external environment and the challenges faced by the organization through an assessment of the competencies and weaknesses of the organization
Section 3	**CRITICAL SUCCESS FACTORS**
	Defining the areas of the organization that must be proactive in responding to opportunities and challenges by matching what needs to be done with what can be done
Section 4	**"CORPORATE" AND "OPERATING" STRATEGIC GOALS**
	Defining how the organization will take advantage of opportunities and overcome challenges to achieve the mission from a corporate and operating view

CHAPTER SUMMARY

This chapter introduced strategic planning by focusing on the goals that the plan will develop. Goals are the ultimate objective of strategic planning, so it is useful to see where the planning process is going before we see how we get to that point in the planning process.

CLOSING REMARKS

Now that we have seen an overview of the strategic planning process, the remaining chapters will focus on each dimension of the process. Chapters 2 to 5 will deal with the elements that cause effective goals to be developed. Chapters 6 to 9 will deal with implementation issues such as decision-making, and Chapters 10 to 12 will focus on setting controls, measuring and managing performance.

TERMS INTRODUCED IN THE CHAPTER

Action	Doing something about achieving your goals.
Best available practice	Excellence in a business practice, found in any business in any industry.
Business	Any organization, public or private, profit or non-profit.
Buy-in	The level of commitment a person has to a concept, or rather, how enthusiastically he or she believes the concept to be true.
Corporate view	High level, long term, results oriented.
Decision	Choosing between alternative courses of action in the future.
Goal	A target for achievement that has a measure and a timeline.
Investment/ resources	More than just money, this represents everything we must give up in order to achieve a goal.
Long-range	Impacts that are felt over 1–50-year planning horizons.
Objective	An outcome that will be achieved when goals are met (our objective is to win the game, our goal is to score more points than the other team).
Operating view	Tactical activities and tasks performed to achieve goals.
Performance management	Using measurement to learn how to make the people and the system perform better.
Performance measurement	Counting things that people and systems have done.
Planning	Matching resources to goals.
Review	Applying measures to your goals and feeding back results so that progress can be determined.
Safety	Minimizing the likelihood and severity of physical or emotional injury faced by stakeholders of your business.
Satisfaction	Having your stakeholders realize that what they give for your products and services has been exchanged for good value.
Short-range	Impacts that are felt immediately.
Stakeholder	Any interested person or group that stakes a claim on how the business operates.
Stewardship	Voluntarily taking on responsibility for taking care of the environment.
Strategic	Long-range and high-level thinking.
Sustainability	Recognizing that economic, social and environmental issues must be addressed for you to stay in business in the long run.
Systematic approach	Doing something the same way every time so that errors and omissions are less likely to occur.

QUESTIONS FOR CLASS DISCUSSION

1. Develop a goal for your college or university. What is it trying to accomplish in the long run? Then develop a goal for yourself. What are you trying to accomplish in the long run? Presumably going to college or university will help you achieve your personal goal.

   Start a discussion with your classmates.

   > Are the goals of your institution consistent with your personal goals?
   > Is it logical for an organization to have goals that don't meet the needs of their customers?

2. Develop some measures of success for your college or university. How will management know they are achieving their long-range goals? (five years down the road). Then develop a set of measures for yourself: How will you know that your stay at your college or university will have been valuable (five years down the road)? Finally, ask your instructor to recite his/her goals for the class, in the short and long run.

   Start a discussion with your classmates.

   > Are all three (university management, you, and your instructor) working towards the same goal?
   > Does the success of one of the goals positively or negatively impact the success of the other goals?
   > If there is a conflict among goals, which set of goals should be most important to serve?

A CASE FOR STRATEGIC PLANNING: MALCOLM AND RUBY'S NEXT STEP

This is an ongoing case that will be developed in each chapter throughout the book.

Fitzrite Computers has been a small supplier of personal computers for the last 10 years, working out of a small industrial complex in Richmond. Malcolm Fitz started the business as a hobby. He was 40 years old when he opened the business. He was able to finance the start-up costs with the proceeds of Uncle Harry's estate.

Business has been average, he has provided for his family, and paid for his daughter, Ruby, to complete a university degree in information technology. He has ten employees. Six assemble machines and pack and ship, three are in sales and one is the accountant.

Ruby just returned from university with her term project on a floppy disk. She has developed a piece of software that will enable people to download movies to a small box on their TV. The movie can be watched twice before it erases itself. The fee for the movie would be included in the cablevision bill. What is completely revolutionary about this technology is that the download takes about 15 seconds for a two-hour movie. Ruby has applied for patent protection for her new product, and has applied for the right to use the trade name "Movie ZAP." Ruby said she would share the profits with Malcolm, because he had paid for her education.

In the interests of testing the marketability of the concept, Ruby let the word out that she had made this discovery. The results were amazing. Offers and suggestions poured in. For example, a major cable company wants to pay $1 million as a base fee and a user royalty for each download, another wants to pay

$15 million for the whole thing, with no royalty for use. TV manufacturers are calling about a deal to incorporate the box into the chassis of new TV's so they could be factory-equipped with "Movie ZAP" capability. Meanwhile, Ruby, who is fresh out of university and anxious to prove herself, wants to keep control of the product, develop the capacity in Richmond to meet local demand, develop the capacity to manufacture and distribute the boxes and get control of a small local market. She then wishes to use her local success as a pattern for rolling out the system worldwide using franchises and strategic alliances.

Malcolm is confused. While he understands Ruby's desire to control the whole thing, he sees many pitfalls along the way. He is very tempted to accept the $15 million and open the garden shop he always wanted. Malcolm and Ruby get into a heated discussion about the situation and they decide to contract with a recent business graduate who can offer some advice on how to approach their problem.

REQUIRED:

Malcolm and Ruby do not want you to prepare a strategic plan. They want an answer to a question:

> *We have heard that writing a strategic plan will help us to identify and resolve some very significant issues we are facing. What are the main issues we are facing and how will preparing a strategic plan help us resolve those issues?*

CHAPTER ENDING CASE: A CASE ABOUT CORPORATE GOALS

Provincial Power Company is an electric utility that serves your province. For the past 75 years, the utility has been a government crown corporation and though it has effectively met the power needs of the province, there has been some criticism about the apparent lack of efficiency in delivering power. The province next door privatized their power company five years ago and they have power production costs that are about 6% lower than in your province.

Your provincial government has been very opposed to privatization in your province because they feel that even though power costs are lower next door, they believe that the private corporation is not doing as effective a job in achieving social results such as economic stimulation for the province and environmental stewardship. Debate in the legislature has been enthusiastic because the opposition is in favour of privatization.

In a recent election, the party in power was replaced by the opposition because one of the planks in their platform was that they would privatize the utility. They won by a landslide! The people had spoken.

At the new government's first cabinet meeting, you, a strategic planning consultant, were invited to come and give them some help. They want to offer the utility for sale but they want to give a very clear picture to prospective buyers about how they want the utility run. They have decided to develop a set of corporate goals that will define their expectations of a private power utility. Then they can evaluate prospective buyers against how they plan to deliver on those objectives.

REQUIRED:

Your job is to develop the set of high-level corporate goals that will define what is expected of the utility in at least five dimensions.

CHAPTER 2

VISION, MISSION AND VALUES

"If you don't know where you are going, any road will take you there."

LEARNING OBJECTIVES

After reading this chapter, engaging in class discussion and doing the exercises at the end of the chapter, you will be able to:

1. Understand how vision, mission and values relate to goal-setting activities.
2. Understand the range of stakeholders in a business, the nature of their claims and how planning is a reflection of stakeholder needs.
3. Understand the composition of a "Vision Statement" and how that statement provides the "Primary Planning Path" of an organization.
4. Understand the composition of a "Mission Statement" and how that statement guides everyone in an organization on how to realize the vision.
5. Understand the composition of organizational values and how they guide everyone in an organization as to how they will behave with customers and each other.

YOUR RESPONSIBILITY

To get the most from Chapter 2 you need to raise your awareness of how businesses and other organizations in your community present themselves to you and how they behave as corporate citizens.

Watch for signals that help you understand how an organization wants to be perceived. Pay attention to advertisements that are not selling you a product, but rather selling you on how the organization is being socially or environmentally responsible. Find out which charities a corporation sponsors. Find out what they do to support a sports team or a social project.

Think about why organizations do these things. There must be more than just a profit motive.

Bring your findings to class and be ready to discuss them.

INTRODUCTION TO CHAPTER 2

In Chapter 1 we discussed the basics of setting goals. We did that first because we wanted a clear view of where this process is going, because, after all, having good goals is the goal of strategic planning.

In this chapter, we will begin a discussion of where goals come from, or rather, what is the foundation that makes goal setting possible.

Recall the first portion of the strategic planning model introduced in Chapter 1.

FIGURE 2.1 The Planning Model

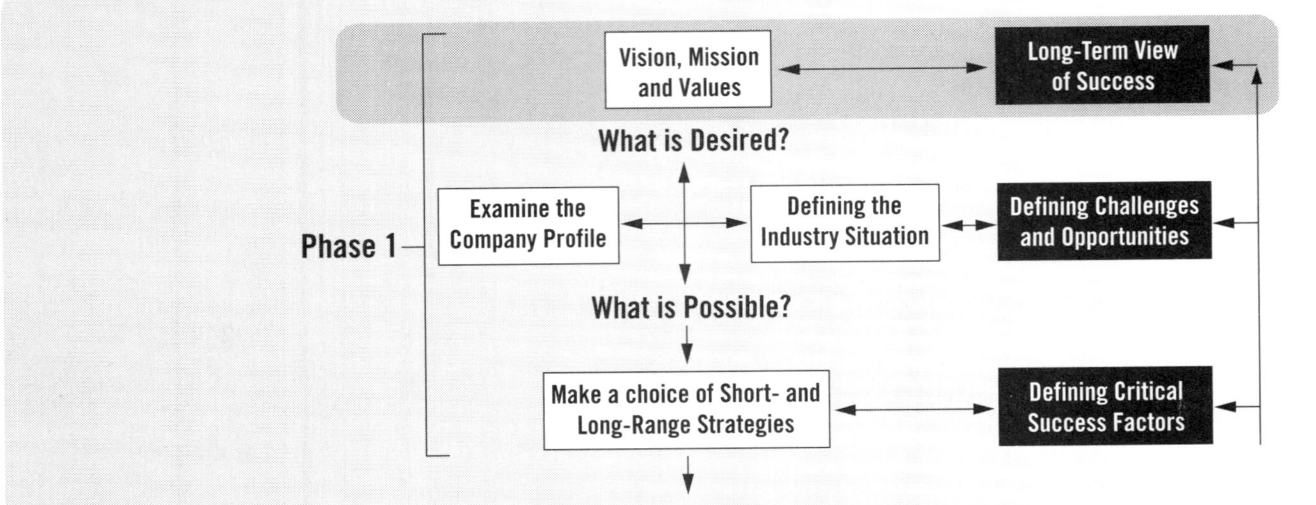

The first portion of the model deals with an organization's long-term view of success. This is in answer to the question, "What is Desired." As you can see, the next step will be to define "What is Possible" and then match them together to begin the detailed part of the plan. You will also recall from Chapter 1 that the goals will come further down the model. In other words, defining the vision, mission and values begins the process of being able to set goals.

This process, and in fact the whole model of strategic planning seems to be sequential, i.e. go from step 1 to step 2 etc. While there is some aspect of a series of steps, keep in mind that the process is also very dynamic. This means that discoveries made later on in the model might just change the vision or mission statements. Remember, each step is set in gelatin, not concrete.

Many authors and practitioners of strategic planning suggest that you need a vision and a mission before goals can be set. Other authors and practitioners of strategic planning say that you need a goal to provide direction in creating vision and mission for an organization.

Frankly, I am confused. I have yet to hear the definitive argument about what comes first, the vision or the goal. Both arguments have merit, depending on the situation. For the purpose of this book, I am going to sit firmly on the fence and suggest to you that setting goals and developing vision and mission are at least parallel tasks.

I can at least get all of my clients to agree that the act of setting goals sometimes changes the vision and mission because of discoveries made in the goal-setting process, and goals sometimes change because of discoveries in writing vision and mission statements.

As a first step, let's examine how visions and missions are written and reserve judgment about the order of things until we have more experience.

DEFINING "STAKEHOLDERS" SO A "VISION" CAN BE WRITTEN

A "Vision Statement" is an expression of how the organization will be perceived by its stakeholders. It is a long-term view of success that takes into account the needs of all constituents to an organization. A vision statement is developed in response to the perceived needs of stakeholders. Therefore, it is important to identify the whole range of potential stakeholders in an organization.

In general, "stakeholders" represent interest groups that have a claim against the organization and how it functions as an economic entity as well as a member of the community and society in which we all live.

Organizations are not inanimate objects that exist for the sole purpose of financial profitability. Obviously, non-profit and public service organizations exist for other reasons, but traditional "business" also exists for reasons other than financial gains. It is true that the most powerful driver for business is the potential for financial return, but we would be negligent as leaders in business if we did not factor other issues into the formula for success. Our society simply won't allow an organization to continue operations if that organization does not recognize that it must be socially and environmentally responsible.

Responsibility is the key word. Stakeholders hold the organization "responsible" for operating in the best interest of stakeholders' needs. A new concept in today's business world is the notion of "Triple Bottom Line." The old adage, "What's the bottom line?" used to mean, "How much money are we making?"— one-dimensional, financially focused. Today, "What's the bottom line?" means, "How are you performing from an economic, social and environmental point of view?" This expanded perspective came from a realization that all stakeholder needs have to be dealt with for continued, long-term prosperity.

Following is a list of potential stakeholders and the responsibility and accountability they place on an organization.

FIGURE 2.2 Stakeholders and their Claims

STAKEHOLDER	RESPONSIBILITY AND ACCOUNTABILITY
Stockholders/ Investors	To provide long-term financial returns that fairly compensate investors for the specific business and general economic risks they are taking by investing in the business.
Customers	To provide high-quality and safe products and services that represent fair value for the price paid.
Employees	To provide a safe and nurturing workplace that fairly compensates people for the value they bring to the organization and to provide people with the opportunity to realize their personal potential.
Suppliers	To provide a professional relationship in contracting for and purchasing supplies and services, and a prompt completion of trade obligations.
Creditors	To ensure that debts are secure and protected and that payment obligations are met promptly.
Competitors	To observe fair business practices and to treat the competition as the business itself wishes to be treated.
Government	To adhere to the letter and intent of laws governing business practices such as fair competitive practices and anti-trust laws, and to honestly calculate and pay promptly all forms of taxes.
Local Community	To involve employees in community initiatives, to employ people from the local community and to conduct business in the best interest of the livability of the community by minimizing the impact of the business on noise and environmental pollution.
General Public	To participate in and contribute to society as a whole by assuming a fair proportion of the burden of government and society and by promoting the growth of the economic system.

The list is not all-inclusive. In the future, as the nature of our social systems changes, the list will change and the claims of stakeholder groups will change. It is the responsibility of the organization to constantly monitor stakeholder groups to ensure that their changing needs continue to be met. Knowing the identity of stakeholders and knowing the nature of their claims is a necessary step in the development of a vision.

DEVELOPING THE VISION

Many organizations have held "Strategic Visioning" retreats where senior management and select interest groups go to an executive retreat for a number of days and immerse themselves in pondering the vision for the organization.

The rules governing these retreats are very simple.

- Everything can be challenged,
- Nothing from the past is assumed to continue into the future,
- No idea is a bad idea,
- Everyone will be heard,
- Creativity will be fostered, and
- Everyone will "own" the vision when it is finished.

Usually an independent facilitator is brought in to conduct the session so that personalities and historical relationships among the group play a minimal role in the process. The facilitator creates an environment where creativity abounds, opinions are heard and challenging ideas is safe and functional. The facilitator usually begins with a definition of what will be accomplished in the visioning exercise.

A vision represents the big picture about where the organization will be on long-range planning horizons. It should state a goal and provide a "picture of success." Vision statements can be fairly general because the specific details of how this will be accomplished will be discovered in later phases of the planning cycle.

The vision statement should define:

- who you are and what business you are in,
- what you provide to your customers, not in terms of specific products, but more in terms of their experience, and
- how you provide your products and services
  - AN IMPORTANT NOTE: Vision statements (as well as missions and values, to be discussed later) should be as simple as possible, stating what needs to be said and not stating what is perfectly obvious. You will notice in some of the examples that follow that some of the suggested elements are not mentioned in the example. This is because those elements are implied in the name of the organization or are defined in the nature of the business. For example, a vision should define the business the organization is in. If you prepare a vision statement for a monopolistic electric utility it might seem redundant to say you produce electricity.

The vision statement sets the stage for the development of the rest of the plan. Therefore, particular care must be taken to ensure that the right planning path is created. For example, if a video rental store were to have a vision of becoming the most effective producer of vine-ripened tomatoes, their management team should do some serious thinking about the business they are in! They may well decide to sell the video store and buy a greenhouse because "everything can be challenged" but to be effective in developing a vision the team must at least understand and agree on the core business they are in. The vision statement will come once they have agreed whether it will be tomatoes or video rentals.

Some organizations have used this visioning exercise to change the very core concepts of the business they are in, which is a healthy analysis. The key is to know when to stop. The video store might better challenge the "rental" part of their business by stating that they are in the business of providing "movies at home" or "home entertainment" and then use this planning path to determine the most effective way to achieve the vision. Perhaps in the technology of the future movies won't be rented in cassette form. Maybe they will be downloaded over the Internet.

ON THIS TOPIC

A Real-World Example

The Firestone tire company began business before the development of the automobile. It was a producer of buggy whips, used to motivate horses to pull in the right direction.

While Firestone might have believed that customer service and satisfaction was important, it wouldn't be here today if it had confined its planning to being the best buggy whip producer in the land.

To survive in a changing world, Firestone needed to define its business at a very high level so that the planning path reflected stakeholder needs.

Firestone saw itself as being in the transportation industry and as transportation needs changed, so did Firestone.

http://www.bridgestone-firestone.com/

The purpose of a vision is to enable the organization to be proactive in meeting the business needs of the stakeholders of the future. Therefore the vision cannot be limiting or confining; it must be challenging and broadening.

One useful tactic for writing a vision statement is to ask the organization to complete the following sentence:

I wish to be viewed by my stakeholders as.....

This will prompt responses that force members of the organization to "put on their customer's hat" and define their customers' expectations. An operator of a skydiving company will use words like exciting and safe, while a bakery will use words like freshness and quality.

The result of this process might be as follows:

Example: ***Sporting Goods Store***

We are aggressive sporting goods retailers offering the ultimate shopping experience to our customers through leading-edge distribution channels.

Example: ***City Management Team***

We strive to have the most appealing, livable and well managed city in Canada

Example: ***Dairy Farm***

Quality and freshness are the core of our business, which involves providing the complete range of dairy products to wholesale markets.

The primary planning path for the sporting goods retailer will be to examine the needs of the marketplace and to research alternative distribution channels such as e-commerce. The primary planning path for the city will be to define "appeal and livability" and to examine management practices to improve efficiency. The dairy farm will need to define quality and freshness and determine how to keep wholesale channels open.

You can see at this point in the planning process that these vision statements are set just in gelatin. When the vision is cascaded down to operating and functional plans, new discoveries might cause the organization to revisit and revise the vision statement because those operating realities are not known at the time the vision is stated. For example, dairy farms produce and sell through marketing boards and cooperatives that set quotas and prices for wholesale goods. If these marketing boards were discontinued, the dairy farmer would become a more traditional supplier of goods through competitive marketing channels and the vision of the dairy farm would change dramatically.

It is safe to assume that the evolution of e-commerce will have significant visionary impact on the retailing practices of all organizations!

ON THIS TOPIC *A Real-World Example* — *Vision Statements*

Quiznos
To be a leader in the sandwich segment by serving the best sandwich in the marketplace: one successful store and one "wowed" customer at a time. (www.quiznos.com)

Citizens Bank of Canada
To engage people in a different way of banking to create a better world. (www.citizensbank.ca)

Microsoft
At Microsoft, we see no limits to the potential we all might reach because we see no limits to human imagination. That is what inspires us. And that is why we create software that helps people and businesses reach their potential. It's not just our purpose. It's our passion. (www.microsoft.com)

PUMA, the running shoe company
To be the brand that mixes the influences of sports, lifestyle and fashion. (www.puma.com)

Sears Canada
Canada's most successful retailer... providing total satisfaction for our Customers, opportunities for our Associates to grow & contribute, and superior returns for our Shareholders. (www.sears.ca)

Coca Cola
To provide a moment of refreshment to thirsty Canadians. (www.coke.com)

As you can see, the range of vision statements is quite wide. In each case they are explaining the customers' view, and they are establishing a cultural tone for the organization so it can begin its planning and management processes.

Once a vision is resolved, the next step is to develop an organizational "Mission Statement."

DEVELOPING THE MISSION STATEMENT

A mission statement defines the fundamental purpose of an organization, which distinguishes it from other organizations of its type. The statement defines the scope of operations in product or service and market terms and it sets an expectation for the results that will accrue when the mission is successfully accomplished. Mission statements have been used to provide organizational direction for centuries.

Organizations want to achieve "buy-in" and commitment to the realization of organizational goals by creating mission statements that bind people together and create a unanimity of purpose.

The creation of a mission statement will, if it is developed and reinforced properly, provide an improved focus on organizational goals and will improve the likelihood and value of future successes.

Organizations develop mission statements because they want:

- to consolidate efforts around one purpose,
- to motivate the effective use of resources, both financial and non-financial,
- to clearly define the planning path,
- to provide a framework for decision making and control,

- to set expectations for results and outcomes, and
- to establish a functional organizational tone and climate.

And yet most of the list of things they want will not be delivered by the mission statement itself. The mission is not an end, it is a means to an end. Don't expect that efforts will be consolidated once the mission is written. Efforts will only be consolidated when the mission is followed by action that produces results that are then recognized and reinforced.

ON THIS TOPIC

A Real-World Example

Employees are often sceptical of senior management efforts in writing mission statements. For one of my clients, (who wishes to remain nameless) before we began the strategic planning process, I surveyed employee opinion about the level of confidence they had in the organization's ability to manage into the future. Predictably they said they lacked confidence because they could see no evidence of senior management engaging in a planning process.

We then began a very public and visible planning process, inviting opinion on the development of vision and mission, expecting that perceptions among employees would improve.

After the vision and mission were approved by all parties, the employees were surveyed again and asked the same question about the organization's ability to manage into the future. I was surprised when the organization scored lower than before!

I followed up with personal interviews and found that from the employees' point of view, all we had accomplished with the vision and mission was to raise the expectations of senior management that wonderful things were about to happen. Yet there was no evidence shown to employees that they would get any more authority, control, or resources to do these wonderful things. They felt that accountability and responsibility had been delegated, but authority and control had not.

One employee put it clearly: "Strategic planning is dangerous to me. The boss has figured out what he wants, and when he doesn't get it, he will blame me!"

The message from this anecdote is to be sure to set the expectation among employees that the mission will be followed by changes in business practices, which will make it possible to achieve the mission.

DEFINING THE MISSION STATEMENT

The Mission Statement is a reflection of the "Statement of Vision" in that the Mission Statement clarifies and refines the vision by providing a distinct definition of the core business.

The Mission Statement should define:

- products and services provided,
- customers that will be served,
- how the products and services will be provided,
- the results that are expected.

In short, the mission defines "What We Do, Who We Do It For, How We Do It and Why We Do It." This enables the organization to define its self concept, make statements about social responsibility, growth potential, future market development, attitudes towards risks, level of commitment to following technological change etc.

The mission statement is used to inform employees, customers, stockholders, competition, in fact the whole list of stakeholders, about the core issues that are important to an organization. It is a marketing tool for strategic change. As such it should be complete and concise.

The following table identifies the primary issues in a mission statement and offers some examples of how those primary issues are defined.

FIGURE 2.3 Elements of a Mission Statement

	What is Defined?	Example
What we do	Defines the primary product or service	• We sell real estate • We manufacture and sell professional quality cameras • We harvest, process, and distribute wood products
Who we do it for	Defines the customers and the market, who the customers are and where they are located	• To customers from worldwide sources who wish to locate in Vancouver • To customers in every city in the world • To wholesale distributors in western Canada
How we do it	Defines the principal technologies used, the ethics and business principles and the organizational philosophies	• By employing the highest ethical principles • By treating every customer with respect • By using e-commerce to its fullest potential • By valuing employees, their diversity and their contribution to the organization • By remaining committed to continuous growth in new markets
Why we do it	Defines the results expected from a variety of dimensions	• Which will maximize the financial value of the organization for stockholders • Which will minimize the impact of operations on the natural environment • Which will ensure a solid foundation of satisfied customers for years to come • Which will maintain our position as leading-edge service providers

Using the above template, you might see the following mission statements developed:

Example: *Sporting Goods Store*

Mission:

To provide high-quality, leading-edge sports equipment and clothing to the aggressive North American sports enthusiast in a convenient, dynamic and service friendly environment that will create a loyal and satisfied customer base, which will ensure the long-term prosperity of the company.

Example: *City Management Team*

Mission:

To protect and enhance the economic and social well being of the city for generations to come by engaging in responsible decision-making, being fiscally accountable, striving for excellence in program and service delivery and consulting openly with community stakeholders on every aspect of our business. We are, above all else, committed to maximizing the satisfaction of taxpayers in our city.

Example: *Dairy Farm*

Mission:

To create a long-range financially stable organization by effectively using technologies that minimize operating costs and maximize product quality and availability to the local wholesale market while at the same time exploring revenue opportunities outside of the local market.

Mission statements can be as simple as one or two words and as complex as multiple paragraphs dealing with each element of the organization. I have a client in the public sector transportation business whose mission is "Safety, Reliability and Efficiency," and a client in the private sector petroleum business whose mission is several pages long with detailed descriptions of what they do, who they do it for, how they do it and why they do it.

Mission statements say what needs to be said. The public organization is not concerned with profitability as it is subsidized by government, its customers are defined by the geographic region and it serves social agendas defined by government. Therefore, its primary concern is "how they do it" efficiently and effectively.

The private company has many more strategic drivers and therefore a more complex mission. The private company also has the ability to change many parameters of the organization while the public company operations may be very limited in what it can change.

ON THIS TOPIC

A Real-World Example — *Mission Statements*

Quiznos

We believe that our Quiznos product is our single best asset as we focus on our quest to be a national market leader in the sub sandwich segment. In addition, we are committed to:

Our corporate employees, who provide the dedication, insight and hard work necessary to grow this chain.

Our Franchise Owners and Area Directors, whom we strive to make successful through our Franchise Support Services.

Citizens Bank of Canada

To be a democratic, ethical, and innovative provider of financial services to our members. Through strong financial performance, we serve as a catalyst for the self-reliance and economic well-being of our membership and community.

Microsoft

To enable people and businesses throughout the world to realize their full potential

PUMA, the Running Shoe Company

To become one of the most desired brands in the world. In order to achieve its mission, PUMA maintains a strong focus on the following three cornerstones: Product, Marketing, and Sales. Our never-ending quest for perfection results in continuous adjustments to these three elements to ensure that quality, innovation and distinctiveness are present in all the products that bear the PUMA name and logo. This tripartite approach is the hallmark of PUMA's ability to be the brand that mixes it up.

Sears Canada
Sears Canada is a multi-channel retailer dedicated to providing its customers with quality merchandise & exceptional service, coast to coast.

Coca Cola
To sell more of our superior products, through the customer, to the consumer, at a profit.

The interesting thing about these example mission statements is that some are deficient in defining what they do, who they do it for, how they do it and why they do it. For example, Microsoft sounds more like a vision, Sears doesn't mention why they do it (profitability), and Quiznos doesn't mention how they do it.

On the other hand, the Coke mission is succinct, easily understood and complete.

- What it does — sell superior products
- Who it does that for — customers and consumers (interesting that Coke recognizes that those who buy its products, i.e. customers, are not necessarily those who use its products, i.e. consumers)
- How it does it — through the customer to the consumer
- Why it does it — for a profit

Again, the range of mission statements is quite broad. Each organization developed its mission statements for the same reason, to provide unanimity of purpose in realizing corporate goals. Each organization is successful today. Time will tell if these mission statements provide sufficient direction for the organizations to continue to be successful in the future.

DEVELOPING VALUES

Values define the essential elements of organizational culture. They determine how the people in the organization will interact with employees, customers and the rest of the stakeholders. Values represent the desired cultural environment which the daily operation of the organization should embody.

It is imperative that the values that are critical to the efficient and effective operation of an organization be shared by everyone in the organization. It is also imperative that personal values not critical to operations be respected. We all develop family, religious and ethical values in our personal lives and we bring those values to the workplace. If personal values conflict with the essential values of the business operation, we have problems. These problems are manifested in employees who work counterproductively because they are in a value conflict: they are trying to make the organization change to meet their personal needs rather than using their personal values to complement and improve the organization.

Many organizations have engaged in cultural programs aimed at "Valuing Diversity." These ask people to identify the values that are critical to the organization and to people and pinpoint areas where there is potential conflict. The exercise is culturally valuable because in many cases, we have assumed that someone whose values are different is someone who is not a member of the team or "mainstream" in our organization. These prejudices are dysfunctional because they represent opinions about effectiveness that are not based on organizational requirements. Rather, they are based on some illogical reference to personal values.

I have very strong and very personal family values, and the people I choose to socialize with share those values. At work, I run across people who don't share those values, and I choose not to socialize with them, but I do choose to respect them at work because we share the values that are important to our work.

The relationship between personal values and organizational values needs to be addressed so that people can know which values are relevant to the organization and the job to be done, and which are not. More important, values should be addressed so that people can change their views about how personal values and organizational values match together.

In valuing diversity we discover that our differences are valuable in themselves. If an organization was made up of a collection of identical people, they would make identical decisions, yet the markets we serve are both socially and culturally diversified. If an organization wants to get a handle on the market and to take advantage of market opportunities, the mix of people in the organization making decisions should be the same as the mix of people the organization is trying to serve.

The statement of values for an organization is the product of a process of discovery and negotiation where people inside the organization identify what is important to the market they serve, and also identify what is important to them. The statement, then, is a list of the values that serve the market, define the culture of the organization, define how the people in the organization will behave and define the set of values that must be shared by everyone.

Value statements are unique to every organization. A religious organization might state that sharing that religion is an important value for all employees. A sports organization might say that having a love for the sport is important. A police department might state that all employees must share the values of "protecting and serving." Accounting firms might make statements about honesty and integrity.

There is no single accepted list of values that would be applicable to all organizations, but, as the following figure (Figure 2.4, Examples of Organizational Values) illustrates, value statements should at least refer to:

FIGURE 2.4 Examples of Organizational Values

	EXAMPLE
How employees are treated and how they treat each other	• Employees will be recognized for the contribution they make to our success • Employees will be provided with opportunities for advancement based on skill and commitment • Wherever possible promotion will occur from within • We care for and respect the rights of our fellow employees
How customers and stakeholders are treated	• We ensure that our customer's positive experience is a priority in every encounter • We will consult with stakeholders and we will listen to their views • We will make every effort to operate in the best interest of all stakeholders
Which values people use to govern how they work	• We will be open with each other so that petty differences don't go unresolved • We will strive to keep our work fun • We will challenge what does not make sense • We will be open and receptive to the views of subordinates and superiors • We will be willing to try everything that makes sense
How the values relate to organizational success	• We will constantly strive to enhance the efficiency and effectiveness of our organization • We will nurture and develop our shared values for the benefit of the organization

When organizations develop value statements, sceptics will comment that these statements are generic "pie in the sky" things to say, just "words," and they will be quick to discredit the process.

Unfortunately, the sceptics are right. They are just words. But if organizations actually do what they say they will do and follow these words with action, so the words actively provide governance for the daily interrelationships of people, then maybe even sceptics will realize that when important values are shared, and unimportant values are ignored, the organization can focus on improvement without the baggage of unproductive behaviours.

ON THIS TOPIC

A Real-World Example — *Value Statements*

Quiznos
- Integrity, trustworthy, profitable, successful, responsive, dependable, leader, innovative, interdependent, professional, efficient, and fun.

Microsoft
- Integrity and honesty.
- Passion for customers, partners, and technology.
- Open and respectful with others and dedicated to making them better.
- Willingness to take on big challenges and see them through.
- Self critical, questioning, and committed to personal excellence and self improvement.
- Accountable for commitments, results, and quality to customers, shareholders, partners, and employees.

PUMA, the running shoe company
- PUMA plans to evolve the organization through the fostering of unique and shared company values, all compatible with the personality of the brand. These can be best summarized in four words: Passion, Openness, Self-belief and Entrepreneurship.

Sears Canada

Innovation
- Leadership in meeting our evolving business needs
- Reinvent to meet the challenges of the evolving marketplace
- Stay ahead of the competition
- Ensure our offer continues to inspire our customer
- Calculated risk taking for profitable growth
- Profitably grow our market share

Customer
- Competitively priced
- Quality merchandise
- Exceptional service
- Seek out customer ideas
- Highest standard of integrity & ethical behaviour
- Maintain customer trust and respect

Associate
- Open environment
- Motivated to perform at their peak
- Given the opportunity to grow
- Authority to do what is right
- Encouraged to contribute to the success of the company

Shareholder
- Growth within our market segments
- Rate of return on invested capital that makes our shares attractive to buy and hold
- Results comparable to the most successful companies in the industry

Coca Cola
- Customer Driven
- Highly Focused
- Accountable
- Never Satisfied
- Good Team Players
- Ethical

As you can see, the range in value statements is less broad. Vision and mission statements tend to differentiate organizations but value statements tend to cover all organizations. Integrity, honesty, passion etc. are values that should be present in all organizations. Quiznos, Microsoft, Puma and Coke would probably be happy using each others' statements of organizational value. Sears is a different story.

Some work needs to be done on Sears value statements because there is quite a mix of values, mission, vision and tactics all on the same list. For example, it's not a value to "stay ahead of our competition" or "grow our market share."

Let's take a closer look at Sears. The highlighted points are clearly "values;" the remaining points are either tactics or goals.

FIGURE 2.5 Values and Tactics/Goals: Sears Canada

Sears Canada	
Innovation • *Leadership in meeting our evolving business needs* • Reinvent to meet the challenges of the evolving marketplace • Stay ahead of the competition • Ensure our offer continues to inspire our customer • Calculated risk-taking for profitable growth • Profitably grow our market share **Customer** • Competitively priced • Quality merchandise • Exceptional service • Customer ideas sought out • *Highest standard of integrity & ethical behaviour* • *Maintenance of customer trust and respect*	**Associate** • *Open environment* • *Motivated to perform at their peak* • Given the opportunity to grow • Authority to do what is right • *Encouraged to contribute to the success of the company* **Shareholder** • Growth within our market segments • Rate of return on invested capital that makes our shares attractive to buy and hold • Results comparable to the most successful companies in the industry

The risk in mixing vision and tactics is that internal users might be confused. This confusion will reduce the power of the statements. Sears should revisit their value statements and clarify them to increase the likelihood that there would be buy-in from staff, employees and other stakeholder groups.

CHAPTER SUMMARY

We began this chapter with five learning objectives. All the objectives started with the word, "Understand."

The theme of this chapter has been to understand the high-level forces that shape a strategic plan. The high-level forces were defined as the long-term view of success, from the customers'/stakeholders' view (the vision), the organization's view (the mission) and the people's view (the values).

If we can understand that all three — stakeholders, the organization and the people in the organization — must be aligned on one planning path to maximize success, then we have a very solid foundation for future planning efforts.

CLOSING REMARKS

MISSION, VISION AND VALUES — Where to from here?

At this point in the strategic planning process, the organization has defined, in very broad terms, where it wants to go and how it plans to get there. If you stopped at this point it is most unlikely that you would make any progress in achieving your long-term goals.

The investment made so far is an investment in organizational culture and attitude. That is, you have defined the objective of the game, and the code of conduct of the players, but you have yet to define the specific rules for the game and you don't have a playing field or equipment!

If we visualize the evolution of the game of basketball, it began with the idea that an inexpensive game could be played with only a basket and a ball, two or ten could play, lines on the floor should be painted, they should mean something, a hole should be cut in the basket so the ball would fall through and a time clock should be used. And we should have the NBA and a billion-dollar industry.

Evolution is very clear in hindsight. Our challenge is to begin an evolution relying only on foresight. The beginning of any evolution is founded in the principles and practices that govern how we behave, and a general description of the goals we wish to accomplish. As we evolve, we revisit these foundation principles and revise them to meet the discoveries of time and experience. While the core principles of basketball have not changed since its beginning, the activities and rules certainly have. While the core principles of the computer industry have not changed in 20 years, the technologies used certainly have.

Using Vision, Mission and Values, we must now create implementation plans that deliver measurable results so that we can become a dynamic and proactive organization that will take advantage of opportunities and effectively deal with the challenges that the future has to offer.

TERMS INTRODUCED IN THE CHAPTER

Mission A definition of how the organization plans to meet the needs of stakeholders, what they do, who they do it for, how they do it and why they do it.

Planning path The overall focus of an organization on how far it will look to meet the needs of stakeholders in the future.

Stakeholders Any group or individual that has an interest in how an organization is run, the products it produces or the impact it has on the social and environmental system.

Values A definition of how the people in an organization will conduct themselves in their interrelationships with stakeholders and each other.

Vision A definition of how the organization will be perceived by its stakeholders.

QUESTIONS FOR CLASS DISCUSSION

1. Make a list of stakeholders for your neighbourhood video rental stores and for a national manufacturer of lawn and garden fertilizer, then prioritize the list according to who would be the most important stakeholders to serve. Finally, comment on how knowing your stakeholders might influence business practices.
2. Develop a set of values that might be used in your local police force. List your values in two groups. One group will deal with the values that govern the treatment of members of the police force in terms of how they deal with each other. The other set of values relates to how the general public will be treated by all members of the police force. Comment on any potential conflicting values that you see.

3. Polaroid recently went bankrupt. The new Polaroid has evolved. Printed below you will find the vision statement for Polaroid prior to the bankruptcy and the new vision statement for today's Polaroid.

    Polaroid vision 1990
    Polaroid manufactures and sells photographic products based on inventions of the company in the field of one-step instant photography and light polarizing products, utilizing the company's inventions in the field of polarized light. The company considers itself to be engaged in one line of business.

    Polaroid vision 2000
    The vision is a very simple one. Polaroid will be to digital imaging what it was to optical imaging. It will provide simple, easy to use, instant picture-printing devices — and specifically the consumable media for instant digital printing.

    Comment on how and why the vision statement has changed.

4. The following is a vision statement for Ford Motor Company from 1916.

    To do as much as possible for everyone concerned, to make money and use it, to give employment, and send out the model "T" where people can use it...and incidentally, to make money...Business is a service, not a bonanza.

    To employ a great army of men at high wages, to reduce the selling price of the model "T" so that a lot of people can buy it at a cheap price, and give everybody a car that wants one.

    If you give it all that, the money will fall into your hands, you can't get out of it.

    Comment on the appropriateness and content in terms of today's expectations of vision and mission statements.

A CASE FOR STRATEGIC PLANNING: MALCOLM AND RUBY'S NEXT STEP

Ruby is so excited. Malcolm has agreed to give her five years to prove herself with this Movie Zap idea. Recall from the case first presented in Chapter 1 that one of the options was described as:

> *"Ruby, who is fresh out of university and anxious to prove herself, wants to keep control of the product, develop the capacity in Richmond to meet local demand, develop the capacity to manufacture and distribute the boxes and get control of a small local market. She then wishes to use her local success as a pattern for rolling out the system worldwide using Franchises and strategic alliances."*

Malcolm has agree to defer his plant nursery plans and is willing to do whatever it takes, financially and otherwise, to make Ruby's dreams come true.

He hopes he will get paid back in five years. Then he can buy his nursery.

REQUIRED:

Make a list of stakeholders, prioritize the list and develop a vision and mission statement for Malcolm and Ruby.

CHAPTER ENDING CASE: A CASE ABOUT STAKEHOLDERS

PetroCanada sold 3,000 litres of gasoline to Taylor Smith, a construction contractor who has a storage tank on his property in northern Ontario. A PetroCanada truck delivered the gasoline and filled his storage tank last Tuesday.

The storage tank is the private property of Taylor and when it was installed 10 years ago, the local building inspector passed the structure as being in compliance with the building code in the local area. Recently, the building code changed, requiring all storage tanks to have a spill retaining wall built around them in case of a tank failure. Taylor was exempt from this because his tank was constructed before the change in building code.

Larry, the PetroCanada driver, noticed there was no retaining wall and did not deliver the fuel until he had phoned his supervisor, Louise, for permission. Louise looked in the Taylor file, noted that Taylor was exempt from the retaining wall requirement and instructed Larry to deliver the fuel.

On Wednesday, Louise got a panic call from Taylor. He told her that the tank was failing, the fuel was leaking at a rapid rate, the fuel on the ground was getting close to the creek, a fish spawning ground, and the mayor of the town, the local officer of the department of fisheries and oceans and the chief of the local Aboriginal council were at the property. No one in the community had the equipment necessary to deal with a spill.

Louise phoned her manager (that's you), and said, "You won't believe this. We have a customer that thinks his gasoline still belongs to us, and he thinks that his spill is somehow our problem! I am just giving you a heads up because I am going to phone Taylor and tell him that he is on his own and he should quit trying to make us responsible for his problem. I mean, if we go and clean up his mess the next thing is he will be phoning Kellogg's to come and clean up the breakfast cereal he spilled on his kitchen floor."

You have a crew, equipped with spill clean-up tools, about 100 miles away. They could be brought to the site in two hours at a cost of $5,000 to hire a helicopter.

REQUIRED:

You are Louise's manager from PetroCanada. What do you do?

In your response, be sure to cite elements of the PetroCanada stakeholder analysis, vision statement and mission statement that will help you rationalize your choice. You are not provided with the stakeholder analysis, vision or mission statements. Part of this exercise is to develop those statements yourself.

Also, be sure to deal with this situation from both a short- and long-term view.

CHAPTER 3

CHALLENGES AND OPPORTUNITIES

LEARNING OBJECTIVES

After reading this chapter, engaging in class discussion and doing the exercises at the end of the chapter, you will be able to:

1. Understand the need to examine the business environments that impact how an organization runs.
2. Understand the three business environments: remote, industry and local.
3. Identify the characteristics of each of the three environments.
4. Understand the need to examine the profile of an organization.
5. Identify the characteristics of every dimension of an organization's profile.

YOUR RESPONSIBILITY

To get the most from Chapter 3, you need to become aware of how an organization deals with the pressures of our very complex economic system. It is oversimplifying to say that video stores compete with other video stores, and that's it! Beat your competition and you are the winner...That's not how it works.

This chapter challenges you to think at a very high level, and very thoroughly. You need to read the business section of the newspaper as well as business magazines. Find out about industry trends. Find out why organizations spend so much time and money trying to understand their industry.

INTRODUCTION TO CHAPTER 3

Recall the planning model introduced in Chapter 1.

Note from Figure 3.1 that the highlight has been moved to include two new boxes in the planning model.

FIGURE 3.1 The Planning Model

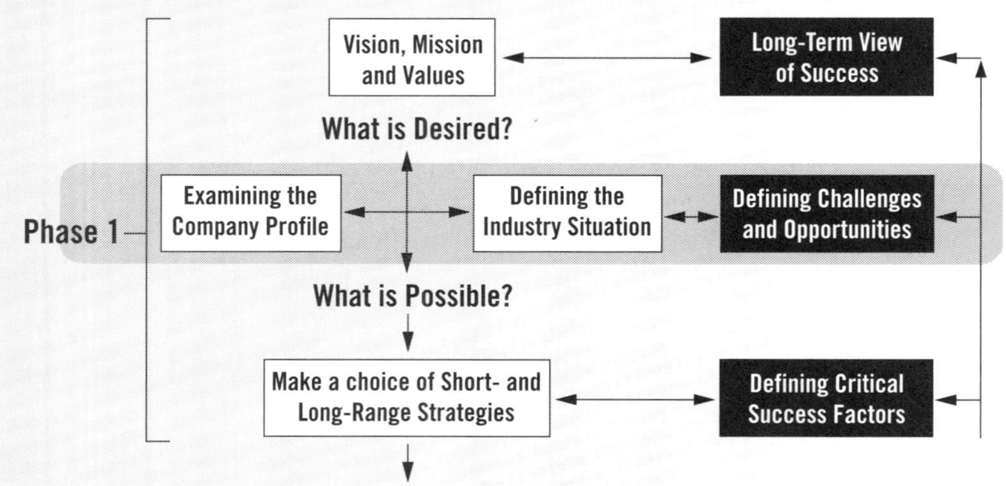

In Chapter 2, using Vision, Mission and Values, we developed a broad description of **"What is Desired."** We did this by creating a long-term view of success. Now we will focus our attention on **"What is Possible."**

In order to define "What is Possible," we match what **can be done** with what **should be done**. In other words, we carefully examine the environment the organization **lives in**, and we carefully examine the profile of skills and resources the organization **lives with**.

As Figure 3.2 illustrates, this process is actually a comparison between the needs of the marketplace and what an organization brings to the marketplace. This comparison is a very effective tool in helping an organization set its path and it is a very effective tool to use to stimulate the enthusiasm of people towards achieving their goals.

FIGURE 3.2 What Do We Have, What Do We Need?

Matching the Profile to the Environment		
Examining the environment	Matching what needs to be done ←	**Examining the organizational profile**
What do we need to succeed?	With what can be done →	What do we have to offer?
What makes the industry work?	In all aspects of the business	What strengths do I have, and what weaknesses must I overcome?

Imagine the resolve of an organization that has a clear understanding of its market needs, now and in the future, as well as having everything in place to meet that market. That organization is going to be deadly focused, deadly accurate and wildly enthusiastic about moving forward.

The truth is that having that level of knowledge and skill is very difficult, if not impossible. Understanding our rapidly changing environment far enough ahead of time to be effective in changing ourselves to meet the new environment is a noble objective, and we should keep trying, but we are not there yet.

We are in a realm of uncertainty and scientific guessing. That is, even when we use scientific methods to try to predict the future, we are still guessing because even the most scientific methods can't eliminate uncertainty. Unfortunately, getting control of change and understanding the future is so attractive to many people, they will actually lie to themselves. They will understate the changes occurring in the environment, or overstate what strengths they bring to the business or they will ignore their weaknesses.

It is most important that this assessment of the environment and the profile of the organization be done honestly and openly.

An honest examination of the environment will pinpoint all the issues and events from the environment that will impact an organization. This examination makes it possible to identify opportunities and challenges/threats provided by the environment, and to identify what needs to be done to take full advantage of the opportunities and minimize the risk and impact of the threats.

An honest examination of the profile of the organization will reveal its strengths and weaknesses. These are then matched to the opportunities and challenges of the environment so that choices about what to do in the short and long run can be made.

The definition of "what is possible" is the cornerstone of goal setting at the corporate and functional levels. Defining what is possible is a systematic process involving three steps. The first two steps are to examine the organization and the environment independent of each other. The third step is to bring the two analyses together for evaluation and decision making.

The remainder of this chapter will focus on the first two steps, analyzing the environment and the organization. Chapter 4 will deal with the third step, matching them to finally understand what is possible.

WHERE DO WE BEGIN, THE ENVIRONMENT OR THE ORGANIZATION?

In most cases, analysts prefer to examine the environment before they examine the organization so they can determine what is required to be successful before they are bogged down with organizational issues. Keeping an open mind is essential. If you have already assessed the profile of the organization before you look at the environment, you might go looking for environments that fit the organization, thereby missing critical realities about the existing environment.

Some analysts prefer to examine the organization first so they can evaluate the environment based on what they already know about the organization. This approach is useful in situations where the organization is limited in what can be done, such as:

- Legal aspects, such as the right to do business in a certain region, might limit the organization.
- Union/management relationships might limit the flexibility of an organization as to working conditions and hours of operation.
- Peculiarities of the marketplace might limit where the organization can operate or what it can do, such as a city bylaw that restricts business activities of certain types.

In these cases, it might be more effective to fully understand the organization before an environmental analysis begins.

ON THIS TOPIC — *A Real-World Example*

I have several clients who are municipal and city management teams. They spend a lot of time trying to anticipate the changing needs of people who live in the community. They are often guided by politicians as to what their priorities should be.

At the end of the day, though, they are severely limited by ever declining resources, falling budgets and staff reductions. The reality is that they are constantly trying to prioritize their spending so they can do the most with the least resources.

These organizations focus on their profile of capability and then try to react to the changing environment. They are driven by what they have.

Where you start is a matter of personal preference. The only condition is that in this stage of the process, you are simply developing a list of potential issues with an open and honest mind. You will have a chance to immerse yourself in organizational issues in the next phase of the process, which is discussed in Chapter 4.

We will begin by examining the environment because we wish to create an analytical framework where change is possible and all aspects of the operation of the organization can be challenged. Thus, first we need to carefully define the environment.

EXAMINING THE ENVIRONMENT

Our view of the environment is much broader than fish and birds. While the physical environment is important, so are the other environments that impact an organization. Being a good steward of the environment is meeting the needs of society at large and being a good corporate citizen. In addition to good citizenship, organizations need healthy, efficient and profitable operations so that all aspects of the life of the organization, financial and non-financial, can be prolonged and enhanced.

Our study of the environment is very broad. We need to carefully examine every single issue that has an impact on the organization, the industry the organization is in and the world the industry is in. Therefore we will study the environment from an "Impact" point of view. We will gather information about the various issues that come into play during the operations of an organization, and seek to understand those issues by looking at the impact they create.

The environment is broken into three broad categories:

THE REMOTE ENVIRONMENT

- Contains issues that impact all industries and all of the organizations in the industries. Those issues are largely out of the direct control of the organization or the industry in which the organization exists. An example is the federal taxation system.

  We must determine the extent to which these issues impact the industry and, specifically, our organization.

THE INDUSTRY ENVIRONMENT

- Contains issues that directly impact an entire industry and all the competitors in that industry. Those issues **could be influenced** by the collective efforts of all organizations in the industry. An example would be the health and safety regulations that apply to everyone in the industry.

  We must determine the extent to which these issues impact the organization, and examine the strength of the industry to combine efforts to change these issues.

THE LOCAL ENVIRONMENT

- Contains issues that impact how each individual organization in the industry deals with customers, other organizations and the rest of the stakeholder groups, where those issues **could be influenced** by the direct efforts of a single organization. An example would be the access to suppliers of your product or the advertising you and your competitors choose to do.

  We must determine the extent to which these issues impact our organization and the strength of the organization in managing these issues.

All the issues combine to have an impact on the operation of the organization. It is necessary to evaluate and monitor all three levels of environmental issues. An organization that becomes too preoccupied with local competition might lose out on global opportunities, and an organization that thinks only about global issues might lose ground against the local competition.

The following diagram, Figure 3.3, sets a framework for this analysis.

FIGURE 3.3 The Three Levels of the Environment

REMOTE ENVIRONMENT

Changes in the global marketplace
The economic system
Changing social views
Political regulation and economic policies
Technological change

INDUSTRY ENVIRONMENT

Business practices among all players in the industry
The availability of supplies needed in your business
The availability of substitute products and services to take customers from your industry
The resources consumed in competitive rivalries

LOCAL ENVIRONMENT

Other organizations competing for your customers
The daily practices of dealing with:
Customers
Competitors
Creditors
Employees
Suppliers
Ecological issues

The three levels of the environment also help to define stakeholders and the various levels of stakeholders that lay claims against an organization. The remote environment contains stakeholders such as government and the community at large, the industry environment contains stakeholders such as competitors and interest groups who govern fair industry practices and the local environment contains stakeholders such as employees and suppliers.

Analyzing these issues causes an organization to model practices and process based on the requirements of dealing with the issues. In some cases, the issues represent opportunities; in other cases, they represent challenges (or threats).

It is important to remember that there is no common definition that enables any one of the issues to be regarded as a challenge or an opportunity. Whether or not the issue is an opportunity or a challenge depends on the competencies of the organization and the nature of the impact of the issue on the organization. For example, in some industries the presence of a severe economic recession represents an opportunity, in other industries, it's a challenge.

ON THIS TOPIC

A Real-World Example

I have a client in the automobile painting business. He specializes in high-end automobiles such as BMW and Mercedes. When the economy is bad, his business is good! He tells me that owners of high-end automobiles traditionally trade them in for the new model every four to five years. When the economy is bad and they can't afford the new model, they become willing to invest in a paint job to spruce up the old one.

I have another client in the video rental business who says business is good during a recession because people choose less expensive entertainment. My client in the travel business sells exotic and expensive vacations in boom times and inexpensive local vacations in bad times.

At this point in the planning process, we are not trying to determine whether or not the issue represents a challenge or opportunity, we are simply trying to thoroughly list the complete set of issues. We will evaluate the issues in Chapter 4.

THE RIGHT "MINDSET" FOR THE JOB

To be effective in the task of examining the environment, you need to have a very clear mindset. You must be:

Willing to hear all points of view
Take the blinders off. Listen to everyone. Sometimes the best ideas come from the most unlikely people!

Not limited by past practices
Don't let past failure or success impact your analysis. Things that worked well yesterday may not work as well today because of changes in the environment.

Aware of prejudices
Try and separate opinions based on good evidence from opinions based on gut feel or intuition. While intuition can be powerful, good evidence is normally more reliable and accurate.

Completely honest
There are things you need to hear, and things you would like to hear. If you are honest with yourself, you will know the difference. If you only hear what you want to hear, you will define the environment according to what you want it to be.

Our study of the three levels of the environment begins with the remote environment.

EXAMINING THE REMOTE ENVIRONMENT

From the definition described previously, the Remote Environment:

- Contains issues that impact all industries and all of the organizations in the industries. These issues are largely out of the direct control of the organization or the industry in which the organization exists.

  We must determine the extent to which those issues impact the industry and our organization in the industry.

To understand the remote environment, we must gather information about a variety of issues, such as:

Economic Issues

Global economic trends, inflation and recession, and regional economic trends may have a significant impact on the organization. The key is to determine if those economic trends directly influence the industry being analyzed.

Social Issues

An organization is a member of the society in which it lives. As social values change regarding crime, family values, attitudes towards work and leisure time, pollution, health and fitness and basic rights and freedoms, the organization must change along with them.

Political Issues

Governments can extend commercial advantages to organizations that add value to the social fabric, and they can put barriers in front of those that harm the social fabric. Tax incentives for high-tech industry might stimulate investment and economic activity, and trade embargoes or import restrictions might protect failing industries.

In addition, environmental law, employment law and laws governing competitive practices, all designed to protect the community at large, can have an impact on the range of activities an organization can undertake.

These government programs can result in a significant impact on the attractiveness and profitability of an industry.

Technological Issues

The impact of today's technologies on business is incredible. Most organizations are being forced to redesign the very basics of their practices, ranging from how employees communicate with each other to how customers place orders and pay for goods and services.

It is also true that decision makers are being inundated with volumes of information. Their biggest problem is sifting through the information to find what is relevant to the decision they are making.

Any organization that fails to monitor technological change and factor those changes into the planning system is destined to fail!

Sources of Information

Examining the remote environment requires primary research into:

- government publications,
- university research papers,
- trade association articles,
- economic and social forecasts,
- publications by consulting firms and financial institutions.

The availability of information is not the problem. The problem is understanding and interpreting the information to make meaningful observations about how the issues impact an organization.

At this point, we are simply gathering as much information as we can to identify potential remote impacts. In Chapter 4, we will use a tool that helps define the nature of those impacts on the industry in question.

Example Scenario

Let's use a snow skiing area to demonstrate an examination of the remote environment.

A ski area can attract customers from worldwide recreational markets and from local neighbourhoods. Like community ice rinks, community ski hills are attractive to those who live nearby, while worldclass resorts like Whistler and Aspen are destinations for world travelers taking expensive holidays.

Before the environment can be analyzed, we need to identify the industry. A ski area is in the **recreation industry**, sharing markets with golf courses, tennis courts, walking paths and mountain bike clubs. In the context of the remote environment, the industry is very broadly defined, capturing a variety of organizations delivering value to customers. The one dimension that binds the industry together is the demographic of the customer. It is true that a skiing customer is different than a golfing customer in many respects, but it is their similarities that enable us to define the recreation industry and to further identify the ski area as a member of that industry.

The most powerful similarity of all customers in the industry, whether they are served by providers of golf or providers of skiing, is that they are all interested in recreation. They are willing to spend their disposable income to do it, and the vast majority of them will do it over and over again. They are committed customers of the industry.

As we look at the three environments, the industry definition will become more precise.

- At the remote level, the ski area is broadly defined as being in the recreation industry.
- At the industry level, the ski area is more accurately defined as a sub-industry of the main recreation industry, now referred to as the **ski area industry**.
- At the local level, each ski hill is a **small market division** of the **ski area industry**, which is in the larger **recreation industry**.

To assess the remote environment facing any industry, we take the economic, social, political and technological issues and describe specific issues or events relating to each issue. Then we identify a potential impact that issue might have on the organization.

From a **remote environment** point of view, we would identify the following as issues that should be considered in assessing the impact of the remote environment on the recreation industry and the snow skiing area as an organization in the industry.

FIGURE 3.4 The Remote Environment for a Ski Area

Remote Environment for a Ski Area		
Type of Issue	**Description**	**Possible Impact**
Economic	The amount of disposable income available for recreation, in the hands of customers.	As available income increases, demand for expensive holidays will increase.
Social	The perception of people regarding health and wellness and the use of recreation to achieve those ends.	As the personal need for exercise increases, demand for skiing should also increase.
Political	Government regulations regarding development of parkland and the environmental impact of the development of recreation areas.	If we already have a ski area, government could protect our competitive position by not allowing development permits. Or it could harm our competitive advantage by opening opportunities for new ski areas to join the market.
Technological	Internet-based advertising systems and reservation systems.	We could attract a more diversified market from global sources.

All the issues mentioned above will have an impact on the total recreation industry, including ski areas, parkland, camping areas, etc. Clearly the list of potential impacts is not complete, but it gives you an idea of the type of analysis that is done at the remote environmental level.

The next level is to focus on the factors coming from the industry environment.

EXAMINING THE INDUSTRY ENVIRONMENT

From the definition described previously, the Industry Environment:

- Contains issues that directly impact the entire industry and all of the competitors in the industry. Those issues **could be influenced** by the **collective efforts** of all organizations in the industry.

We must determine the extent to which the issues impact their organization, and to examine the strength of the industry in combining efforts to change those issues.

Forces That Shape an Industry

Industries are characterized by both competition and cooperation. While organizations in an industry have a need to beat the competition in earnings, market share, product innovation and returns to stockholders, frequently the whole industry needs to cooperate to ensure that the industry itself survives.

For example,

- Industries might band together to lobby government for incentives or protection for an industry. (Farmers lobby government to ensure that an overproduction of potatoes in Washington State is not dumped in the British Columbia market at a low price).
- An industry might create standards of measurement or engineering design to enable products to be interchangeable. (Tire manufacturers and auto makers have agreed to use the same wheel sizes, manufacturers of CD players and manufacturers of CDs have volunteered to use the same engineering standards).

While there are some examples of industry cooperation, there are thousands of examples of industry competition, vying for the top spot, takeovers and mergers and winners and losers. At the industry level, competition can be fierce as organizations try to deal with the power held by a variety of competing issues.

Michael E. Porter, in his book *Competitive Strategy: Techniques for Analyzing Industries and Competitors* (1980) developed a model for analyzing an industry structure as part of the strategic planning process. Porter suggested that a company should strive to meet opportunities and deal with threats coming from the industry environment, so we need a method of identifying those opportunities and threats.

The industry environment consists of five basic issues that put competitive pressure on the organization, thus these five forces will determine how fierce competition will be in a particular industry.

The following diagram represents a view of the five forces.

FIGURE 3.5 The Five Forces that Impact Competition in an Industry

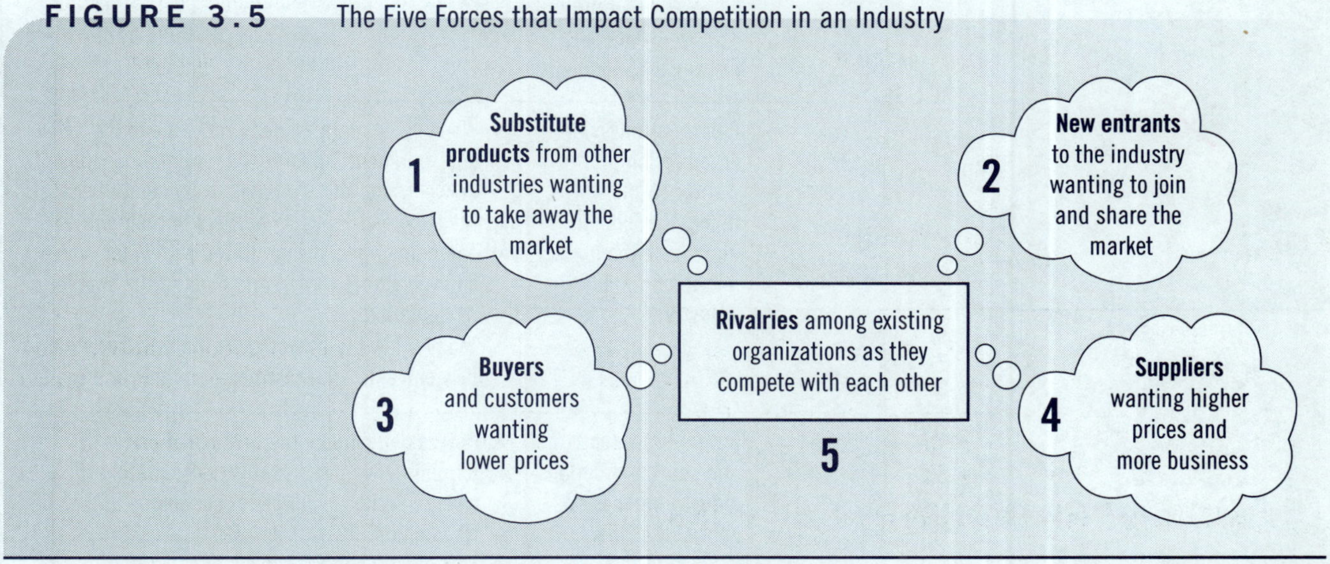

Each of these forces will impact an organization in varying degrees depending on the strength of the organization and the extent to which the forces exercise the power they have over an industry.

Analysts are constantly assessing these five forces to determine if any of the forces are changing to the extent that they represent a new threat or a new opportunity in an industry.

In addition, one must be sure the forces remain in balance. Repeatedly, history has shown organizations becoming preoccupied with competition at the local level while a substitute or new entrant joins the market virtually unchallenged.

The industry environment is constantly changing and in many cases the changes are revolutionary. In other words, industries don't change in cycles by repeating the past, drawing up old methods and putting them to use again. Industries change by doing something innovative and brand new. Change is active and dynamic, and sometimes not particularly well thought out!

It is usually true that industry leaders are the ones who innovate and set the stage for change that others will follow. It is not always true that industry leaders lead from a profit point of view. In some situations, sticking your neck out provides a great chance to get your head chopped off. The message is that innovation and change is essential to survival, but forging ahead without careful evaluation and planning is dangerous.

Understanding the relative impacts of the forces that govern an industry is a useful starting point in making the change process safer and increasing your chances of success.

To begin the analysis, the following table (Figure 3.6) defines the forces that impact competition and offers a brief example of how each force has impacted an industry in the past.

FIGURE 3.6 Examples of the Five Forces

Issue	Definition	Example
Threat of Substitute Products	A substitute product provides the same value to a consumer as the product supplied by the industry, but the product does not come from the current set of competitors in an industry	• Car stereo makers focused on competitors who produced cassette systems for years until CDs were introduced to the market. • Snow ski manufacturers enjoyed years of competition with each other until the snowboard was introduced. The industry has not been the same since.
Threat of New Entrants	A new entrant is an organization that is waiting in the wings to join the industry and divide the market and the profits of the industry	• When video rental stores first came to the home entertainment industry, there were thousands of new entrants in the market every month because there were virtually no barriers to their entry. • The market became saturated with video stores on every street corner, and most of the smaller shops failed. • Today a few big names have multiple outlets and new entrants are scarce because they are scared.
Power of Buyers	Buyers draw goods and services from an industry when they believe that there is value in their purchases	• Buyers can change the balance of power by forming buying groups and consolidating the purchase of a large number of customers under one transaction. • This can be done at the customer-to-retail level (groups of people on vacation expecting reduced price from hotels because they are block booking). • This can be done at the retail-to-wholesale level (groups of competing auto repair shops getting together to place one large sparkplug order so they can all gain some buying advantage).

Issue	Definition	Example
Power of Suppliers	Suppliers deliver goods and services to an industry as long as they receive prompt payment and as long as they see the industry has a chance of surviving	• If you have a retail home electronics store that carries a variety of brands of stereo, television, CD player, video etc. products, you have relatively weak suppliers in that you could shift brand names with minimal impact on your market position. • If you have a "Sony Store" where the only products sold are Sony products, you have a very strong supplier since your success as a retailer is a function of Sony's success as a manufacturer and marketer.
Rivalries Among Existing Organizations	There are very powerful forces that impact how organizations compete with each other and how their rivalries can govern their lives	• For the past 30 years there has been a small family owned golf course near where I live which has enjoyed peaceful, profitable operations. Five years ago, a new course opened next door. The total market for golfers has not changed so now there is an intense rivalry for each course to protect as much of the market as they can. • They have turned one very profitable golf course into two marginal golf courses!

Each of the five forces gets their power from the organizations in the industry. Some characteristic of the industry allows the issue to gain control, and when industry forces gain control, they can be hazardous to the health of the industry.

Just as a germ in your body left unchecked will eventually make you sick, any one of the forces left unchecked in your industry will eventually take profits away from the industry and/or reduce the security of the organizations in the industry.

When something has "power" over you, that power was not taken from you. You willingly gave it up! The bullies in the schoolyard have power because their victims give it to them. You can deal with bullies by teaching victims how to not give power to bullies. The same holds in an industry. For example, suppliers have power because the practices of the industry or a specific organization in the industry allow the suppliers to have power. Industries can limit the power of suppliers, and any of the five forces, by learning where power comes from, and how to not give it to anyone who wants it.

Each of the five forces has characteristics of either the marketplace or the business practices of the organizations in the industry. These influence the amount of power each of the forces can exert on the operation of the industry. In order to limit the amount of power, we must first understand where the power comes from.

Figure 3.7 illustrates some of the characteristics that make each of the forces powerful.

FIGURE 3.7 What Makes the Forces Powerful?

Characteristics That Make The Forces Powerful		
Threat of Substitute Products	**Demand is high for the total industry relative to supply**	If customers can't be served by the supply of the existing industry they will look to substitutes to meet demand. This means lost sales for the primary industry and increased opportunity for the substitute industry. *(If a person's need for fitness products can't be met by your industry, they will look to other industries to meet their needs).*
	Customers are not product sensitive	Substitutes fill a need with products that deliver the same utility to a customer, although the products themselves are different. If customers are **very** attracted to filling the need but are indifferent as to how the need will be filled, then a substitute product will be successful. *(A person's need for fitness can be satisfied with a very diverse set of products).*
Threat of New Entrants	**Profits are high**	New entrants are attracted to industries with high profits because the risks are lower. A new entrant will usually cause existing competitors to lower prices in order to retain market share. When profits are high, there is more room to move in pricing strategies. *(When video rental stores were first introduced, they charged large membership fees and high rental fees. The high profit margin attracted new competition and the market was saturated while profits were skimmed).*
	Small capital investment is required	New entrants are attracted to the market when the initial capital investment is low, and where there is a low investment in employee training or research and development costs. If it is easy to enter the market, and if there is low risk in entering the market, the new entrant will be there! *(A lawn cutting service has low capital investment and low training costs. A new entrant could enter the market easily).*
	Customers are not brand sensitive	Where there are no fences around product brand names, a new entrant can easily achieve equal status with the existing brands in the market place. *(We don't pay attention to the brand name of our telephone. A new telephone on the market will be perceived as simply another telephone).*
	Demand exceeds supply in the industry for the product or service	A new entrant may go unchallenged by existing competitors if there is sufficient room in the industry for the new entrant. *(The present golf course has a waiting list that is long enough to more than fill the new golf course).*

Characteristics That Make The Forces Powerful		
Power of Buyers	**Buying groups are formed**	Buyers are most powerful when combined in numbers. A supplier is at the mercy of a buying group if that group represents a large enough portion of the supplier's business. *(Retail ski shops placing one collective order for long underwear from one supplier for all of the shops in Western Canada.)*
	The product doesn't add value for the buyer	Buyers become very price sensitive when they buy goods and services out of necessity where they see limited value added for them. *(Paying an accountant to prepare statements that meet government regulations, which the owner of the business never looks at.)*
	The buyers are not brand sensitive	Where wholesale, retail or end use customers are not brand sensitive, they are price sensitive, and price sensitive buyers are very powerful because they will switch suppliers over price, which leaves supplier profit margins low. *(The brand of milk used for breakfast cereal in a restaurant.)*
	They could integrate backward	Buyers are powerful when they pose a threat of backward integration, *(producing their own products for sale)* thus eliminating the supplier. *(The furniture store that begins to make its own furniture.)*
Power of Suppliers	**A small number of suppliers for the industry**	Suppliers are powerful when there are few of them. They call the shots on price, quality and delivery because buyers have few alternatives. *(The local pub buys beer from a small number of suppliers.)*
	The product supplied is important to the quality of the buyer's product	When buyers assemble components that suppliers provide, and if those components are important to the quality of the buyer's product, then the supplier has power because the buyer does not want to contaminate product quality by buying from another supplier. *(INTEL INSIDE)*
	Low profits are earned by the suppliers	Suppliers exert power when they have a lot to lose, and if the profit margins are low in the supplying industry, those suppliers will protect margins and keep customers using, whatever tactic they can. (Vegetable farmers supplying the CO-OP)
	They could integrate forward	If there is a real threat of integration into the retail market where suppliers open their own retail outlets, those suppliers can exert a great deal of pressure on buyers to ensure that the integration does not occur. *(Factory outlet stores)*

Characteristics That Make The Forces Powerful		
Rivalries Among Existing Organizations	Industry profits are low	Where margins are low, suppliers will use whatever tactic they can to attract and retain customers because there is a small margin of safety. *(Grocery stores have a low profit margin. They must maintain a high volume of sales through a loyal following of customers to protect their small margins.)*
	Customer growth rate is low	Serving a market where the only new customers are the ones becoming old enough to use your product means that your growth rate is linked to population, which in many regions is growing at a fairly slow rate. *(One store selling diapers for babies in a very small town is probably enough. When a second store opens, the rivalry is intense because there is not sufficient market to sustain two stores.)*
	Customers are not brand sensitive	Price is the most important criterion for the buying decision, therefore the supplier who is willing to take the lowest profit will win the customers' business. *(Crude oil supplied to gasoline refineries is highly price sensitive.)*
	Switching costs are high	Sometimes it is too expensive to leave a market. *(Switching from a bowling alley to a squash court requires a heavy capital investment.)*

Now that we know how the forces are defined, and how the forces acquire the power that makes the issue a limiting factor on an industry, we can take some action to control that power.

Given the unique nature of each industry and the dynamic nature of change in industries, it is not possible to list **all the options** you have in dealing with situations. That would be like teaching someone the 3,000 things to do in the face of a schoolyard bully, and while you are thinking about all of the options, you get punched in the nose!

We are better off learning about how to figure out what to do, rather than being told what to do in each instance of a situation.

Figure 3.8 illustrates some of the tactics that are available to manage the power in an industry for the benefits of protecting the interests of the organization or creating new opportunities for the organization. The list is not complete, but it does show that there are things that can be done to manage each of the forces.

FIGURE 3.8 What Can We Do About "Power" in the Industry?

How is the Power "Managed" for the Five Forces?	
Threat of Substitute Products	Create a strong awareness of your industry with customers by cooperating in industry-based advertising.

How is the Power "Managed" for the Five Forces?	
Threat of New Entrants	Build a fence around the brand name so that it would be too expensive for a new entrant to gain market acceptance. Make it necessary for a new entrant to invest large amounts of capital to gain production efficiencies. By securing trademarks and patents, make it necessary for a new entrant to invest large amounts in research and development to achieve a similar product or service. Lobby government to regulate the number of competitors allowed in a market.
Power of Buyers	Diversify the customer base so that you do not become too dependent on one customer or one group of customers.
Power of Suppliers	Diversify suppliers by expanding the number and changing primary suppliers so that no one supplier becomes too powerful.
Rivalries Among Existing Organizations	Buy out the competition or form joint ventures to reduce the competition for a limited size market. Develop co-operative advertising among rivals to expand the market size for the benefit of all competitors.

The most important thing to note is that your reaction to reduce the power in any of the five forces of an industry will be met with a reaction from that particular force trying to regain the power. A lot of energy is spent managing this balance.

I wonder how much more we could accomplish if we could use the energy we spend trying to protect ourselves in more effective areas, such as improving efficiency or capacity?

Sources of information about the Industry Environment

The most valuable source of information about an industry is the industry association. There are hundreds of industry associations ranging from the Independent Grocers Association and the Automobile Retailers Association to the Lawn and Turf Growers Association. If you can name an industry, you can probably find an association for that industry.

An association is a collection of competitors in an industry that pay a fee to create an association. The association hires professional researchers and lobbyists who work for the association and its members to research and share with the members the best practices of the industry, and to lobby government to protect the industry if necessary.

These association researchers constantly publish information about the characteristics of the industry, and the new trends in the remote and industry environment. These associations are therefore very valuable sources of information surrounding environmental concerns.

Continuing the Ski Area example at the "Industry Environment" level

Back to the ski area example: if we assume the ski area is in the "recreation industry" we might reach the following conclusions (See Figure 3.9).

FIGURE 3.9 The "Industry Environment" for a Ski Area.

Industry Environment for a Ski Area	
Substitute Products Alternatives to skiing that provide recreation needs to customers	Suppliers of substitutes waiting to take away the ski area market would include holidays to expensive and exotic locations or tennis and golf in the customers' own neighbourhood. The prospect of a substitute attacking the market is very great because the recreation market can be served by a wide variety of suppliers. Ski area management must be constantly on the lookout for what customers are choosing to do when they are not choosing to ski.
New Entrants to the Market Recreation providers of *all types* who are wanting to join the market	New ski areas will face barriers getting access to land and having to acquire huge capital resources to construct the runs and put in the lifts. It is very difficult for a new ski area development to suddenly appear, surprising the existing operators. The public consultation process ensures that everyone has sufficient time to plan for dealing with a new entrant. However, given that the industry includes recreation alternatives that are not ski areas, you need to consider the ease of entry into the market of tennis courts, travel agents and mountain bike rentals etc., all of which could enter the market with relative ease.
Buyers Customers range from transient single day skiers to travel agents buying bulk accom-modation packages	Buyers exert pressure by trying to reduce the price by organizing groups and getting special discounts. Weekend and transient skiers are normally price sensitive to restaurant and retail services, while skiers on an extended holiday are price sensitive to the whole package, including accommodation and lift prices. Travel agents are constantly negotiating for special group and off-season discounts while regular customers are pressuring for lower season pass rates.
Suppliers Suppliers include travel agents, fuel and electricity, high-ways, food and chair lifts etc.	Suppliers exert pressure by keeping their prices as high as they can so that profits are eroded from the ski area rather than the suppliers as the pressure from buyers becomes successful in reducing package prices.
Rivalries Among Ski Areas Ski areas situated close enough to each other that they are attractive to the same group of customers	Rivalries among ski areas have been intense because there is only one market and that market needs to be shared by many ski areas. Vancouver enjoys access to three local ski hills within 30 minutes travel time from the city, 3 more within two hours, and 4 more within 4 hours. Those ski areas that are worldclass destination points have rivalries in world markets, and those that serve local markets have rivalries in local markets. Fortunately, there are enough skiers to fill the hills on good skiing weekends. Unfortunately, there are not enough to fill the hills on weekdays, and there are not enough good skiing weekends.

The industry environment provides a multitude of opportunities for the dynamic organization, and a multitude of threats for the complacent organization. Understanding the dimensions of the industry and where industry power comes from is a good starting point to turn the complacent organization into the dynamic organization that will meet the challenges provided by the industry.

Now we need to move to the third level of the environment, the local environment.

EXAMINING THE LOCAL ENVIRONMENT

From the definition described previously, the Local Environment:

- Contains issues that impact each individual organization in the industry in terms of how the organizations deal with each other. Those issues could be influenced by the direct efforts of a particular organization.

  We must determine the extent to which these issues impact their organization, and the strength of the organization in managing these issues.

The distinction between the industry environment and the local environment is somewhat "soft" because issues at the local level are often driven by issues at the industry level. The most important difference between the two environments is the amount of time management spends giving consideration to the issues in each environment. Managers spend too much time focusing on the local environment and too little time focusing on the industry environment.

The local environment contains the daily routine of dealing with customers, suppliers, employees and today's weather. Most managers spend the majority of their time supervising the tasks done by others, or doing the tasks themselves. Managers then spend too little time analyzing the broader scale of the industry and the global elements of the environment so that the organization can be better positioned to meet the future through effective planning and improving how operations are done.

To create more time for planning, we need to create less time for supervising. We need to delegate more effectively and build systems that enable trust to be transferred from managers to employees so management can assume with confidence that routines are being taken care of while management focuses attention on long-range planning issues.

The best way to understand the local environment is to identify the overall issues, identify a sub-set of issues and then pose some questions that need to be answered about the issues. By the time you have answered all the questions listed in the following table, plus any additional questions you can think of during the process, you will have a thorough understanding of the local environment.

Figure 3.10 demonstrates this approach.

FIGURE 3.10 Characteristics of the Local Environment

Analyzing the Local Environment		
Issue		**Question to be answered**
Customers	**Geographic**	In what region will customers make the buying decision? How many customers are there presently in the region, and how many will there be over the next planning horizon?
	Demographic	What attributes, such as age, sex, income etc., define the customer? Do the features of the product match the demographic of the market?
	Psychographic	What motivates the customer to make the buying decision? Can we predict when the buying decision will take place? Can we predict what the customer will do when he or she decides to not buy our product?

Analyzing the Local Environment		
Issue		**Question to be answered**
Competitive Position	**Market Share**	Where do we fit in with the rest of the competitors in the industry? Do we have a small share of a very profitable market? Do we have a large share of an unprofitable market?
	Breadth of the Product Line	Is the product line sufficiently wide to attract all potential customers? Do we have follow-up products to add to a primary product? Do we have replacement products to meet the customers' changing needs?
	Product Quality	Do customers perceive the product as high value for the price paid? Do we maintain records of repeat customers and their opinions? Do we maintain records of the reasons why customers are not satisfied with our product? If we have these records, do we do anything with the information?
	Advertising Effectiveness	Does the advertising and promotion strategy effectively trigger the buying decision? Do we have the ability to use information about changes in the marketplace effectively?
Competitive Position continued	**Production Efficiencies**	Are production costs as low as possible through the deployment of efficient production methods?
	Financial Efficiencies	Are we profitable in our transactions and do we effectively reinvest profits in financially attractive areas of the organization, including building more capacity, improving efficiency of operations, paying stockholders a fair return on their investment and managing the debt to equity position?
Creditors	**Financial Claims**	Do creditors value the organization's stock as collateral? Is there a sufficient credit line to let operations continue efficiently? Are creditors satisfied with your payment history? Are creditors willing to let the loan serve its purpose?
Employees	**Quality**	Do the employees complete work in the minimum amount of time with the minimum amount of error? Are employees motivated to suggest new methods of efficiency? Are employees dedicated to all the dimensions of the strategic plan?
	Availability	Can the organization attract and hold the right people? Is the rate of turnover of employees equal to or better than the industry average?
	Cost	Are the wages paid at all levels of the organization comparable to industry standards?

Analyzing the Local Environment		
Issue		**Question to be answered**
Suppliers	**Quality**	Are the products supplied to support your system of sufficient quality to meet your customers' needs?
	Quantity	Are suppliers able to meet your present and future demand for their products?
	Timeliness	Do suppliers provide their products before or as they are needed by your organization?
	Cost	Are your supplier's prices comparable to other suppliers in the industry?
Ecological issues	**Impact**	Does a change in the season or a change in the weather impact your operations? Does a change in the natural environment, such as the quantity of salmon in the run if your business is commercial fishing, impact your operations?
	Predictability	Are you able to effectively predict changes in the natural environment? Are you able to modify operations to compensate for changes in the natural environment?

Clearly, answering these questions will enable us to understand the local environment as well as the profile of the organization. Now, what do we do with the answers?

It is tempting to jump ahead at this point. Some people, when a problem is uncovered or an opportunity is discovered, want to deal with it right away. We have to try not to do that at this point in the planning process. Once we have finished this part of the model, which we will do in Chapter 4, we will have a clear understanding of what needs to be done, and we will have a priority order for when things should be done.

Jumping ahead because a better opportunity is coming along might be a waste of resources. Be patient. It will be worth your while.

A set of typical answers is presented in the following figure, Figure 3.11, with the ski area example.

FIGURE 3.11 The Local Environment for a Ski Area

Analyzing the Local Environment for a Ski Area		
Issue		**Answers to the Local Environment Questions**
Customers	**Geographic**	There are a certain number of skiers attracted from the local market, and a certain number from the global market.
	Demographic	The average age, sex and financial characteristics of customers are easily determined.
	Psychographic	The buying decision is made before the day of skiing, and the decision can be reversed if the weather is bad.

Analyzing the Local Environment for a Ski Area		
Issue		**Answers to the Local Environment Questions**
Competitive Position	**Market Share**	Identify the portion of the market the ski area is serving.
	Breadth of the Product Line	Identify the mix of skiing, snow boarding and après skiing activities.
	Product Quality	Conduct an opinion survey among customers to measure their satisfaction with the ski area.
	Advertising Effectiveness	Determine which advertising medium is most effective for each demographic.
	Production Efficiencies	Examine the maintenance and operating costs of the lifts.
	Financial Efficiencies	Measure and report stockholders' returns, and operating profit margins.
Creditors	**Financial Claims**	Determine the level of satisfaction creditors have with the industry.
Employees	**Quality**	Ask customers about the quality of treatment by employees and examine safety records.
	Availability	Compare turnover rates to other ski areas.
	Cost	Do a wage analysis of the industry.
Suppliers	**Quality, Quantity, Timeliness, Cost**	Poll the internal and external customers to ensure that all of the dimensions of the products supplied are being met.
Ecological issues	**Impact**	Good snow...good business!
	Predictability	Snow can be predicted with reasonable accuracy. Alternative use of the facility during the winter if it doesn't snow is minimal.

Examining the Organizational Profile

The purpose of analyzing an organizational profile is to gain understanding about the strengths and weaknesses of the organization. This enables the organization to use its strengths to the best advantage possible, and to do something about reducing the impact of weaknesses, either by directing internal resources to resolve the weakness, or hiring/purchasing external resources to resolve the weakness.

The first step of the analysis is to do a complete, thorough and honest list of every single characteristic of the organization, from the organizational structure to the process used to apply the wrapping on a finished product. Some of the items to be listed have already been discovered in the analysis of the local environment. The task now is to complete the list.

As a starting point, identify the major areas of the organization where strengths and weaknesses might be found.

FIGURE 3.12 Step 1 in Profiling an Organization: Identify the "Major Areas"

Major Areas	
Strategic Planning	
Marketing	
Financial and Accounting	
Production, Operations and Technical	
Human Resource Management	
Organization and Management	

The next step is to identify as many potential issues for each major area as you can. Be creative, record every idea, don't stifle anyone in this process. It should be a complete free-flowing generation of ideas and concepts.

These ideas will be sorted for relevance later. For now, we need a complete list.

FIGURE 3.13 Step 2 in Profiling an Organization: Develop a Complete List of Potential Issues

Major Areas	Potential Issues
Strategic Planning	Quality of long- and short-range objectives Degree of buy-in from employees Degree of buy-in from directors and senior management Can the organization act on the objectives?
Marketing	Breadth of the product line Ability to gather and use information about the market Brand loyalty Customer service, before and after sale Product image Market share Channels of distribution Effectiveness of promotions

Major Areas	Potential Issues
Financial and Accounting	Ability to raise money Financial relationship with owners and investors Leverage and the debt to equity situation Profitability Internal cost control systems Financial planning capability
Production, Operations and Technical	Cost and supply of materials Efficiency of production processes Patents and other legal protection Effectiveness of control systems
Human Resource Management	Employee morale and commitment Employee skills Union/management relationship Effectiveness of programs motivating excellence
Organization and Management	Organizational structure Quality of the strategic goals and objectives Willingness of management to delegate tasks and authority Flexibility of management to respond to changes in the environment

Clearly, the list is not complete. Every organization in every environmental situation will create a unique list of potential strengths and weaknesses.

CHAPTER SUMMARY

This chapter has been about gathering information. We need information about the environment we live in and the skills we have so we can thoroughly and honestly understand our situation and make informed choices.

You might be a little frustrated at this point because we have not acted on what has been discovered. This frustration is understandable because it is exciting to discover an opportunity and people want to do something about it!

Be patient. Acting on opportunities too soon could mean you won't have the ability to act on even bigger opportunities later.

CLOSING REMARKS

Where to from here?

At this point in the strategic planning process, the organization has defined its industry and has defined itself in the industry. The next step is to organize these issues into opportunities and challenges (threats) in the industry and strengths and weaknesses in the organization, and then match them all together in one process that will point the way to the best possible decision.

TERMS INTRODUCED IN THE CHAPTER

Environment Everything outside the organization, including but not limited to birds and fish. The business environment has many dimensions.

Remote Economic, social, political and technological issues that impact the entire economic and social system.

Industry New entrants, substitutes, buyers, suppliers and rivals which determine the level of competition an industry generates.

Local Customers, competitors, creditors, employees, suppliers and ecological issues which govern how things go in the neighbourhood.

Profile The mixture of skills and resources that an organization brings to its daily business of meeting the needs of stakeholders.

QUESTIONS FOR CLASS DISCUSSION

1. If you were helping a manufacturer of compact disks (just the blank disks) write their strategic plan, which environmental issues do you think should be clearly understood and factored into the plan?
2. For each of the five forces of industry competition, identify a company that is **most significantly impacted** by a particular force and comment on how you think they should deal with that force. (You will have one scenario for each of the five forces. For example, identify a company most impacted by the power of suppliers and identify how that company should deal with supplier power.)
3. Identify the remote environmental factors that have impacted the airline industry recently and comment on what you think it should do in response to those events.
4. At a busy intersection in your city, there are four gas stations. Comment on the power of competitive rivalries and offer examples of what these rivals will do to each other.
5. At that same busy intersection, if you could be a consultant to all four gas station owners, what would you suggest they do?

A CASE FOR STRATEGIC PLANNING: MALCOLM AND RUBY'S NEXT STEP

Ruby is so excited. She found a location for the manufacturing process. (Malcolm's old shop just wouldn't be big enough. After all, she is going to take over the world!)

Ruby signed a ten-year lease on a plant in the industrial park just outside of town. She began ordering equipment and placing ads in national newspapers, looking for the right management team.

Ruby and Malcolm had breakfast about a week ago. Malcolm was trying to get Ruby to do some planning using this amazing new strategic planning model he read about. The model suggested they make a list of environmental issues as well as organizational issues. Then they could take their issues and define them as environmental opportunities and threats and organizational… "Enough!" said Ruby. "I don't have time for this. Onward and upward. Never look back. Dad, I think you're turning into one of your plants."

"There is nothing wrong with being cautious," said Malcolm. "Just try this for a few minutes, please."

They started to list the environmental issues, just like the book said. When they got to about the 10th item on the list, Ruby said, "I see what you mean. This is a very valuable tool. In fact, on our list already I see that 6 of the 10 items are terrific opportunities. Well, gotta go." Ruby then went and leased the building and ordered the equipment and started placing ads.

REQUIRED:

Malcolm has come to you for help. He thinks Ruby's enthusiasm is going to destroy them. He needs you to show him how the environment and profile should be examined for his company so he can show Ruby what they should be doing. Develop a list of issues for Malcolm so he can show Ruby.

CHAPTER ENDING CASE: A CASE ABOUT THE 5 FORCES OF COMPETITION

Walter Bradley is the third generation of his family to be the chief executive officer of the family lightbulb-making business. "Bradley Bulbs are Better" has been the motto since Walter's grandfather designed a process that enabled the low-cost mass production of lightbulbs. Within two years, Bradley Bulbs enjoyed 60% of the Canadian lightbulb market.

The family has done very well with the business. Walter's father and Walter himself heeded Grandpa Bradley's advice. Grandpa said, "This business works, leave it alone, and don't do anything stupid. People will need lightbulbs forever so just do what I did and you will be successful."

Walter's son, William, a recent graduate of a college business program, approached his father and said, "Have you noticed our sales are down 45%, that we are losing our wholesale customers, that consumers are buying the new halogen and fluorescent lights?" "Yes," Walter replied, "I noticed, the sales manager told me, but I think he is just getting lazy. He also told me that while sales are down, we now hold 72% of the incandescent bulb market, so in fact we are doing better than the competition! This confused me a bit so I don't want to change anything right now until I figure it out. Grandpa said not to do anything and that people will need lightbulbs forever. That was good advice for my father, it's good advice for me and it will be good advice for you. This sales decline is just temporary and as soon as I figure this out we will be back on track. We are using the same process with the same tools Grandpa used, and in fact over 90% of the people in the factory have been there for more than 25 years, doing the same thing. I am not about to change now."

William decided to try and get his father's attention by preparing an analysis of the new business environment. He has decided to use Porter's model of five forces. This is important to William. He wants to inherit something of value!

REQUIRED:

Give William some advice on how he should start this exercise, how detailed he needs to be, how wide the range of issues is he should examine and how he might present this information to his father.

CHAPTER 4

Critical Success Factors

I used to be indecisive, but now I'm not so sure.

LEARNING OBJECTIVES

After reading this chapter, engaging in class discussion and doing the exercises at the end of the chapter, you will be able to:

1. Organize issues raised in the environmental analysis of the previous chapter into "Opportunities" and "Challenges or Threats."
2. Organize the issues raised in the analysis of the organizational profile into "Strengths" and "Weaknesses."
3. Use a SWOT analysis to compare and contrast opportunities and challenges with strengths and weaknesses
4. Identify the set of issues that represents "Critical Success Factors" for an organization.
5. Arrive at a conclusion from the SWOT analysis as to what the overall grand strategy should be for an organization.

YOUR RESPONSIBILITY

To get the most from Chapter 4, you need to develop your understanding of how people and organizations deal with their environments by using their strengths to take advantage of opportunities and reduce the impact of their threats.

Study a sports team or an elite athlete. How did they get to be perfect? At some point in their development, they must have decided **what they wanted to be**, found out **what was needed** to be one, figured out **what they were lacking** and set about to **get what they didn't have**, **develop what they did have** and **worked towards their goal**.

It has been proven over and over again that to be an elite athlete you need focus, commitment and good information about your sport.

The same holds for a business.

INTRODUCTION TO CHAPTER 4

Recall the planning model introduced in Chapter 1. In Figure 4.1 below, we have moved the highlight to "Defining Critical Success Factors." Once we know what is critical for the environment and for our own organizational profile, we will be able to set long- and short-range goals, which we will do in Chapter 5.

FIGURE 4.1 The Planning Model

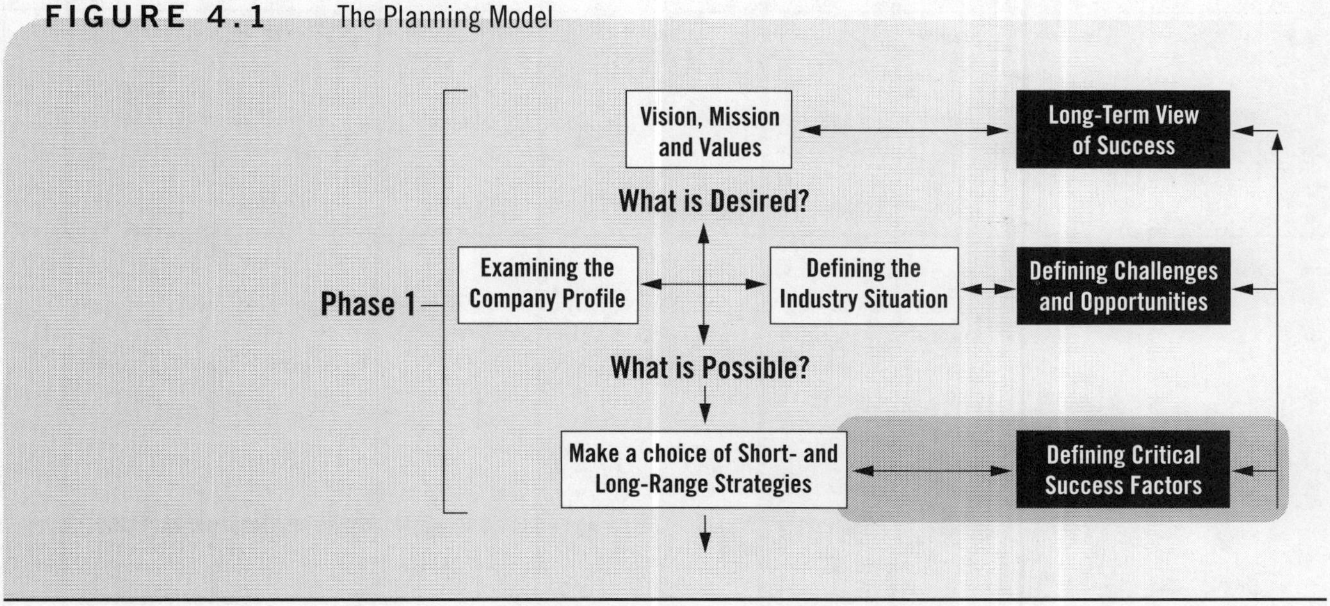

To recap where we are in the planning model: In Chapter 2, we developed some clarity around what we want to accomplish with the development of "Vision" and "Mission" statements. In Chapter 3, we discovered some information for "what we need" to deal with our environment and "what we have" to deal with our environment. Now, in Chapter 4, we need to interpret and act on our discoveries from Chapter 3.

DEFINING CRITICAL SUCCESS FACTORS

To make choices regarding long-range and short-range goals, we need to define the areas where change is possible and desirable. Those areas are called "Critical Success Factors." The factors represent the aspects of the environment at all three levels (remote, industry and local) that are opportunities for business success, and challenges or threats to business success. In addition, there are factors in the organizational profile that represent strengths that should be used to advantage and weaknesses that should be corrected.

At this point, we have a long list of issues from the analysis of the environment and the organizational profile, but they are just issues waiting for further analysis. An issue becomes a critical factor when a failure to act on that factor results in missed opportunities for prosperity or missed opportunities to correct weaknesses. As in the environmental analysis, we view factors in the context of their impact on the organization. Therefore, the critical factors are those that will have the most significant impact if we fail to act.

The model for this analysis was introduced in Chapter 3. The overview of the model is reproduced below for convenience.

FIGURE 4.2 What Do We Have, What Do We Need?

Matching the Profile to the Environment		
Examining the Environment	Matching what needs to be done ← With what can be done → In all aspects of the business	**Examining the Organizational Profile**
What do we need to succeed?		What do we have to offer?
What makes the industry work?		What strengths do I have, and what weaknesses must I overcome?

Earlier it was suggested that this analysis involves making tradeoff decisions, prioritizing issues and developing action plans that are consistent with the findings of this analysis.

To take this analysis to a new level of complexity, Figure 4.3 identifies how the model relates to more specific dimensions of the organization.

FIGURE 4.3 Matching the Profile to the Environment

Matching the Profile to the Environment		
Examining the Environment	**Doing an independent and honest review of each aspect**	**Examining the Organizational Profile**
Determining the level of competence required to operate effectively in this environment as to:		Determining the level of competence the organization has as to:
Marketing and sales	Matching what needs to be done ← With what can be done → In all aspects of the business	Marketing and sales
Production		Production
Financial Management		Financial Management
Research and Development		Research and Development
Human Resource Management		Human Resource Management

To make informed choices, we must deal with the organization in as many dimensions as possible, not losing sight of the fact that all the various dimensions need our attention. If we are good at production and nothing else, we had better find a way to get the marketing, financial and human resources cared for, otherwise we fail.

ON THIS TOPIC

A Real-World Example

New York Seltzer was the first soft drink to enter the market with a soft drink that was clear, but came in multiple flavours.

Its advertising was brilliant, it covered the media, it put free samples on doorsteps, it created huge demand for its product. However, it did not have sufficient coverage at the wholesale and retail distribution end.

Everybody wanted the product but retailers weren't carrying it. Demand went unmet until substitute products entered the market and capitalized on the demand that had been created by New York Seltzer.

ANALYZING THE ENVIRONMENT, OPPORTUNITIES AND CHALLENGES/ THREATS

The Terms Defined

Opportunities present themselves in all three levels of the environment. An opportunity is something that, if taken, **will** result in something positive for the organization. The range of opportunities is unlimited: opportunities for new customers, cost savings, a secure future, improved public perception, reduced probability of loss of life or personal injury etc. The bottom line is that if you do not respond to an opportunity, or if your response is ineffective, the positive outcome that could have come your way is gone.

A challenge/threat is quite different. Out of the environment, something with a negative consequence to your organization **is going to happen** unless you act in some way. You can act to eliminate the threat entirely, or to reduce the impact or likelihood of a threat, but a failure to act means that you are willing to accept the negative consequence.

You can ignore opportunity, and you might survive, but you can't ignore challenges/threats unless you have lots of resources to be able to lose!

I have had some difficulty with clients trying to identify their threats. While we all agree on what a threat is, we need to further clarify the term we use to describe negative consequences coming from the environment. Many authors refer to the potential for negative consequences as "threats," using the single term. I prefer to use both terms, challenges and threats, to describe these issues because, to me, something is threatening if you don't have the ability to respond to the threat, and something is challenging if you do have a response ready. It is a matter of positive thinking. If a boxer feels challenged, he will try hard and rise to the occasion. If a boxer feels threatened, he will make mistakes and lose the fight, or not fight at all.

What Goes First, Environment or Profile?

Now that we are about to turn our list of environmental issues into opportunities and challenges/threats and our profile issues into strengths and weaknesses, there is one major point to make about the order we choose: it is very difficult to distinctly separate the environment from the profile because some issues in the environment will be a challenge to the organization that lacks strength, while the same issue might be an opportunity to an organization that has a strength in that area.

Many people argue that they can't understand their strengths until they know what is in the environment. Others argue that they can't assess the environment until they know their strengths and weaknesses. The truth is that the two sets of analyses are so closely linked that they must be done almost simultaneously, letting discoveries from each part of the process alter perceptions from the other part of the process, so that at the end, a realistic opinion evolves.

To begin, we will examine the three levels of the environment first. Then arrive at some conclusions about the profile and finally, merge the two together.

THE REMOTE ENVIRONMENT: OPPORTUNITIES AND CHALLENGES/THREATS

The remote environment contains issues that impact all industries and all the organizations in the industries. Those issues are largely out of the direct control of the organization or the industry in which the organization exists. An example is the federal taxation system.

We must determine the extent to which these issues impact the industry and specifically, our organization.

The remote environment consists of economic, social, political and technological dimensions. In Chapter 3, we developed a list of issues that fit each of the dimensions. To determine if an issue represents an opportunity or a challenge (threat), we need to have some basic knowledge of the industry we are working with. For example, economic issues will impact the recreation industry differently than vegetable growers.

We will take the issues raised in Chapter 3 and examine their impact relative to the industry we are in to try to categorize the issue as an opportunity or a challenge (threat).

Using the ski area example introduced in Chapter 3, we would examine the remote environmental issues as follows:

FIGURE 4.4 The Remote Environment for a Ski Area

Remote Environment for a Ski Area			
	Description	**o/t**	**Explanation**
Economic	The amount of disposable income available for recreation, in the hands of customers.	T	Disposable income is declining and as an exclusive ski resort our package is too expensive. Sales have declined.
Social	The perception of people regarding health and wellness and the use of recreation to achieve those ends.	O	As the personal need for exercise increases, demand for skiing should also increase.
Political	Government regulations regarding development of parkland and the environmental impact of the development of recreation areas.	T	The provincial government has embarked on a very aggressive promotion trying to bring new ski area developers to the province. Large land reserves have been rezoned because recreational and tax relief is being given to new developers.
Technological	Internet-based advertising systems and reservation systems.	O	Our industry is just beginning to attract customers from world markets for destination, exclusive ski resorts because of the impact of the Internet.

The classification of opportunity (O) or challenge/threat (T) is a matter of judgment, and related specifically to this particular business in this particular industry. Perhaps in another region of the country, a decline in disposable income would have no effect on a particular ski area. The point is that if the analysis is thorough and realistic, then recognizing an opportunity or threat should be very informative for the planning process.

There is also some question about whether or not the issues relate to the remote environment or the industry environment. Sometimes the distinction is a little grey. Politicians sometimes create industry opportunities and sometimes technological change is generated by the efforts of an entire industry. Don't worry too much at this point about clarifying the distinction. It will either become clearer later in the analysis or the lack of distinction will continue. Either way, there is no harm in being a little confused about the category.

THE INDUSTRY ENVIRONMENT: OPPORTUNITIES AND CHALLENGES/THREATS

The industry environment contains issues that directly impact an entire industry and all the competitors in that industry. Those issues could be influenced by the efforts of all organizations in the industry. An example would be the health and safety regulations that apply to everyone in an industry.

We must determine the extent to which these issues impact the organization and examine the strength of the industry to combine efforts to change these issues.

As with the remote environment, the classification of opportunity or challenge/threat is often subjective. Some knowledge or assumptions about the organization's strength and weaknesses is needed to clarify the classification. For example, the issue of substitute products might be relatively weak for a maker of automotive CD players and relatively strong for a maker of automotive cassette players.

To the customer, both these businesses are in the "music in my car" industry. In the total industry, there has been cooperation in standardizing the technology used to produce and read CDs, but there may be new technology on the horizon that makes the CD redundant and still provides "music in my car." The maker of cassettes has a substitute that already exists and the CD maker has a substitute on the horizon.

A similar type of analysis would take place for each of the five forces as they relate to a particular industry.

Following from Figure 3.7 in Chapter 3 where "what makes the forces powerful" was discussed, here is an example of how the analysis might be applied to the ski area.

FIGURE 4.5 Opportunities and Challenges from the Five Forces Applied to the Recreation Industry (Ski Area)

Force	Issue	o/t	Explanation
Substitute products Alternatives to skiing that provide recreation needs to customers	Demand is high for the total industry relative to supply	T	If a person's need for fitness or recreation products can't be met by your industry, they will look to other industries to meet their needs.
		O	On the other hand, this signals room for expansion for you.
	Customers are not product sensitive	T	If customers are ***very*** attracted to filling the need but are indifferent as to how the need will be filled, then a substitute product will be successful. A person's need for recreation can be satisfied with a very diverse set of products.
New entrants to the market Recreation providers of ***all types*** who want to join the market	Profits are low	O	This industry is characterized by big investment and fairly low profits. This is an opportunity to those already in the market because few competitors are attracted to join the industry.
	Large capital investment is required	O	The large capital investment is a powerful barrier to new entrants, therefore existing competitors see this as an opportunity to continue in their marketplace.
	Demand exceeds supply in the industry for the product or service	T	Perhaps not ski areas, but the recreation industry in total has demand exceeding supply. Ski areas need to be concerned about golf courses and tennis clubs, which fill the need for recreation.
Buyers Customers range from transient single day skiers to travel agents buying bulk accommodation packages	Buying groups are formed	T	Travel agents doing block bookings will drive the price down or they will go to other suppliers.
	The buyers are brand sensitive	O	High-end ski areas have a clientele that likes their mountain and likes the service they get and they are unlikely to switch unless an attractive alternative comes along.

Force	Issue	o/t	Explanation
Suppliers Suppliers include travel agents, fuel and electricity, highways, food and chair lifts etc.	There are a large number of travel agents	O	Travel agents have limited power because there are thousands of them, and in fact the Internet is rapidly replacing what they do.
	There are a small number of suppliers of chair lifts and equipment	T	These suppliers are very powerful. Because of limited supply, they call the shots on price and availability.
Rivalries Among Ski Areas Ski areas situated close enough to each other that they are attractive to the same group of customers	Industry profits are low	T	Ski areas depend on customers, fixed costs are high, operating costs are high. Each area will aggressively try to attract customers from the whole recreation industry, not just other ski areas.
	Customer growth rate is high	O	As a demographic, more people are enjoying recreation because they have more leisure time (but not more disposable income) and they are enjoying recreation in later years of their lives due to improved lifestyle.
	Customers are not brand sensitive	T	Among ski areas there is some brand sensitivity, but in the whole recreation industry, customers are fickle. If the snow is no good, they will play tennis or golf.
	Switching costs are high	T	A ski area can only be used for skiing and unless you find ways to attract customers in the off-season, you are limited to winter and the weather is the most important contributor to your revenue stream.

From this analysis, you can see that the ski area faces a very broad range of issues. You can also see, referring to Figure 3.7 in Chapter 3, that not all the issues raised were analyzed in this example. That is because we only deal with the issues that are relevant to a ski area in the recreation industry.

It is also logical that you might disagree with some of my classifications of issues as to opportunity or challenge/threat. In practice, this type of analysis would take place in an open discussion involving a broad cross-section of people from the organization. No issue would be classified until it had been thoroughly discussed and there was consensus about its classification.

THE LOCAL ENVIRONMENT: OPPORTUNITIES AND CHALLENGES/THREATS

The local environment contains issues that impact each individual organization in the industry: how the organization deals with customers, other organizations, and the rest of the stakeholder groups, where those issues could be influenced by the direct efforts of a single organization. An example would be the access to suppliers of your product or the advertising you and your competitors choose to do.

We must determine the extent to which these issues impact our organization, and the strength of the organization in managing these issues.

In Chapter 3, Figure 3.10, "Characteristics Of The Local Environment" was introduced to demonstrate the breadth of issues in the local environment. The figure identified issues in the local environment and then proposed that analysis would begin by posing some questions about the issue.

To classify the issue as an opportunity or a challenge/threat, we need to answer those questions. At this level of analysis, the distinction between the environment and the profile of a company becomes very slight. It would be very difficult to answer the questions without a working knowledge of the profile. In most cases, we would call it an organizational weakness if we couldn't answer one of the questions because they need to be answered.

Following from Figure 3.10 in Chapter 3, I have selected one question from each of the areas of concern to demonstrate how the analysis might be done.

FIGURE 4.6 Characteristics of the Local Environment

Analyzing the Local Environment				
Issue		**Questions and Answers**	**o/t**	**Explanation**
Customers	**Demographic**	Do the features of the product match the demographic of the market? *Yes, R&D has done a great job of product design.*	**O**	Having the right product is critical. Now we just have to market it effectively.
Competitive Position	**Product Quality**	Do customers perceive the product as high value for the price paid? *No, feedback is that our price is too high.*	**T**	They will go to the competition or a substitute.
Creditors	**Financial Claims**	Are creditors willing to let the loan serve its purpose? *No, they are constantly pressuring us for principal repayment.*	**T**	Losing flexibility in our financing is very detrimental.
Employees	**Availability**	Can the organization attract and hold the right people? *Yes, we have a loyal and skilled workforce.*	**O**	Having confidence in our people makes us confident in our goals.
Suppliers	**Quantity**	Are suppliers able to meet your present and future demand for their products? *No, the suppliers total industry is failing.*	**T**	Huge threat. Unless we can find a new industry to supply, or integrate and be our own suppliers, we are dead.
Ecological Issues	**Impact**	Does a change in the season or a change in the weather impact your operations? *No, we can operate efficiently no matter the season or weather, (except extreme weather).*	**O**	Not depending on the physical environment is a huge advantage. As long as we can create revenues, those revenues will not be interrupted by natural forces.

Continuing with the ski area example introduced in Chapter 3, the following table presents answers to the questions and classifies the issues.

FIGURE 4.7 Analyzing the Local Environment for a Ski Area

Analyzing the Local Environment for a Ski Area				
Issue		Answers to the Local Environment Questions		
		Response	o/t	Explanation
Customers	Geographic	80% of our skiers come from the local market.	T	We are seen by our customers as a community hill, not the high-end destination we want to be.
	Demographic	The average age of our skiers is 51.	T	Not the profile of our target customer.
	Psychographic	Most of our customers look out the window in the morning to make their buying decision.	T	Not the profile of our target customer.
Competitive Position	Breadth of the Product Line	There has been a 25% increase in snowboarders in the last two years.	O	The marketplace is changing which means we can change too.
	Product Quality	87% of skiers are very satisfied with the terrain and the maintenance of the runs.	O	Our physical location is good.
	Advertising Effectiveness	Travel magazines are the most effective medium for our target market.	O	We have ready access to several travel magazines.
	Production Efficiencies	We are in line with industry on hourly operating costs.	O	Our ski operations are efficient.
	Financial Efficiencies	Our operating profits are 30% below industry average.	T	Our restaurant, rentals, lessons and après ski are not efficient.
Creditors	Financial Claims	Creditors are willing to invest in the growth of the industry.	O	Our creditors can be our partners during growth.
Employees	Quality	Customers view our employees as surly and uncaring.	T	We hire poor quality people.
	Availability	Our employee turnover is twice the industry average.	T	There is no incentive to stay.
	Cost	Our wages are 20% less than industry average.	T	Cheap people are not necessarily good people.

Analyzing the Local Environment for a Ski Area				
Issue		Answers to the Local Environment Questions		
		Response	o/t	Explanation
Suppliers	**Quality, Quantity, Timeliness, Cost**	There is a ready market of suppliers for everything we need.	**O**	We can easily acquire what we need to change operations.
Ecological Issues	**Impact**	In the last 50 years, 10 years presented insufficient snow to open the chairlifts.	**T**	Our environment is not reliable.

By the end of this process, an organization should have a clear understanding of its environmental situation.

Before any action can be taken on these discoveries, we need to identify the issues in the profile of the organization, label the issues as strengths or weaknesses and match them to the discoveries in the environment.

THE ORGANIZATIONAL PROFILE, STRENGTHS AND WEAKNESSES

The "profile" of an organization is the list of characteristics owned and controlled by the organization that it uses to meet its marketplace. In addition, the profile is another list of things the organization doesn't own or control that it should have to meet the needs of its marketplace.

The profile is defined through identifying what an organization has or doesn't have, as being a strength or a weakness. We need to understand strength and weakness before we can proceed.

The textbook definitions read:

- A strength refers to a situation in which an organization can, with little effort and no additional investment of time or resources, respond to a situation with the results of the response equal to or better than the results achieved in other organizations in the industry.
  A strength means you are already equipped to handle the situation and you are using state of the art procedures.
- A weakness refers to a situation in which an organization must invest resources to acquire the ability to respond to a situation, and it is uncertain if, as a result of responding to the situation, the response will achieve the minimum standard set by the industry
  A weakness means you don't have the tools to deal with the issue.

The practical definition is:

- A strength is something you have that you need,
- A weakness is something you don't have that you need.

Things that you have and don't need are waste, and things that you don't have that you don't need are irrelevant.

What you "need" is defined by the analysis of the environment, what you have is defined by an analysis of your profile and what you have and don't need can be abandoned. You should not acquire things you don't need.

Figure 3.13 from Chapter 3 introduced the second step in profiling an organization. This step was to generate a list of potential issues. Now we need to take the next step, which is to identify each issue as a strength or weakness.

I have selected one from each category of the list of issues from Chapter 3 to demonstrate how the analysis might take place. Every organization will be unique in the issues raised, and every organization will be unique as to why the issues are strengths or weaknesses.

The results are in the following table (Figure 4.8):

FIGURE 4.8 Step 3 in Profiling an Organization: A Partially Complete Organizational Profile

Major Areas	Potential Issues	S/W	Explanation
Strategic	Planning Quality of long- and short-range objectives	S	We hired a college graduate to facilitate the development of goals.
Marketing	Market share	W	We hold a small market share of a rapidly growing market. We are not growing at the same rate.
Financial and Accounting	Profitability	S	We earn a rate of return that is significantly higher than the industry average.
Production, Operations and Technical	Efficiency of production processes	S	Our unit production costs are lower than industry average because we have state of the art machinery and equipment.
Human Resource Management	Union/Management relationship	W	Four of the last five rounds of negotiations were resolved after a work stoppage, two strikes and two lockouts.
Organization and Management	Willingness of management to delegate tasks and authority	W	Management is willing to hold others responsible and accountable, but they are not willing to delegate authority and control.

At this point, the picture is beginning to become clear. This organization has a good production process but some weaknesses in management practices. To make the picture even clearer we need to rank the strengths and weaknesses in priority order so that our most powerful strength is known and our most significant weakness is known.

Prioritizing can be difficult unless you consider the environment at the same time as you rank your profile issues in order. A strength is not a strength on its own. It is only a strength when it has been matched to a need in the environment.

A useful tool to help prioritize strengths and weaknesses is the "Stages of Industry Evolution."

Stages of Industry Evolution

In the study of marketing management we use the "Product Life Cycle" diagram to describe how products evolve through their lifespan in the marketplace. Products go through four phases, introduction, growth, maturity and decline. Marketing managers then develop strategies to make the introduction phase as short as possible, the growth phase as fast and as big as possible, the maturity phase as long as possible and the decline phase as unlikely as possible.

FIGURE 4.9 Product Life Cycle

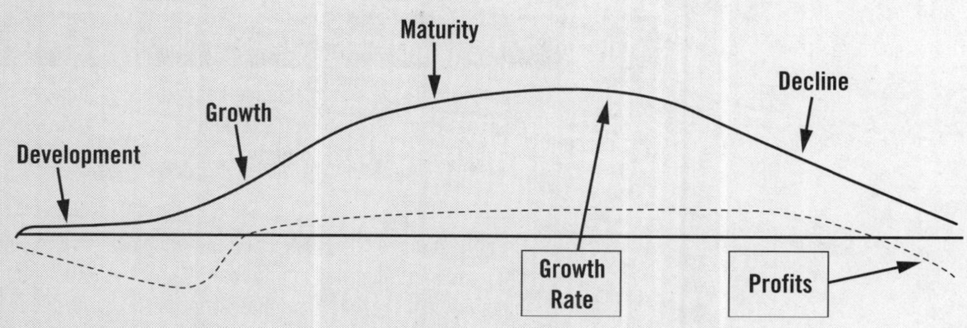

Note that in development and early growth, profits are usually negative. This is because of the large investment required to create awareness and gain access to distribution channels.

When products mature, we work to extend the life cycle by introducing product variants: "new and improved" or additional add-ons or features.

When products decline, we sell them off and start again with new products and new innovations.

The same logic holds for entire industries rather than just individual products in an industry. If we consider that an organization operates in an industry, and that industry has its own cycle of evolution, then we can pinpoint the critical factors that are needed to succeed at each phase of the industry evolution. We would then be able to match our organizational profile to those factors, which will help in planning.

Figure 4.10 illustrates the linkage between industry evolution and the factors that must be present in an organization to succeed in that stage of evolution.

FIGURE 4.10 Critical Success Factors at Each Stage of Industry Evolution

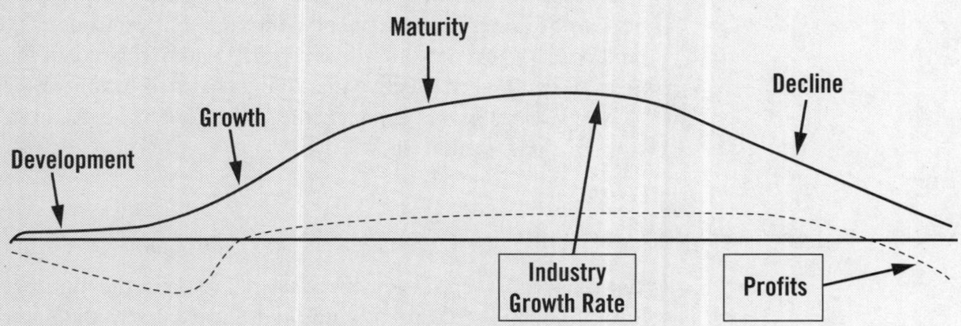

Function	Development	Growth	Maturity	Decline
Marketing & Sales	Create widespread awareness.	Establish brand recognition. Find effective marketing channels.	Hold existing markets and promote to new markets. Introduce successor products to extend maturity.	Focus on the best channels. Replace old products with new ones.
Finance	Finance initial R&D losses.	Finance expansion and net cash outflows.	Reinvest profits and employ cost controls.	Prune the product line and harvest the resources from liquidation.

Function	Development	Growth	Maturity	Decline
Production	Limit number of designs. Use standards.	Increase capacity while retaining quality.	Improve the product and reduce operating costs.	Redeploy unused equipment, simplify processes and reduce product variants.
R&D	Be able to make changes and take the bugs out.	Focus on quality and ability to make product variants to satisfy customers.	Improve processes to reduce costs and introduce successor products.	Commit resources to new growth products.
Human Resources	Be flexible in staffing and training.	Employ motivated and loyal workforce with excellent product knowledge and selling skills.	Reduce workforce and increase efficiency.	Reduce and reallocate personnel.
Focus Area	Engineering and Marketing	Sales and Market Share	Production Efficiency and Successors	Finance and Investment Recovery

To use Figure 4.10, we simply identify the position in the life cycle where our industry is situated, and then review (and add to it if necessary) the critical factors for that position in the cycle. Then we can match what needs to be done with our profile to see if those things can be done.

At the bottom of the table, the "Focus Area" identifies the two most important things that need to be done in that stage of evolution. For example, if you have a product that will replace CDs, you need to prove it works and that you can mass produce it (engineering). You need access to very effective marketing channels to quickly create widespread demand.

Many decision makers have found this tool to be useful in identifying and prioritizing their strengths and weaknesses.

Back To The Ski Area Example

Ten years ago, the ski industry appeared to be in the maturity phase of evolution. There was a loyal following of customers, and new customers to the market came mostly from people coming of age to ski. The growth rate of the industry was linked to population growth.

The industry has experienced recent dramatic growth by doing exactly what the figure above illustrates. Snowboarding as a successor product, advertising in world markets for worldclass resorts, and increasing the efficiency and capacity of chairlifts have all contributed to extending the maturity of the industry and, in fact, creating new growth.

DEFINING ORGANIZATIONAL CRITICAL FACTORS

Now that we have examined the environment and the profile of the organization, it is time to match what needs to be done with what can be done in all aspects of the business. The result of this analysis will be the definition of critical success factors.

In the analysis of the organizational profile, a variety of strengths and weaknesses were identified. A SWOT (strength, weakness, opportunities and threats) diagram is a useful tool to match the profile to the environment so that choices can be made.

A SWOT diagram is illustrated as follows:

FIGURE 4.11 SWOT Diagram

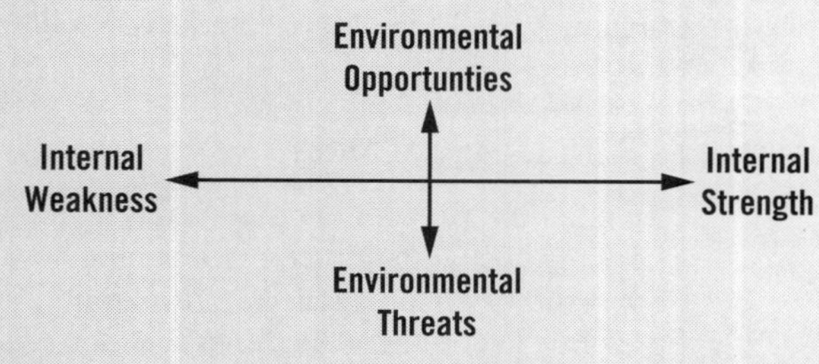

In order to conduct the analysis, you simply place the strengths and weaknesses discovered in the analysis of the organizational profile along the horizontal axis. Then take the opportunities and threats discovered at each level of the environmental analysis and place them on the vertical axis. Finally, use the diagram to locate your organization in one of the four cells.

FIGURE 4.12 SWOT Analysis

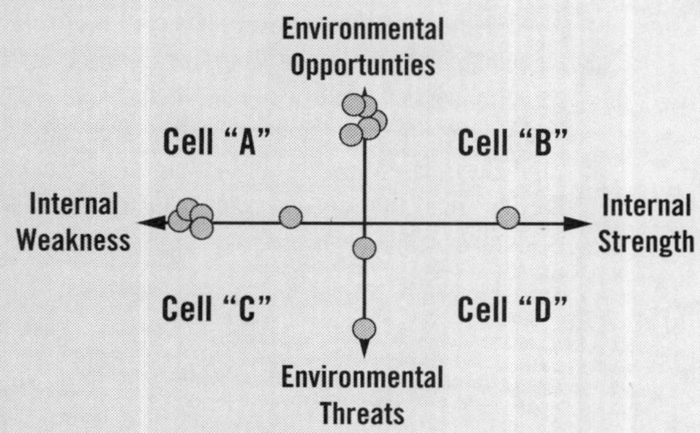

The placement of the dots represents the level of significance or priority of each of the issues. The above organization would place itself in "Cell A" to develop its primary plan and would use "Cell C" to help focus attention on its challenges/threats.

This is a good time to go back to the findings of the environmental analysis and categorize all of the factors identified at each level as "opportunity" or "threat."

An opportunity is a condition presented by the environment, which will result in lost benefits if not acted upon. A threat is a condition presented by the environment, which will also result in lost benefits if not acted upon. The difference between opportunities and threats is that if you fail to take advantage of an opportunity you will continue to have what you already have. If you fail to deal with a threat, you may lose what you already have. It is therefore important to act on both opportunities and threats.

Placing your organization in one of the cells in a SWOT analysis enables you to choose a "Grand Strategy," which is a very broad governing principle of where the organization should be going. This is then further refined into strategic goals.

FIGURE 4.13 The "Cells" of a SWOT Diagram

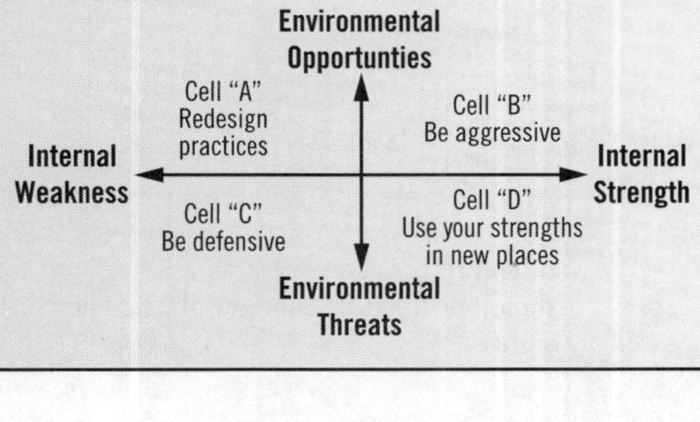

The cells represent a very broad indication of the courses of action available to your organization. The cells are described as follows:

Cell "A" Grand Strategy, "Redesign Practices"

An organization with internal weakness that is facing an industry with numerous opportunities must focus attention on redesigning how business is done to effectively capture the opportunities. This is called a "Turnaround" strategy because the organization takes what it presently has, reduces the things that don't meet the opportunity, creates new things that do meet the opportunity and changes how the organization functions.

ON THIS TOPIC

A Real-World Example

When Apple Computers began to create huge demand for home and educational computers, IBM was far behind. At that time IBM was known as "Big Blue," a mainframe computer company capable of producing giant computing machines for only the most sophisticated business user.

IBM changed their strategy completely, losing the Big Blue image and replacing it with the personal computer image. They began this transformation by recognizing what was needed — personal service, well-designed product, mass marketing etc. Then they recognized what they had — excellent engineering skills, large capital resources and production capacity — and what they didn't have — marketing expertise, consumer confidence, a working product. Then they got what they needed, used what they had, abandoned what they didn't need and the rest is history.

www.ibm.com

Other Cell "A" Strategies

Retrenchment/Turnaround

- Sell or otherwise reduce some portion of the organization and use the money raised in the sale or saved from closing part of the operation to reinvest in a portion of the organization that will continue. (Sell off or close an unprofitable portion of the organization and expand the profitable portion).

Joint Venture

- Join forces with an organization that has the strengths that are your weaknesses so that the combined venture has a better chance of succeeding. (An engineering company with a new invention but no marketing skills or access to distribution channels could join forces with a marketing and distribution company).

Strategic Alliance

- Two companies join forces for a particular customer but remain independent for other customers. A software company with a new point of sale system for hardware stores could form a strategic alliance with a cash register company to bundle their products together to form a turnkey package. Each company would remain independent when dealing with their other customers.

Cell "B" Grand Strategy, "Be Aggressive"

An organization with internal strengths that is facing an industry with numerous opportunities would expand operations into new markets, invest in growth and reproduce success in other areas. Aggressive strategies are born from the realization that the organization is doing the right things in the right places. Therefore, it can proceed with confidence and multiply its success.

ON THIS TOPIC ***A Real-World Example***

For example, McDonalds® has been highly successful in their market for many years, therefore they have focused on growth in new geographic regions, such as Russia and China, and they have focused on new retailing techniques, e.g., McDonalds Express™, and partnerships with WalMart.®

www.mcdonalds.com

Microsoft® is an excellent example of an aggressive strategic organization. Their rocketing success has been a result of being willing to take a risk, make the required investments and push the organization forward.

www.microsoft.com

Other Cell "B" Strategies

Product development

- Add life to an existing product by offering an enhancement or a new attachment. "New and Improved" or "Version 2" often repeats the buying decision from the same market, and it serves the needs of new customers entering the market.

Market development

- Find new geographic regions, or new demographics in the same region to expand the market size. The product is good, customers are satisfied. We are just looking for more of them.

Vertical Integration

- Take on an activity that is a neighbour on the marketing channel. A retailer goes into the manufacturing business or a manufacturer opens a factory outlet retail store.

Cell "C" Grand Strategy, "Be Defensive"

An organization with internal weakness that is facing an industry with numerous threats needs to reevaluate whether or not it is advisable to stay in business. It is a tough road when you need to shore up the organization to take on an industry that keeps delivering more challenges.

ON THIS TOPIC ***A Real-World Example***

For example, Eatons recently tried to meet a very demanding marketplace with an organization that was in need of major overhaul. The result was the failure of the business.

On the other hand, the Chrysler Corporation faced a similar scenario when Lee Iacocca became president. The difference is that Chrysler™ was able to become a market leader and change a threatening environment into an environment filled with opportunities, at the same time changing the practices of the business to meet the new environment.

The result was the most successful turnaround in history!

www.chrysler.com

Other Cell "C" Strategies

Divestiture

- Sell a portion of the organization and use the proceeds of the sale to increase the solvency of the surviving portion of the organization or to return investment to owners so that the risk is reduced. The forest products company sells the video store and uses the proceeds to reduce outstanding debts against the forest product company.

Liquidation

- Assets are sold for cash and the creditors are paid. Anything left after creditor claims is returned to owners. All is lost, there is no hope, you are out of business.

Cell "D" Grand Strategy, "Use Your Strengths in New Places"

An organization with internal strengths that is facing an industry with numerous threats should evaluate whether or not its expertise could be transferred to a new, less threatening environment.

ON THIS TOPIC

A Real-World Example

For example, gas stations used to consist of an auto repair shop and gas pumps. Some had a few chocolate bars and soft drinks. The automobile repair industry began to change when repair shops opened without the gas bar. These included brake and muffler shops, transmission repairs and radiator shops. The result was that demand for repairs at the local gas station declined.

Gasoline retailers realized they had a significant strength in retailing the gasoline, so they used their retail expertise to close the service bays, put in convenience stores and repackage the gas station as a place to refuel your car, and yourself. Some gas companies have found that the convenience store is more successful than the original gas bar!

Other Cell "D" Strategies

Horizontal Integration

- Buy up or open businesses like your own that serve the same market with a different approach and brand name. For example, a sportsbar owner opens a nightclub in the same neighbourhood.

Concentric Diversification

- Buy up or open businesses that are in a completely different industry than yours, but are a good investment. For example, a forest products company buys a video store.

CHAPTER SUMMARY

The objective of Chapter 4 was to define critical success factors. The factors refer to an industry and an organizational perspective.

The "stages of industry evolution" was introduced as a tool to pinpoint the critical success factors from an industry point of view. By matching the stage of the industry evolution to the success factors for that stage, we were able to develop the equivalent of a "shopping list" of things the organization needs to be able to do.

The SWOT diagram was introduced as a tool to match the industry critical success factors with the organizational profile developed in Chapter 3. This process pinpointed the factors that are critical from an organizational point of view.

The SWOT analysis placed the organization, matched to the environment, in a cell, which established a potential grand strategy for the organization. The grand strategy has set the foundation for the strategic goals.

At this point the analyst should be able to make statements like:

> *"Given that our health food industry is in its growth phase, and given that our company has strength in the necessary aspects of producing and marketing health food cookies, we will embark on a grand strategy of market and product development for the coming planning cycle which will put a healthy cookie in every jar in the country."*

Or perhaps

> *"Given that our current industry is in decline, and given that our company still has leading edge expertise in the manufacture of precision tools made of brass and stainless steel, we will embark on a grand strategy to redeploy our resources in a new industry that uses brass and stainless steel tools."*

In either case, the organization is ready to set long- and short-range goals, at a high level for corporate goals and at an operating level for functional goals. The cookie company will use the growth strategy to set goals that target improved market share and improved sales, while the tool business will set goals to attract new customers and design new products.

CLOSING REMARKS

This leads us to the final section of the planning model, developing "goals and action plans," in Chapter 5. Chapter 1 introduced an overview of goals and where they fit in the management process. Chapter 5 will deal with goals in much more detail.

TERMS INTRODUCED IN THE CHAPTER

Challenges Things presented by the environment that if they are not acted upon, negative consequences will flow to the organization.

Critical success factors Issues that must be monitored and managed in order for an organization to be successful.

Focus area The most important attributes an organization must have at each phase of industry evolution.

Grand strategies The product of a SWOT analysis, the grand strategy is the high-level, overall strategy an organization chooses to take.

Industry evolution Like the product life cycle, the transformation of an industry through development to growth, maturity and decline.

Opportunities Things presented by the environment that if they are acted upon, benefits will flow to the organization.

Strengths Things that an organization has and needs in order to be successful.

SWOT A diagram that matches strengths, weaknesses, opportunities and challenges/threats so that a choice of grand strategy can be made.

Threats Potential negative issues that the organization cannot deal with because it lacks the resources or a plan to deal with them.

Weaknesses Things that an organization does not have but needs in order to be successful.

QUESTIONS FOR CLASS DISCUSSION

1. If you were advising an airline on how to deal with its changing environment, what issues should be raised for analysis at each of the remote, industry and local levels and what order of priority would you place those issues in?
2. Given the fast food industry in today's marketplace, compare and contrast the strengths McDonalds and Subway bring to the industry.
3. Identify a company in an industry that is in the development phase of industry evolution and comment on whether or not that company has what it takes to be successful.
4. Identify a company in an industry that is in the growth phase of industry evolution and comment on whether or not that company has what it takes to be successful.
5. Identify a company in an industry that is in the maturity phase of industry evolution and comment on whether or not that company has what it takes to be successful.
6. Identify a company in an industry that is in the decline phase of industry evolution and comment on whether or not that company has what it takes to be successful.
7. Identify a company that has or is using a strategy from "Cell A" of the SWOT diagram and comment on what it is doing or has done to implement that grand strategy.
8. Identify a company that has or is using a strategy from "Cell B" of the SWOT diagram and comment on what it is doing or has done to implement that grand strategy.
9. Identify a company that has or is using a strategy from "Cell C" of the SWOT diagram and comment on what it is doing or has done to implement that grand strategy.
10. Identify a company that has or is using a strategy from "Cell D" of the SWOT diagram and comment on what it is doing or has done to implement that grand strategy.

A CASE FOR STRATEGIC PLANNING: MALCOLM AND RUBY'S NEXT STEP

Ruby is well on her way to starting production. The machinery is in place, materials are arriving daily (although some have to be returned because they don't fit the design, which also seems to be changing daily) and her advertising is really paying off. The phone is ringing off the hook. She doesn't want to turn anyone away so she is making promises for delivery that Malcolm knows she cannot meet.

In order to finance the construction of the plant, Ruby got some short-term financing but has now run that to the full extent and still needs $100,000 to finish the plant. Her $100,000 estimate is based on her intuition. (She didn't do well in accounting at college.)

Malcolm has also discovered that another company, "Homeshow," is about three months away from perfecting a system that is about the same as the "Movie Zap." He heard that Homeshow had been approached by the TV makers to consider including their technology in new TVs. He also heard that the Homeshow people were thinking seriously about selling the technology to the cable company and accepting a royalty on all units sold.

When Malcolm confronted Ruby with this information, Ruby was not surprised. "The head technician at Homeshow was in my robotics class at college. He thinks he has all my notes. He doesn't. Their machine won't work, I guarantee it!" Malcolm then asked if the papers had been returned regarding the patent on Movie Zap. Ruby said she had cancelled the patent application because a friend in law school told her that she would be better off spending the money on advertising. According to the law student, "the best protection in a market is customer awareness of your name."

REQUIRED:

Following from the issues raised in the case from Chapter 3, and incorporating any more issues you see from the above, organize the challenges, opportunities, strengths and weaknesses into a SWOT and make a choice of a grand strategy. Be prepared to challenge their decision to go into manufacturing themselves. Make a recommendation on the basis of the SWOT analysis.

CHAPTER ENDING CASE: A CASE ABOUT SWOT

Mallard Power Company has been working for the past 10 years on a process that transforms animal and human waste into electrical energy. The company got its start when Donald, an engineer, began researching the process using the waste produced by the ducks that inhabited a pond on his property. His original intention was to find an environmentally friendly way to dispose of the waste. It was during this research that he discovered that a byproduct of his process was electricity.

Donald patented the process and began soliciting anyone who would listen to see if there was a way he could get his product to market. Some were sceptical that the machine actually could reliably produce electricity, some were sceptical about the reaction of the public to the source of fuel, some were sceptical about how the machine could be mass produced and some were sceptical about the cost and profitability of the machine.

Everyone was sceptical for one reason or another. Nobody would listen.

For the past 10 years Donald, on a shoestring budget, has been running a small research and development company to work on various applications for his machine so he can demonstrate how it works in a variety of settings. Currently, interest has been expressed by the automobile industry, electric utilities and home improvement stores. All of whom might be wiling to make an investment on the condition that a working prototype can be shown.

Donald has one unit that produces electricity for his office, but the rest of his potential applications for the machine are all on paper or in his head.

REQUIRED:

Prepare a presentation to be made to a group of potential investors that would be a convincing argument for them to invest in the business. In your presentation, you might want to use the industry life cycle concepts to explain how an investment would be used and what investors could expect in return. You might also choose to use a SWOT analysis in your presentation.

CHAPTER 5

Setting Goals And Managing Change

My goal was to be perfect, and now I am.
Perfect in every way, perfect every day.
How did I do this?
Simple… every day I lower my expectations.

LEARNING OBJECTIVES

After reading this chapter, engaging in class discussion and doing the exercises at the end of the chapter, you will be able to:

1. Understand the notion of "Cascading Goals" as they relate to realizing grand strategies.
2. Develop a set of high-level corporate goals that reflect the strategic plan.
3. Develop a set of operating goals that reflect the corporate goals.
4. Develop a set of reasonable expectations around goals so they can be realized.
5. Develop basic measures to track the progress in achieving goals.
6. Understand the tradeoffs that must be made between competing goals.
7. Understand what links goals to performance improvement.

YOUR RESPONSIBILITY

To get the most from Chapter 5, you need to raise your awareness of goals in general. You have personal goals, government has goals, corporations have goals, in fact, having goals is a way of life…as is not reaching our goals!

Pay attention to goals going on around you. You will see them in slogans, "Satisfaction Guaranteed," or "Quality is Job 1," in newspaper headlines, "Air Canada Attempts Cost Savings," in advertising and annual reports.

There are two questions you should ask yourself when you see a goal.

1. Will the people working here be motivated by these words?
2. How will the organization know when the goal has been achieved? (What is the measure of accomplishment?)

INTRODUCTION TO CHAPTER 5

From the planning model introduced in Chapter 1, we have moved the highlight to the last aspect of planning: creating corporate and operating goals.

FIGURE 5.1 The Planning Model

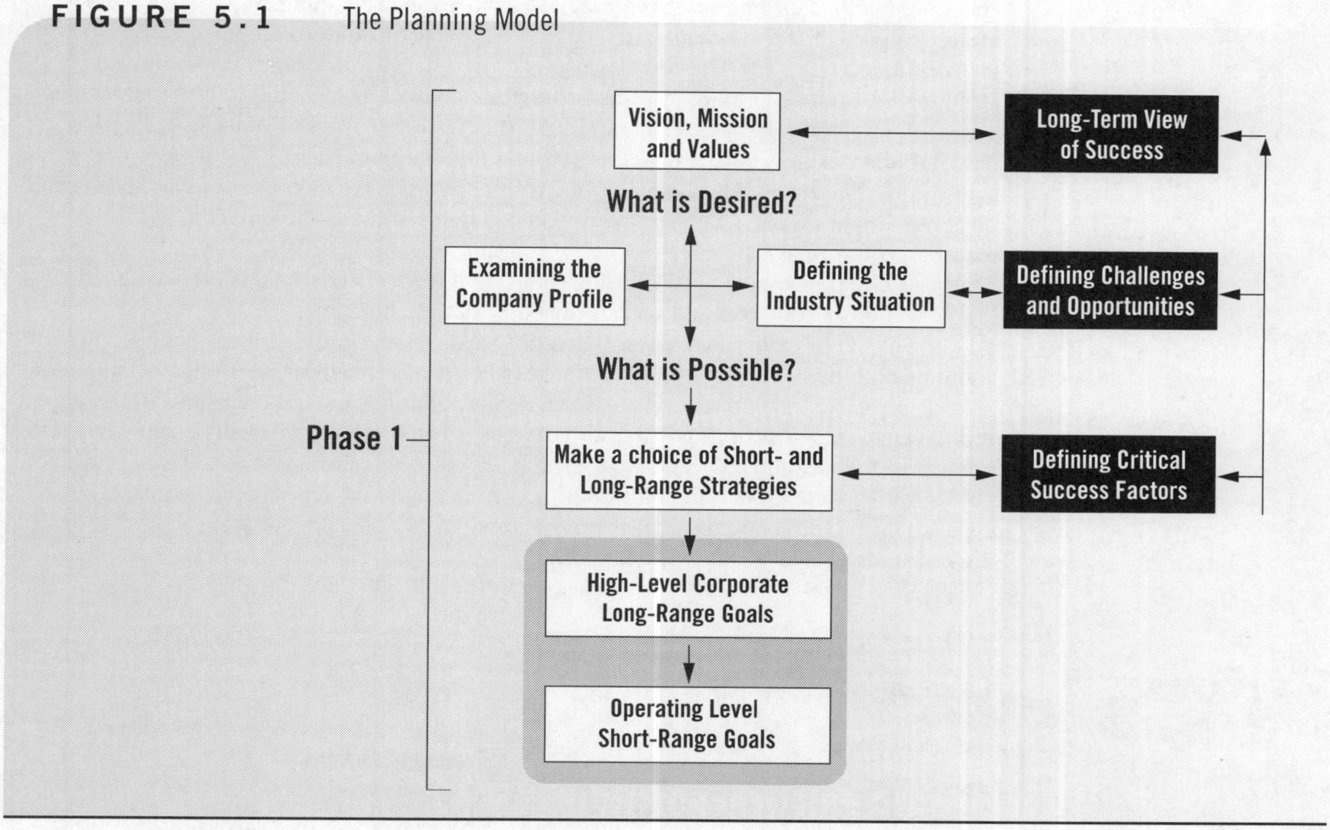

Goals were introduced in very basic terms in Chapter 1 to identify the goal of the planning process, which is to produce effective goals and to put into context where goals fit in the management cycle.

Now we will examine goals in much more detail.

SETTING CORPORATE AND OPERATING GOALS

The first order of business is to deal with a language problem. It seems authors can't agree on what a "goal" is relative to an "objective." Some define the goal as a subset of objectives; others do the opposite.

The following definitions will apply to this book:

Goal	A target for achievement that has a measure and a timeline
Objective	An outcome that will be achieved when goals are met

For example, a hockey team has an objective to win the game and a goal to score more points than the opposition. An objective is high level and results oriented; a goal is a step along the way to achieve the objective.

In an organization, the vision and mission and grand strategy represent the objective and the steps along the way are represented by a challenging and comprehensive set of goals. The most frequent criticism of the wording of a goal is that it lacks measurement. "To be a better person" is something we strive for but unless we are more specific about what dimension of ourselves we need to change to become a better person, we won't know if progress is being made. Perhaps "to be a better person" is more of an objective than a goal.

The "Grand Strategy" developed in Chapter 4 sets a framework for the goals that will govern operations for both the long-range and short-range planning cycles. The Grand Strategy represents the ultimate outcome that is expected from the combined achievement of the corporate-level goals. The corporate-level goals will be realized with the combined achievement of the operating-level goals. To create a visual image, imagine the champagne glasses at a wedding stacked in a pyramid. All the glasses are filled by pouring champagne only into the top glass. As the top glass becomes full, the champagne cascades into the glasses below until they are all filled. I tried this, and after wasting several bottles of champagne and breaking several glasses, I came to the conclusion that setting up the model so it will work requires professional expertise.

A well-designed model of "Cascading Goals" will work effectively; a poorly-designed model will waste resources and will not meet the desired outcome.

The concept of cascading goals is that at the top level, the grand strategy defines a general planning path that the organization will take over the next planning horizon. Out of that one guiding principle, corporate-level goals will define about five to ten dimensions of the organization where change is both possible and desirable. Those dimensions will become the focal points for organizational development for the next planning horizon. Each of those focal points will become the action items taken up by the operating departments where those departments might, between all of them, set hundreds of detailed operating goals that dissect the corporate goals into manageable pieces.

The path of cascading goals is represented in the following diagram:

FIGURE 5.2 Cascading Goals

Figure 5.2 represents a variety of concepts.

First, the grand strategy comes from the SWOT analysis from Chapter 4, (note the four quadrants).

Second, the corporate goals come from the high-level goals suggested in Chapter 1 (profit, sustainability etc.). The different shapes of the arrows at the corporate-goal level indicates that organizations will place different levels of importance on corporate goals, depending on their situation, but in general, some attention will be paid to all dimensions.

Finally, at the operating level, all the arrows are different sizes. Some intersect with other arrows, some stand alone in an operating area. Operating goals are specific outcomes tailored to each operating unit.

ON THIS TOPIC

A Real-World Example

Visit the Alcan Inc Web site at www.alcan.com

When you look at the corporate information, you will see Alcan has one grand strategy, "sustainability."

Alcan is so committed to sustainability that in addition to the traditional annual report, it publishes a "Sustainability Report" which is about the investment it makes in the community and the environment in order to enable its operation to continue.

Alcan cascades the sustainability concept through corporate goals in each of its business units through to operating goals in each functional area of each business unit.

Now that we have an overview of the cascading concept, let's take a more detailed view, beginning with the foundation of goals: the grand strategy.

GRAND STRATEGIES, THE FOUNDATION OF GOALS

Recall from Chapter 4 that at the grand strategy level, the SWOT analysis proposed four possible strategic paths coming from each of the cells in the SWOT analysis:

Cell "A" Redesign Practices
- Retrenchment/Turnaround
- Joint Venture
- Strategic Alliance

Cell "B" Be Aggressive
- Product Development
- Market Development
- Vertical Integration

Cell "C" Be Defensive
- Divestiture
- Liquidation

Cell "D" Use Strengths in New Places
- Horizontal Integration
- Concentric Diversification

From these grand strategies, senior management develops corporate-level goals, which call for change in an organization. The change being acted upon is clearly aligned to the grand strategy.

Goals define in specific **measurable terms** what end result will be delivered from **efficient and effective operations**. There is some confusion about the distinction between goals and vision. We know this because many organizations publish goals that are clearly not goals at all!

ON THIS TOPIC

A Real-World Example

The following were collected from various annual reports. All were cited as goals:

- To be the most efficient...in North America
- To improve over last year
- To maximize stockholder value
- To improve the morale of employees
- To increase public awareness
- To improve customer satisfaction

These are all important concepts, and if they are achieved, the organization will be better off. However, they are not useful goals until they are clarified further.

Goals must be distinctly measurable. A vision can be general and can lack measurement because a vision is a broad concept. A goal, on the other hand, needs to be measured because it is more than a concept, it is a framework for action, and as such the results of actions need to be measured. For example, from the list above, what evidence will you show in five years to prove that you have become the most efficient organization? What evidence will you show to prove that employee morale has improved?

The answers to these questions will be found when the grand strategy is translated into corporate-level goals and when the corporate-level goals are translated into operating goals.

CHARACTERISTICS OF ALL GOALS, CORPORATE OR OPERATING

All goals, whether they are high-level corporate goals or specific, action oriented operating goals, have the same basic characteristics. They must be S.M.A.R.T.

The SMART acronym refers to a test that should be applied to a goal before it can be accepted as a goal. The test is as follows.

Specific

- Does the goal provide specific expectations? Goals that are too general don't provide guidance to people.

Measurable

- Are the results of achieving the goals expressed in measurable terms so that progress towards achieving the goal can be tracked? If a goal cannot be measured, then it is probably a value or a vision, rather than a goal.

Authority

- Does someone have the authority to do anything about achieving the goal? There must be direct control over all of the characteristics of what we are trying to change. Otherwise, we can blame others when progress is not made.

Realistic

- Is the goal motivating and realistic? It is tempting to set stretch goals that can never be achieved because you believe that the far-reaching target will be motivating. The truth is that people stop trying to reach the unreachable star out of frustration and lack of positive reinforcement. You can keep the unreachable star as a vision, but don't let the same logic flow into operating goals.

TIME LIMITED

- Is the timeframe for achieving the goal clearly stated? This enables milestones to be measured along the way, and it sets an expectation for when the full benefits of the results will be felt by the organization.

In addition to these tests that are applied to the goals themselves, there are two principles that govern effective goals from an overall point of view:

1. Goals Must be Understood by All Parties

- Simplifying goals into a language that the performer understands is a critical element of goal setting. You can't expect people to act on information that makes no sense to them.

2. Goals Must Remain Flexible

- Goals project outcomes into the future, and the future is uncertain. Goals therefore require constant monitoring to be certain that while the goal is being worked on, the goal still applies. If an environmental or operating situation changes the expected result from a goal, the goal needs to be adjusted to reflect the new outcome.

CORPORATE-LEVEL GOALS

In Chapter 1, **top-level corporate goals** were referred to in five dimensions or "Accounts."

The figure that represents the five dimensions of corporate level goals is reproduced for reference.

FIGURE 5.3 Five Accounts of Corporate Goals

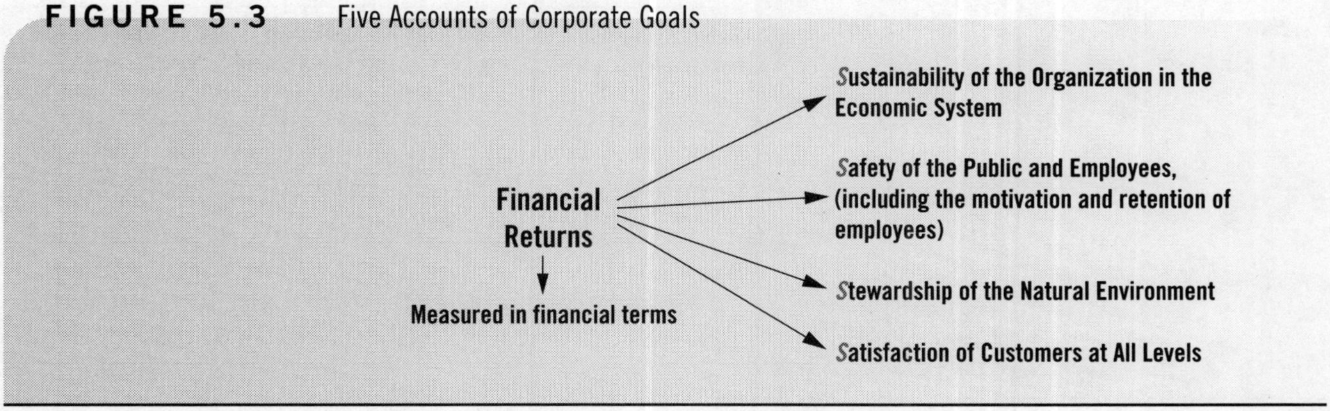

This framework for corporate strategic goals relates to the "grand strategy" for the organization. It enables meaningful operational short-term goals to be prepared.

Assume we have an organization that has adopted an aggressive strategy of new product development in an industry that is approaching its decline phase. The organization will use the Industry Evolution Diagram, the SWOT analysis and The Five Accounts of Corporate Goals (Figure 5.3) to establish a set of corporate goals, as shown in Figure 5.4, following.

FIGURE 5.4 Corporate Long-Range Strategic Goals

Strategic Issues	Objective	Strategic Goal
Financial Returns	Maximize financial returns to stockholders.	Maintain an average return on investment of a minimum of 15% for the next five years.
	Improve market share.	Increase the level of awareness of our product in world markets by 15% over the next two years.
	Reduce unit manufacturing costs.	Reduce the percentage of cost to selling price by 10% within 2 years.
	Improve product quality.	Reduce the reject rate by 5% during the next year while maintaining or reducing sales returns over the same time period.
Sustainability of the Organization in the Economic System	Maximize the impact of the organization on the regional economy.	Maintain continuous employment for our 1,600 people for the next five years.
		Contribute 20% of the local Chamber of Commerce operating budget for the next five years.
Safety of the Public and Employees, (including motivating and retaining employees)	Minimize the probability and severity of employee and public injury.	Maintain an injury rate less than the national average for the next five years.
	Maximize the motivation and retention of employees.	Maintain a 90% satisfaction level of employees and have a retention rate 5% higher than the industry average for the next five years.
Stewardship of the Natural Environment	Minimize the impact of operations on the natural environment.	Reduce the level of solid particulate emissions to the landfill to 3 parts per million by June 2007.
Satisfaction of Customers at all Levels	Maximize the satisfaction of customers at all levels.	Achieve and maintain a 90% customer satisfaction level regarding service, product quality and perceived value by April 2004 and for the next five years.

These high-level goals indicate where the organization will be when results have been achieved in measurable and realistic terms.

The operating divisions of the organization will then take these high-level goals and translate them into operating or action-oriented goals that are more specific as to what will be done, by whom and by when.

OPERATING-LEVEL GOALS

The operating-level goals are cascaded down from the corporate goals by giving the operating division a general direction of performance improvement for each dimension of the organization. Now the operating departments are expected to take each of the high-level goals and initiate action plans to achieve those goals.

Following from the example given above, each of the high-level goals will be taken to the next level where action items directed at departmental tasks and functions will be developed. For example, one of the corporate-level goals from the financial account was:

FIGURE 5.5 Long-Range Corporate Financial Goal

Corporate Long-Range Goal	Measurement Concept
Maximize financial returns to stockholders.	Maintain an average return on investment of a minimum of 15% for the next five years.

In order to achieve this result, operating departments would take the high-level concept and develop short-run goals directed at specific action plans. For example:

FIGURE 5.6 Operating Financial Goal

Operating Short-Range Goals by Department		Measurement Concept
Sales Department	Maximize revenues.	Increase total sales by 5% this year by introducing a new pricing structure that includes quantity discounts and an easy payment plan.
Production Department	Minimize production costs.	Reduce materials, labour and overhead production costs per unit by 5% this year by automating the packaging step in the manufacturing process.

Another example for the safety account would be:

FIGURE 5.7 Long-Range Corporate Safety Goal

Corporate Long-Range Goal	Measurement Concept
Minimize the probability and severity of employee and public injury.	Maintain an injury rate less than the national average for the next five years.

Tactical plans developed by the operating departments would include:

FIGURE 5.8 Operating Safety Goals

Operating Short-Range Goals by Department		Measurement and Tactic
Human Resource Department	Increase awareness of safety procedures.	Train all 150 shop personnel in the effective use of safety equipment by November 15th, 2000.
Production Department	Reduce the probability of injury on the assembly line.	Correct the 17 shortfalls cited by the recent Workers Compensation Board safety audit by September 1, 2000, at the least possible cost.

It is most important that operating goals are SMART.

You can see that at the operating level the goals have become very specific and time limited, that measures are clear and that, ideally, the performer has the authority to act on the goal. You can also see that when each of the corporate goals is dealt with at the operating level, there could be hundreds of goals to work on, so many, in fact, that that the process becomes far too confusing.

ON THIS TOPIC

A Real-World Example

In the early 1990's, the BC Hydro customer services division created a performance measurement system based on operating goals.

There were *16 pages* of performance measures related to operating goals that managers had to check every day!

Managers quickly realized that more time was spent watching than doing!

www.BCHydro.com

Clearly, we need a method to pare down the number of goals so we have a meaningful and manageable set of goals. The following sections will help in this regard.

Goals have three primary elements:

1. The target for achievement,
2. The strategies or tactics to be used,
3. The key result area where the benefits of the activity will be felt.

FIGURE 5.9 Three Elements of a Goal

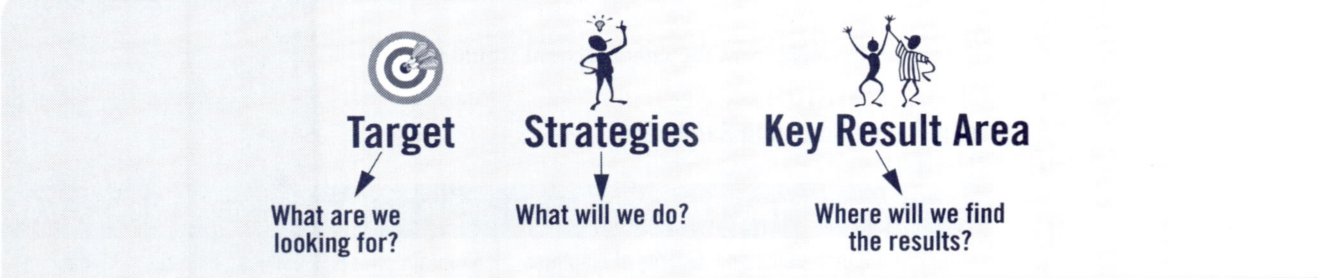

For example, the corporate-level goal,

Minimize the probability and severity of employee and public injury	by maintaining an injury rate less than the national average for the next five years.

has the **target**, to "**Minimize** the probability and severity," and the strategy or tactic, "by maintaining an **injury rate** less than the national average for the next five years, with the **results** being felt by "**employee** and **public**."

Similarly, the operating goal

Maximize revenues	Increase total sales by 5% this year by introducing a new pricing structure which includes quantity discounts and an easy payment plan.

has the **target** "**maximize** revenues," the strategy or **tactic**, "by introducing a **new pricing structure** which includes quantity discounts and an easy payment plan" and a **result**, "**Increase total sales** by 5% this year."

The point of studying these characteristics is that if your goal is missing any of the SMART elements, or any of the three primary elements from Figure 5.1, your goal is deficient, the result you expect probably will not happen and your performers will be confused.

Use the characteristics of a goal to perform a checklist of your goal before the goal becomes public.

THE BASICS OF MEASURING GOALS

Notice that the measurement concept at the operating level has become much more precise. Chapters 10, 11 and 12 of this book deal with the measurement of performance in detail, but at this point it is useful to introduce the basic concept.

It is critically important that there be meaningful measures linked to goals at all levels. A goal without a measure, i.e. evidence that progress is being made, is simply a waste of time and effort. Those who develop effective measures claim two major benefits:

1. I am able to show senior management that their investment is paying off, therefore acquiring more investment becomes easier.
2. I am able to show everyone on my team that progress is being made, therefore acquiring more effort is easier.

The "Key Result Area" defines **where** results will be found. Now we need to know **how** those results will be found. Measurement is the only way to show evidence that progress is being made, and evidence is the only way to justify continuing to try and realize a goal.

There are many performance measurement systems available on the market. Some are very expensive. Most are very complex. Many organizations have had a bad experience trying to measure their work.

This has been a very interesting aspect of research, in preparing to write this book. I have discovered that most applications of performance measurement fail because key players are afraid of measurement. Some are afraid of the costs of a system, some are afraid of the complexity, some are afraid of what measurement might reveal.

There will be much more on this topic in Chapters 10, 11, and 12. For now, let's examine the basic measurement model as it relates to measuring goals.

The SAVI Performance Measurement Tool develops measures of **results and outcomes** using four basic measures: speed, accuracy, volume and investment. The bottom line is that if your operating goal is to deliver goods and services:

- when customers want them (**speed**),
- and the goods and services meet the customers' quality needs (**accuracy**),
- and if you do enough to satisfy all customers (**volume**),
- and you do it at the least possible cost (**investment**),
- then you have an efficient and effective system.

Figure 5.10 depicts the dimensions of the measurement framework using an image of a spinning top.

FIGURE 5.10 The Measurement Model

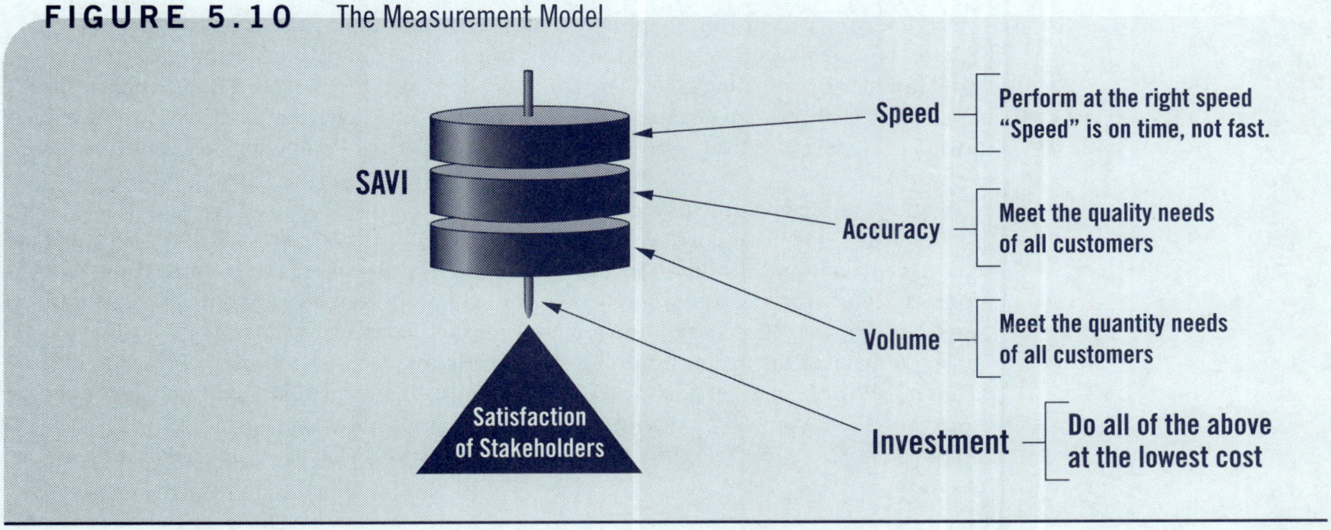

Speed, accuracy and volume are outputs or results of a process, while investment (cost) is an input of a process. All of this is perched atop the groups of stakeholders whose satisfaction is very important.

The significance of the spinning top is that if the output dimensions, (speed, accuracy and volume) are maximized and in balance, while the input dimension, investment, is minimized to reflect financial efficiency, the "top" will spin safely. If any dimension is managed out of proportion to the rest, the balance will be impacted and the top will fall and damage satisfaction.

This performance measurement model becomes the focal point of the operating goal-setting system because we need to track performance in results, most frequently measured in the realm of satisfaction, and we need to track the efficiency of the use of resources, most frequently measured with input side measures of resources consumed in the delivery of results. An illustration of how the model works will use the operating goal set previously:

Reduce the probability of injury on the assembly line	by correcting the 17 shortfalls cited by the recent Workers Compensation Board safety audit by September 1, 2000 at the least possible cost.

- The **Speed** dimension is captured by "September 1st, 2000."
- The **Accuracy** dimension is assumed in the word "Correcting" in that we assume it will be done properly.
- The **Volume** dimension is captured in the number "17."
- The **Investment** dimension is captured in "At the least possible cost."

The bottom line here is that for a goal to pass the SMART test, you need to deal with the "M." Every goal can be measured. Ideally, the SAVI model of measurement will begin your thinking about the measurement of your goals.

We will continue this study in Chapters 10, 11, and 12.

COMPETING GOALS AND TRADEOFFS AMONG GOALS

It is better when people take personal ownership of their goals, and work enthusiastically towards achieving them. But there is one caution. It sometimes happens that realizing one goal might actually damage the results of another goal.

For example, at a corporate-goal level, we advocate financial efficiency and customer satisfaction. An easy way to satisfy customers is to give them more, which of course will impact financial efficiency. Environmental goals are realized by using money with little chance of a financial return. Meeting safety requirements uses up financial resources with little return and so on.

Because managers are trying to serve multiple corporate goals at the same time, and because those goals tend to govern the whole organization, managers need to make effective tradeoffs among competing goals. They can only do that if they have full knowledge of the impact, financial and non-financial, of each goal, and full knowledge of the vision, value and mission of the organization to offer guidance as to how these competing achievements should be prioritized.

At an operating level, the problem becomes more pronounced.

Ownership of goals at the operating level is more intense because the goal is directed at the achievements of a specific division, finance, production, marketing etc. In some cases, the problem is more pronounced when we link the achievement of goals to bonus compensation plans. Now the managers have something to gain from meeting the goals.

The problem at the operating level is that if you leave departments on their own to set goals and allow them to set goals without considering how their goal might impact the rest of the organization, you will have serious competition among the goals.

For example, assume that the primary objectives of the divisions of an organization are as follows:

FIGURE 5.11 Primary Objectives of Business Divisions

Division	Primary Objectives
Finance and Accounting	Make as much money as we can while making business risks of all types as low as possible. Invest profits in improving the security and returns of stockholders.
Marketing and Sales	Create a massive awareness of the product and sell as many products as we can to worldwide markets, meeting every single customer's needs by giving them what they want, when they want it. Invest profits in expanding the market size, moving to new regions and markets, developing new products and increasing customer awareness through advertising and promotion.
Production and Distribution	Simplify the production process to maximize efficiency and reduce the risk of warehousing inventories. Standardize production to focus on a few products that are produced efficiently. Invest profits in improving the efficiency of the production process, reducing distribution costs and improving product quality.

These divisions have a very strong concept of achieving their objectives, and a vested interest in achieving their objectives.

If these three departments could set detailed operating operating goals on their own, without considering the impact on other parts of the organization, the following is what you could get:

FIGURE 5.12 Operational Goals in Business Divisions

	Operational Goals		
Focus of Operational Goals	**Finance and Accounting**	**Marketing and Sales**	**Production and Distribution**
Order Processing	Cheap order processing	Fast order processing	Slow order processing
Product Variants and New Designs	Reduced variants to reduce investment	Very frequent variants to meet changing customer preferences	Standardized production of one product to increase efficiency
Warehousing	No warehousing because there should be no inventory	Huge regional warehouses serving local markets by providing fast delivery to local customers	One warehouse at the factory to take care of production cycles, customers can pick up from there
Credit and Collections	Cash only, paid in advance, to reduce business risk	Liberal credit and extended payment terms to make buying easy	N/A
Use of Financial Returns	Pay down the debt, provide a return to stockholders, invest in sound growth opportunities by acquiring risk free assets	Increased advertising and promotion to maximize product awareness in existing and new markets	Alter the configuration of the plant and replace worn out assets so that product quality and cost efficiency is improved

Divisions of organizations have always had rivalries and competition, sometimes friendly and constructive, sometimes not. Competition and enthusiasm are healthy when the realization of individual goals improves the position of the organization, if all the goals are added together. The competition is not healthy if one goal can harm overall performance, while at the same time reward good performance in the division.

To alleviate this problem, goals need to be set in open forums with negotiations and communications between divisions. Goals that are openly negotiated will actually allow organizational bottlenecks to be discovered before they occur.

WHAT INFORMATION IS NEEDED TO SET A GOAL?

The mere existence of a goal implies that the organization wants results in the future to be better, otherwise the goal would not have been set in the first place. If the results in the future need to be better, then it follows that the present results are not good enough. If we know that present results are not good enough, we must have measured something to arrive at that opinion.

Goals for the future are set through a process called benchmarking, where we measure what is being done at the high level and operating levels of the organization, and then we benchmark something for comparison. The difference between what we are presently doing and what we have benchmarked becomes the ammunition we need to set a goal.

There are three sources of benchmarking data: the past practices of your own organization, the practices of competing organizations and the best available practices used in all organizations. We will deal with the sources individually.

Benchmarking the past practices of your own organization

Yesterday we did something that was not very good. We should improve on that.

- Past practices are a good place to set as a reference point for where the change process began, but they are not a good source of goal-setting information. If you were a fool yesterday, and you improve on that, now you are just marginally better than the fool you used to be.
- Use the benchmark of the past to serve as a reference point for where the change process began, or where you are changing from.

Benchmarking the practices of competing organizations

Our competition does things better than we do. We should copy them and then improve on that.

- If your competitor is perfect, it is wise to follow, but if your competitor is a fool and you improve on that, you are now just marginally better than the fool that he or she is.
- Use a benchmark of competitors' practices to judge if you are beating them, but don't assume they are perfect. You might find a process that is even better by looking elsewhere.

Benchmarking the practices of all organizations

Organizations outside of our industry do something similar to what we do, but they do it much better. We should copy and improve on that.

- A common failing of benchmarking is that people confine their search to similar organizations in similar industries. The fact is that while industries are different, the activities within organizations across industries are the same in many cases. Automobile dealers have parts departments with inventory systems. Hardware stores and bakeries also have inventory systems. Perhaps their systems could be brought to the automobile industry to achieve efficiency gains.

- The idea of best available practice is to compare the function or activity to functions and activities across industry boundaries. When the best possible practice is found, this information will be very useful in setting operational goals.

LINKING GOALS TO MANAGING CHANGE

Realizing corporate and operating goals will cause an organization to change. It is assumed that the planned changes are performance improvements. It is hard to imagine an organization that chooses to be worse in the future than it is now. (*Government critics might say that we are worse off than before, but it is still hard to believe that a government chose to do that out of good planning practices.*)

Ultimately, organizations would like goals to be achieved instantly, but that is not realistic. Change takes time and in fact the organization might go through several rounds of goal setting and adjusting processes before results begin to materialize. Therefore, organizations build goal-setting strategies by making a long-range forecast of where they would like to be, then making short-range forecasts of milestones of achievements that will lead to the ultimate objective.

There are an unlimited number of goal-setting strategies for facilitating change. Two are described below.

PARADIGM SHIFT

One view of setting goals to facilitate change is the paradigm shift. This is a very popular strategy for change because the resulting performance improvement is immediate. The idea is quite simple. You simply identify an old level of performance that is undesirable, then identify the new level of performance you want, and then you change the organization by putting in place what you need for the new performance.

The shift in paradigm is that old practices will be abandoned and new ones put in place; the old paradigm goes out and the new one comes in. Figure 5.13 shows how this performance gain appears.

FIGURE 5.13 Performance Improvement Through Paradigm Shift

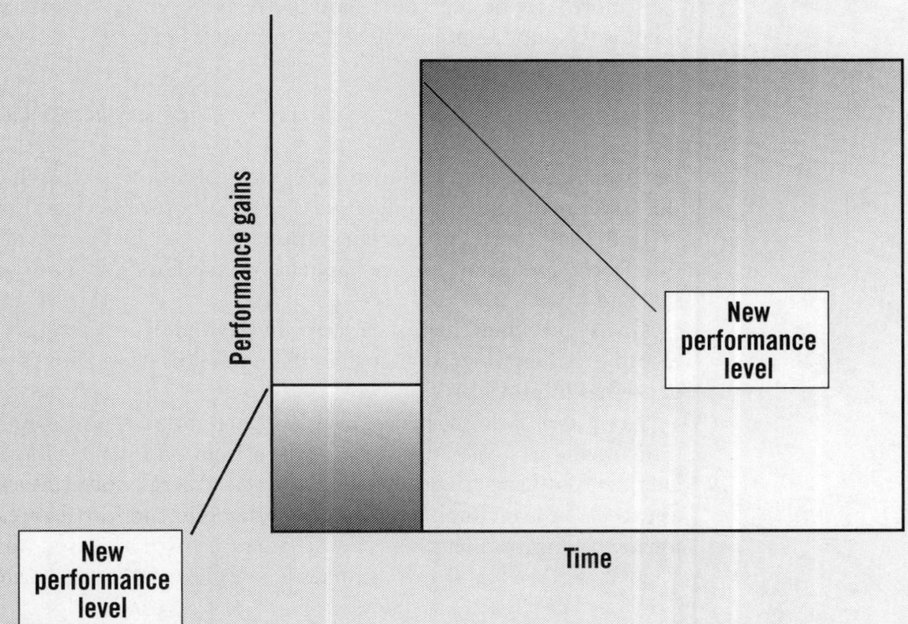

If we can clearly see the operating characteristics that should be in place to achieve excellence, we could move there immediately. This involves dramatically realigning resources on short planning horizons. For example, an organization might abandon a department to achieve cost savings, or create a new department to bring in a new revenue stream.

The advantage to the paradigm shift process is that performance change is immediate. The disadvantage is that performers do not feel many of the reinforcement benefits. In fact, most paradigm shifts are so disruptive that performance actually falls in the short run.

ON THIS TOPIC

A Real-World Example

In 1998 the City of Vancouver management was instructed by Council to change their paradigm and create new revenue streams for city coffers.

This meant that the city now had to charge for things they had not charged for before. The management team decided to charge for parking in Stanley Park, one of Vancouver's premier tourist attractions.

The result was an immediate inflow of cash. And an immediate negative reaction from the public.

www.vancouver.ca

If a paradigm shift creates immediate improvement, then why isn't every corporate and operational goal cast in terms of a paradigm shift? Because the paradigm shift seldom works!

Many organizations use the concept of a paradigm shift to rationalize a corporate reorganization. The thinking is that this new organization will immediately be a better performer. Aubrey Daniels, in his book, *Bringing Out The Best In People* recited an interesting statistic. Apparently 917 U.S. corporations were surveyed 18 months after they had reorganized for immediate performance gains. They were asked, "Did you receive any measurable gain in performance coming from the reorganization?" Only 4 of the 917 reported a performance gain.

A complete reorganization applies to the whole organization, while operating goals apply only to segments of an organization. While some paradigm shifts at the operating level do create immediate gains, most do not. My experience has been that paradigm shift can work in places where money is the predominant measure of success, but when you are looking for changes to customer satisfaction, service quality, sustainability or employee morale, the process of change takes place over time.

A more realistic expectation around realizing goals and measuring organizational improvement is to adopt a notion called "Performance Shaping."

Shaping

Performance shaping, as shown in Figure 5.14, involves achieving sub-goal targets that lead to the attainment of the overall target over an extended period of time.

In the early stages of a change process, the marginal gains will be small while the organization learns about how change happens. We tend to be cautious and take on initiatives that are safe and small.

Goals and achievements are larger in the middle range because performers have a track record of achievement that enables them to take bigger bites of progress, because their confidence has improved.

As we approach excellence, goals are pared down because marginal change becomes more difficult and less cost-effective at near perfect performance. Most people will redirect their energies to other performance areas that need greater improvement. This is desirable as long as excellence is maintained. Figure 5.14 demonstrates the relationship between time and performance improvement.

FIGURE 5.14 "Shaping" as a Strategy for Change

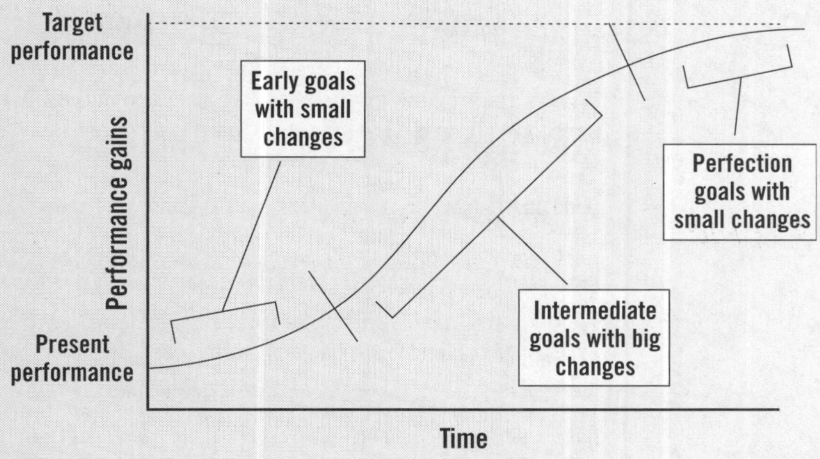

Shaping offers frequent reinforcement for each marginal change in performance. Performance changes all along the graph are measured and recognized frequently to enhance the behaviour of performers, by rewarding success in achieving improvements.

This concept is very useful in defining realistic goals for achievement. If the process you are trying to change is presently very inefficient, you should set short-term goals that call for small gains. If you have had some recent success in improving efficiency, you can set bigger goals for improvement. If you are getting close to excellent performance, you should lower your expectations for improvement.

CHAPTER SUMMARY

Of the seven learning outcomes stated at the beginning of this chapter, three began with "understand" and four began with "develop." Most of the learning outcomes from the previous chapters were to "understand." To "develop" means that you should have enough of an understanding of the theories so that you can start using them.

Corporate and operational goals have been sufficiently described so you can take an active role in helping in developing goals in your organization. Proceed with confidence and proceed with caution. When goals are carefully developed using the principles described in this chapter, they can be very powerful tools to manage change, but when they are poorly developed, they can be very harmful to morale and enthusiasm.

A goal is a contract between an employee and his or her organization. The contract states that if the employee is given the resources, the authority and the control to initiate change, then the results from the change will be measured by the goal itself.

Stakeholders will be given notice of the value that will be added by the organization if the short- and long-range goals are realized. Goal setting is thus more than just a method of managing change. It is also an advertising plan to be used with stakeholders so their expectations can be managed.

CLOSING REMARKS

Chapter 5 plays an important role as part of the set of chapters forming Section 1 of this book. This chapter brings all the pieces of goal setting together into one functional, systematic model. This model also sets expectations among members of an organization that these goals, when realized, will make the organization more effective and efficient and even more prosperous.

That is Chapter 5's key point: setting expectations about future prosperity. There may even be great excitement about those expectations and the rewards that will follow once this new prosperity is achieved.

Starting with Chapter 6, we will discuss how to move an organization towards that new prosperity.

TERMS INTRODUCED IN THE CHAPTER

Benchmarking Comparing an organization's operation to itself, its competition and best available practice.

Cascading Moving from one grand strategy to a few corporate goals to many operating goals, all of which network together and swerve the organizational vision and mission.

Competing goals The notion that within the same organization it might be that an operating goal in one department is detrimental to the operating goal in another department.

Corporate goals High-level expectations about how the organization will change.

Operating goals Milestones of achievement that are directly related to operating functions in the organization.

Paradigm shift The instantaneous improvement of performance by replacing old practices with new, improved practices.

Profitability Financial health in terms of net income, cash flow, debt/equity. Earning per share etc. in both the short and long run.

Safety Ensuring that operations reduce the likelihood and severity of physical and emotional injury suffered by employees and the public.

Satisfaction Ensuring that the value given in exchange for goods and services is perceived to be fair value.

Shaping The notion that performance will improve over time with small performance gains in the early going of the change process and bigger gains coming later.

SMART Five test questions about goals that improve the quality and understanding of goals.

Speed, accuracy, volume and investment Four dimensions of a measurement model that help in measuring the outcomes of goals.

Sustainability Efforts made by the organization to be active in the social and environmental system so that a good corporate citizenship will assure long-term prosperity.

Stewardship Being a diligent operator in reducing the impact of operations on air. Aquatic and vegetation health.

Tradeoffs among goals The informed decision to minimize results in one function of the business so that results can be maximized in another function of the business.

QUESTIONS FOR CLASS DISCUSSION

1. Distinguish between a goal and an objective.
2. Explain each part of the SMART acronym and then prepare an operating goal for the meat department in a grocery store showing how the SMART dimensions are used.
3. Explain, by using an example, the relationship between a corporate and an operational goal.

4. Explain how, within one organization, there might be conflicting goals between departments. Explain how you would conduct the tradeoffs that need to be made.
5. Explain, using an example, how the concept of "sustainability" should be embraced by organizations.
6. Given that the satisfaction of stakeholders is the ultimate objective of any organization, explain how the satisfaction of the "customer group" could be measured and then explain how the satisfaction of the "local community environmentalists" could be measured.
7. Develop an example of the paradigm shift logic of change management.
8. Develop an example of the shaping logic of change management.

A CASE FOR STRATEGIC PLANNING: MALCOLM AND RUBY'S NEXT STEP

Malcolm finally found a consultant Ruby would pay attention to. They had a very informative discussion about SWOT and now Ruby is more convinced than ever that her idea can work. Fortunately, she is also quite a bit more cautious and sensible in her planning activities.

Ruby has embraced a two-phase plan. In the short run she has to deal with environmental opportunity and critical internal weakness, but as soon as the weaknesses are dealt with (six months from now), she plans to aggressively go to market by matching her strengths with the environmental opportunities.

REQUIRED:

Prepare a grand strategy and a set of corporate goals that reflect both the short- and long-run aspects of the business.

Prepare a set of operational goals for finance, marketing, human resources, production and research and development and demonstrate how cascading works.

CHAPTER ENDING CASE: A CASE ABOUT GOALS AND CHANGE

Dave's grocery store has been serving your neighbourhood for 20 years. Dave has a reputation for freshness and good value. He has been meeting all the grocery needs of the neighbourhood.

In the next town, Dave's friend Larry, who also runs a grocery store, was forced to close recently because he just couldn't compete with the Super Megastore that came to his town. The Super Megastore chain has already been nosing around Dave's town looking for business potential.

The Super Mega store has decided not to locate in Dave's town. It feels that the region could not support two megastores. However, Super Mega will be providing a free shuttle service from Dave's town to the megastore in the next town, about 30 minutes away. Super Mega has done this before, having found that providing the shuttle for the first six months of a store opening changes buying patterns: people will travel for 30 minutes to get their groceries because of all the other things the megastore has to offer.

Dave conducted a small survey among his customers and has discovered that what his store is most lacking is a pharmacy. Other than that, he seems to have everything they need to keep them from going to the megastore.

REQUIRED:

Develop a grand strategy, a set of corporate goals and operating goals for Dave.

In terms of change management, help Dave understand what the introduction of a pharmacy will do to his employees and customers. Can he expect immediate success?

SUMMARY OF PART 1

The first five chapters if this book dealt with a planning model that reflected the needs of stakeholders by using the SAVI acronym:

Stakeholders need Added Value from their Investments

At the end of the planning cycle, there will be a clear understanding of where the organization wants to go, why it wants to go there, how it plans to get there and what benefit there will be in being successful in achieving the Vision, Mission, Values and goals.

The plans are set, the targets are identified and there are great expectations about what the future will bring. Now it's time to do something about it.

You don't realize goals by writing them down. Goals are realized by making decisions and then doing something about those decisions.

The next section of the book will deal with the process used to make the necessary decisions to ensure that goals are met.

Part 2

DECISION-MAKING TO REALIZE GOALS

Screening **A**dded **V**alue **I**nitiatives

INTRODUCTION TO CHAPTERS 6 to 9

The SAVI Decision Making and Control tool follows the goal-setting tool because the next step, after goals are set, is to **S**creen **A**dded **V**alue **I**nitiatives. In other words, we need to select the projects and initiatives that will maximize the returns promised in the goal-setting process.

The figure below indicates where we are in the management cycle.

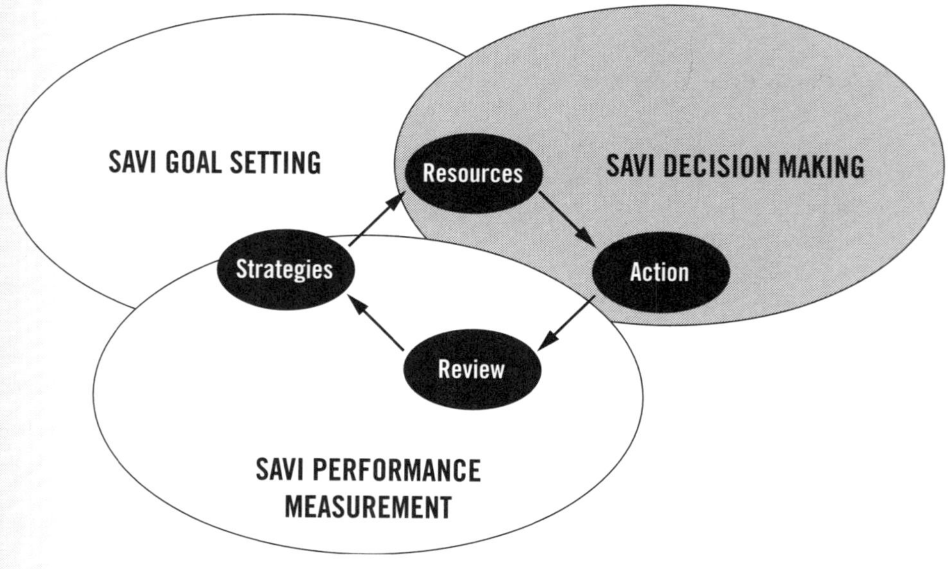

Decision Making and Control has two distinct parts. Decision Making involves making a choice between alternative courses of action to be taken in the future, and Control involves monitoring the resources used as the course of action is underway.

Making the correct decision is particularly important when an organization has limited financial, human and operational resources. It would be nice to implement **every good idea** that comes along, but most organizations have limited resources, which means that we need to choose the best ideas and pass on the bad ones. In addition, we have to be sure that once we have made a choice to do something, we control the use of resources and monitor the results so that we can continue to enjoy the benefits of a good idea. Left uncontrolled, the benefits, even from good ideas, can erode if we are not careful.

In Chapters 6 to 9, we will be dealing with the decision-making process. We will be examining a systematic model for decision making that uses a close linkage to strategic and operational goals as we have developed them in the first five chapters. Once we have finished the decision-making process in Chapter 9, we will be able to close this book with some discoveries in performance measurement (tracking project results).

The decision-making model we will be studying is called the "*Total Impact*™ Business Case Analysis." Preparing a business case to support a new or ongoing project is nothing new. We have been preparing business cases for years. What is new is the need to prepare a very comprehensive business case that encompasses more than the financial impact of a project. The "triple bottom line" concept and the "sustainability initiative" are new issues being faced by today's organization. Stakeholders want to see the financial, social and environmental impact of the operations of the organization. Various stakeholders closely monitor the dimension of the organization that is important to them.

The "*Total Impact* Business Case Analysis" is coming from the new realities faced by organizations in today's economic and social environment. Some of the realities of this environment are described as follows.

The Realities We Face

Regardless of whether your organization is a private company dedicated to maximizing financial returns for stockholders or a public service organization dedicated to maximizing service levels, you face basic realities. These realities govern the decision-making process by defining the constraints around resource allocation decisions.

1. **Resources are Limited**
   - There is not an infinitely large pool of resources to draw from. Therefore, we cannot act on every good idea that comes along. Instead, we need to rank the ideas in descending order of attractiveness from financial and non-financial points of view.

2. **There is Competition for Funds**
   - Managers who propose new initiatives will have those initiatives compared to other ideas in the organization. Like all competition, there will be winners and there will be losers.

3. **Sometimes the Winner is the Best Sales Person**
   - Some people seem to have figured out how the game is played, so they get resources flowing to them on the basis of the quality of their presentation rather than the quality of their idea. Unfortunately, there are a number of excellent ideas in the hands of people who don't know how to play the game, so the ideas go unnoticed.

4. **Financial Decision Rules Don't Always Match Operating Decision Rules**
   - The financial evaluation system puts monetary values on benefits and costs. In fact, there is pressure to attempt to "monetize" all benefits by expressing everything in financial terms.

Sometimes the true benefits of an initiative, such as safety, aesthetics, impact on a community's way of life etc., are non-financial, so a useful language is needed to describe the non-financial returns of a project.

5. **Financial Returns And Efficiency Will Continue To Be Powerful**

- While strategic customer satisfaction and broad social returns are important to stakeholders, it will continue to be true that financial results, either in the form of profitability or efficient use of resources, will be the most powerful decision criteria in an evaluation process. We are looking for the best return we can find in both financial and social terms, but we can't accept any project that has an excessive cost.

Dealing with these realities can be a very complex task. Using a systematic model that considers these issues and others in the analysis of alternative courses of action, will make the decision-making process more thorough and will improve the quality of the decisions that are made.

The SAVI model demonstrates where in the management process decision making and control takes place.

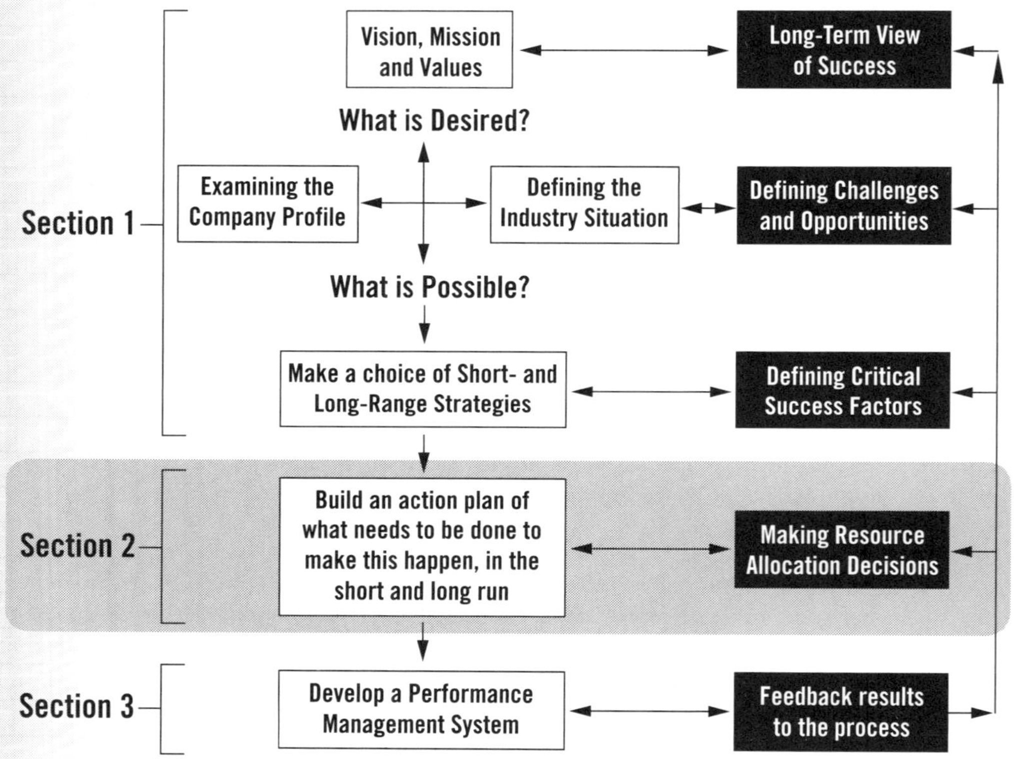

Let's begin our study of "**S**creening **A**dded **V**alue **I**nitiatives" by examining the most important part of problem solving...defining the problem to be solved!

CHAPTER 6

The Problem-Solving Model And Defining The Problem

If common sense is so common, why is there so little of it?

LEARNING OBJECTIVES

After reading this chapter, engaging in class discussion and doing the exercises at the end of the chapter, you will be able to:

1. Understand the link between the evaluation and initiation of a project and the realization of strategic goals.
2. Understand and use a systematic model for problem solving.
3. Describe the components of a complete "business case."
4. Distinguish between a problem and an opportunity.
5. Understand the four levels of problems or opportunities.
6. Use the principles of goal setting from previous chapters in the context of setting goals for projects.

YOUR RESPONSIBILITY

To get the most from Chapter 6, you need to raise your awareness of how people do things to solve their problems. This also means that a failure to do something means the problem continues!

News headlines are a great source of information about the problems we are trying to solve. Most of the time the headline is very clear. "Communications industry is seeking new cost savings" or "Hotels face increased vacancies." Sometimes a headline can be curious: "Plane too close to ground, crash probe told." (Apparently, it was very close to the ground.)

Your task is to take the business section of the newspaper and read each headline. Before you read the article, ask yourself if you understand the problem it is trying to solve, then quickly imagine what you think the proposed solution is.

In some cases, you will find that the problem is clear and the solution obvious. In others, you will find there are more questions than answers, that the problem is not understood or the solution doesn't relate to the problem.

INTRODUCTION TO CHAPTER 6

Two of the difficult issues facing today's manager are:

- Finding the optimal solution to a problem
- Communicating the findings to a decision maker.

Finding a solution to a problem that may not be the best solution is easy. If choices were made using financial returns, reliability, safety, or customer service as single criteria, then problem solving would be simple, because we would select the options that best suit the *single criterion*. Problem solving becomes difficult when multiple criteria are applied to the choice. When we merge these criteria and try to identify which one is stronger, show the tradeoffs to each other or show which one is going to deliver benefits to people outside the organization, the decision process becomes more complex.

The major shift in thinking for today's manager is to integrate issues and impacts of decisions from both inside and outside the organization. People need to identify the impacts of solutions to problems on the whole range of stakeholders in an organization, the same way we identified the impact of long-range and short-range strategic goals on stakeholders. The framework for this integrated analysis in decision making is called *Total Impact* **Business Case Analysis**, the intent of which is to capture the effects of a decision across a variety of social and financial accounts.

As introduced in the SAVI Goal-Setting Tool, there are five accounts relating to strategic goal setting issues, particularly at the corporate level. The accounts are: **financial efficiency and effectiveness, sustainability of the economic environment, stewardship of the natural environment, safety of employees and the public and service to the customer**.

The same five accounts (or impact areas), that were used to set goals will be used to evaluate decisions. The decision maker identifies how each alternative course of action impacts the organization through the five accounts, and then uses the accounts as decision criteria to rank the alternatives in order of attractiveness.

The *Total Impact* framework is a useful decision tool. Traditional problem-solving processes will be significantly enhanced by using the *Total Impact* approach, because the breadth of analysis includes an examination of issues that are relevant to the organization, its customers and the members of society at large.

This presentation of a decision-making tool describes traditional problem solving processes and demonstrates the application of *Total Impact* concepts in the decision process. If this tool is applied to analysis and decision-making activities, the quality of decisions will improve. Financial and non-financial returns to the organization and society will also improve, as will the effectiveness of the organization.

LINKING BUSINESS CASES TO STRATEGIC PLANS

Many organizations devote management effort to a strategic review of their purpose so they can realign resources to better serve customer needs. Sometimes a strategic review reveals that customer needs are being met by current operations. The reaction is to control operations to ensure that these continue to be met. Sometimes the business process must change to meet customer needs. The reaction is to alter the process and improve it.

Most organizations have discovered several areas where improvement is possible and desirable. The strategic path for an organization includes initiatives that call for change and improvement in five general areas of corporate objectives. As stated previously in the context of *Total Impact*, the broad objectives are to improve performance in the areas of:

- financial efficiency and effectiveness,
- sustainability of the economic environment,
- stewardship of the natural environment,
- safety of employees and the public, and
- service to the customer.

The corporate objectives represent the broad areas of operation where improvement is both possible and desirable. The purpose of decision making and business case analysis is to identify and report the financial and non-financial effects of projects and initiatives so that expenditures best meet the needs of the organization.

Decision making and business case analysis is one element of a management cycle that is a continuous loop of **needs assessment**, preparing **operating plans, action/implementation** and **review**. The following diagram was used to explain the position of strategic goal setting in the management cycle. The same diagram is used to explain the position of decision making (business case analysis), in the management cycle.

Developing Mission, Vision and Values and the development of long- and short-range corporate and operational strategic goals begins the management cycle and sets a framework for decision making. The framework of "strategies" is expressed as organizational needs. In other words, the organization needs to accomplish short- and long-range goals in order to satisfy all the stakeholders.

The "Total Impact Business Case Analysis" follows the decision-making path that has been created by the strategic phase of the cycle.

FIGURE 6.1 The Management Cycle and Business Casing

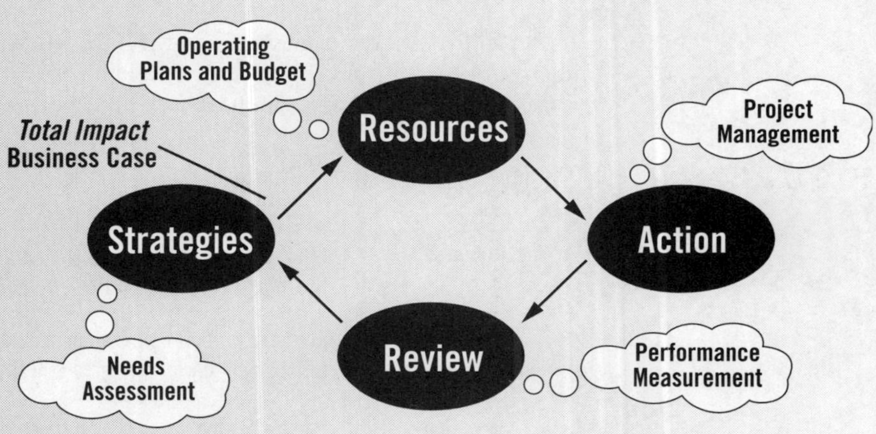

ON THIS TOPIC

A Real-World Example

The British Columbia Railway, BC Rail, has embraced the Total Impact™ approach to justifying capital and operating projects.

Before any project, new service, new capital addition or even the abandonment of existing services or assets, can be considered, it must be presented in a business case format. BC Rail has taken the process one step further by also embracing a concept called "report card," which means that, built in to the proposal for a project, there must be a report card of performance measures, a measurement timetable and clearly stated goals for performance improvement.

Not only is the linkage to realizing strategic goals an important philosophy at BC Rail, it is also built into the budgeting and performance measurement process.

www.bcrail.com

This example demonstrates the level of importance BC Rail places on ensuring that project results are part of the initial proposal to spend money.

What is a Business Case?

A completed business case is a report (a document or an oral presentation) that a decision has been reached regarding a particular problem or opportunity being faced by the organization. The report makes the decision maker understand that the problem **needs to be solved**, it **is solvable** and the solution recommended in the report makes the **best use of limited resources**. To make the best possible decision, we need the best possible analysis. In addition, the decision maker must **believe** that the best possible analytical process was used to make the decision being proposed.

Decision makers rely on a business case to provide them with sufficient, relevant and accurate information about the situation from a variety of "impacts," so they can make an informed choice about going with the recommendation presented in the business case, or rejecting the proposed idea for some "impact" reason.

Decision makers are usually happy when the case is:

Complete
Consistent
Concise
Not **C**ontrived
Using **C**ommon Sense

These "five C's" of business casing are fundamental principles. If followed, they will improve the quality of the business case and increase the likelihood that someone in a decision-making capacity will understand and approve the proposal.

FIGURE 6.2 The Five C's of Business Casing

Complete	Tell the whole story. Don't let your decision-makers ask you "if you considered this alternative." Make them understand that your analysis was very thorough.
Consistent	Everyone in your organization should use the same format so that case presentations can rely on the content of the case rather than the presentation style.
Concise	Don't offer too much information. Keep the analysis closely linked to the problem, because too much information can confuse your audience.
Not Contrived	A case is an expression of what will happen if the case is approved. Therefore, you are expressing relationships between benefits and costs. Be careful that those relationships are logical.
Use Common Sense	If you can convince yourself that the solution proposed is the best possible solution, then you will also be able to convince others of the same thing.

What is a Business Case Analysis?

A business case analysis is a systematic process of evaluating a cross-section of alternatives against criteria that match strategic goals, to arrive at the best solution to a problem. The **business case document** is a product of the *Total Impact* **business case analysis** approach to problem solving. Therefore, any flaws in the analytical process will be discovered in the reporting process if the decision maker is smart and/or lucky enough to see the flaws in the analysis. If not, the flaws will be seen when the decision doesn't deliver as promised!

The best place to discover a flaw in your thinking is at your own desk. The worst place is in the hands of the customer. Good decision analysis will reduce the possibility of a poor quality decision getting to the point where it negatively impacts the strategic goals of the organization. Good decisions will have a positive impact on realizing strategic objectives.

Two Related Steps
The bottom line is that there are two steps:

Step 1: Find the best solution to a problem by preparing a complete business case analysis using a decision model.

Step 2: Put the findings of the analysis into a report that will be convincing for a decision maker.

We begin with the first step.

FINDING THE BEST SOLUTION

THE PROCESS AND CULTURE OF REALIZING GOALS

The goals for change coming from the strategic goal-setting activity have both **process** and **culture elements**. The process element is the business practices used to achieve goals. The culture element is the people in the organization, their attitudes towards change and their enthusiasm and dedication while striving to achieve goals.

A goal could be partially realized by forcing a change in business practices, by writing a new "policy statement" which outlines the new business practice and sets an expectation for performance improvement. There may be some performance gains, but they will be short term and will not be maximizing. If we integrate a **culture change** among people with the new "policy statement," we have an opportunity to raise the value and the life of the outcome.

For example, using a "financial returns strategy," the organization might have an objective to "raise unit cost efficiency." A short-term performance gain could be realized if we eliminated some management positions, forced the survivors to work harder and sacrificed some customer satisfaction. In contrast, a healthy management culture would cause a manager to carefully balance the tradeoffs in the situation, make the choice that best suits all of the stakeholders, and make the choice work by nurturing and promoting success with all impacted parties. We want to ensure that long-term gains are not sacrificed for short-term gains.

Each strategic goal calls for a significant change in the business processes used, and each of the new business processes calls for a change in the culture of the team and the style of management to be used. It is important, therefore, to see the linkage between changing processes and changing people.

Business case preparation is not intended to be another layer of corporate bureaucracy, but rather is a thought process that expenditure and project initiators should use to help them make decisions on all types of expenditures.

COMPONENTS OF A BUSINESS CASE

Business case preparation is a structured problem-solving approach. We must clearly understand that a structured approach is not meant to stifle creativity or put the blinders on while people develop solutions to problems. A structured approach is used to ensure that all dimensions of a problem or opportunity situation are considered in the analysis. This structured approach:

- Identifies all aspects of a proposal in enough detail to give a decision maker confidence that the analysis is complete.
- Provides justification for the recommended solution by evaluating and choosing from alternative courses of action.

The initiator of an expenditure request must convince those with the authority to approve it that:

- The problem or opportunity is real.
  - *The problem requires a reaction because it will not resolve itself and the impact of letting the situation continue negative and large.*

- The alternative chosen is the best available.
  - *There is a range of alternative solutions, but the one recommended provides the best returns.*
- The investment makes the best use of limited resources.
  - *In comparison with using resources on other projects, this project shows the best results.*

To further complicate the problem-solving process, an expenditure decision must consider some or all of the following factors:

- The possibility of multiple goals that conflict with each other.
  - *You might not be able to maximize financial efficiency while also minimizing environmental impact.*
- The fact that projects have life cycles.
  - *Most solutions are not permanent. They require investment in the future to maintain the flow of benefits.*
- The range of alternatives getting wider as technology improves.
  - *Solutions that didn't even exist yesterday must be factored into the analysis for problems that will occur tomorrow.*
- Impact of the expenditure decision across organizational boundaries.
  - *Customers don't recognize the departments of an organization. The customer's view is horizontal. Organizations might achieve gains in one area of the organization that actually cause losses in other areas.*
- Dynamics of the change process, and the need to address risks and uncertainty in a rapidly changing world.
  - *As we learned from "paradigm shift" and "shaping" as goal setting strategies in Chapter 5, in most cases, change is not immediate.*

We can see the need for a systematic model. With so much going on in the process of trying to propose a solution to a problem, we are going to need a systematic and structured model just to keep information organized.

The optimal solution to a problem or the optimal reaction to an opportunity is one that maximizes benefits and/or minimizes costs over the total life cycle of the project. This may be difficult to show because all business cases involve evaluating hypothetical outcomes and quantifying uncertain future benefits and costs.

A business case is not a contract to acquire funds from the planning process. It is a contract to deliver a solution to a problem. The finished business case document must convince the reader that careful analysis has been undertaken, that the recommended solution is the optimal solution, that risks have been identified and the expected outcome is clearly understood as to how it will impact strategic goals.

Analyzing and identifying the best solution to a problem uses a systematic and comprehensive problem-solving framework. Problem solving involves a tradeoff between accuracy and speed. In some cases, having conducted a quick review of the situation, we can see a logical solution to a problem. In other cases, an extensive and detailed review might disclose no workable solution to the problem. We should realize that the solution found after a quick review might not be the best solution, and the solution we could not find after an extensive review might still be waiting in the wings.

PROBLEM-SOLVING PROCESS

The structured problem-solving approach illustrated on the following page (Figure 6.3) will lead you through a sequential process of problem solving. This problem-solving model is presented to help managers who find **quick solutions** that may not be the best solutions, to expand their horizons and search for better solutions. It should also help those who can't find a solution to focus their problem-solving efforts more efficiently.

The approach is useful because it prompts the manager to be systematic and comprehensive in analyzing the problem. This often results in the discovery of better-quality solutions.

FIGURE 6.3 Problem-Solving Model

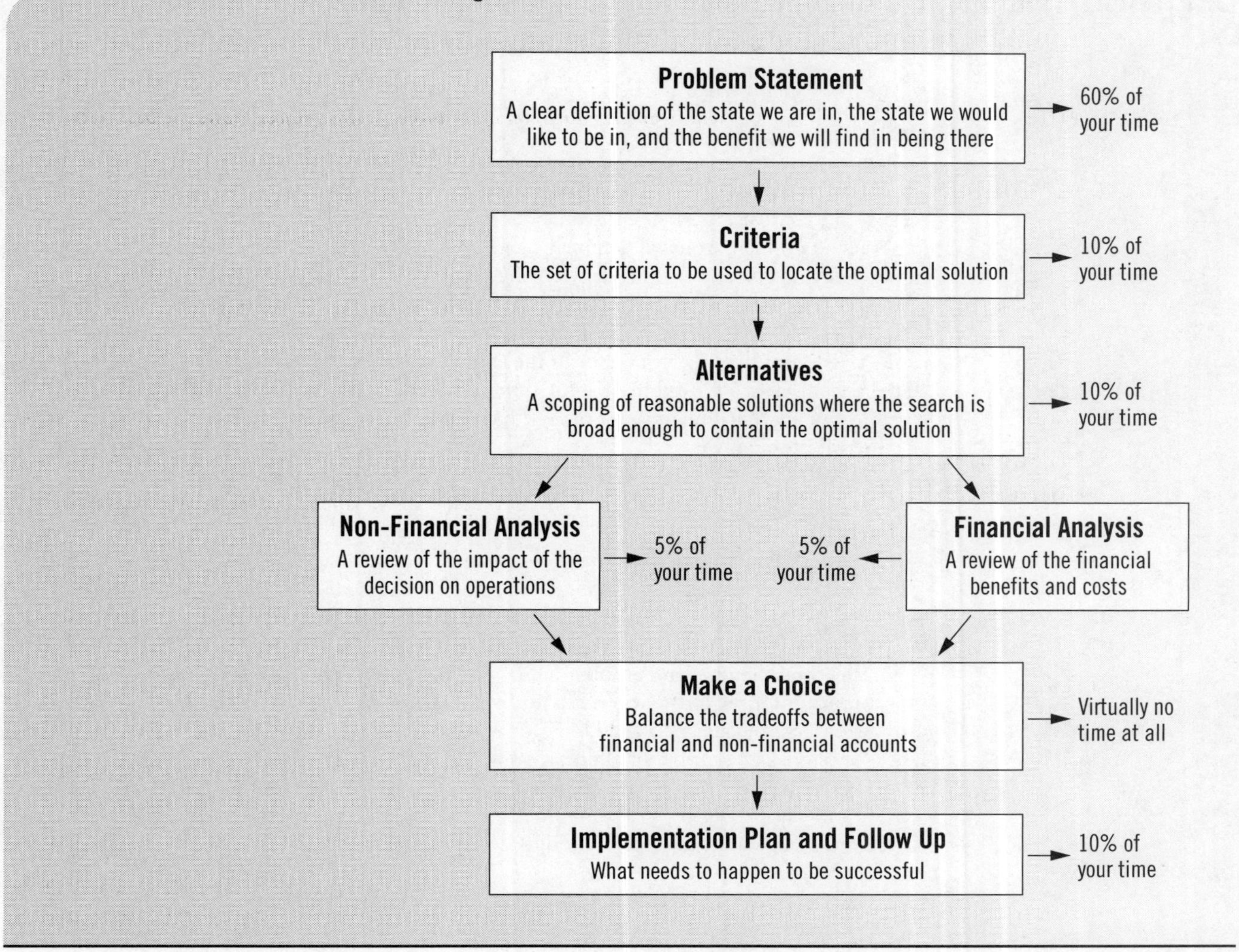

It is important to note that the process is sequential only for its first iteration. Once a complete review has been done, the model becomes dynamic, because discoveries along each step will cause changes in preceding elements of the process. The model is the backbone of the problem-solving process. The remainder of this section deals with the elements of the model in detail.

On the right side of the boxes in the diagram in Figure 6.3, you will find some estimates of the amount of time or energy required to deal with each box. The proportions are not the result of any scientific research. They reflect my observations about problem-solving activity, which I have observed in hundreds of situations. The proportions represent what should be done, not what is being done.

The bottom line is that most of our time should be spent defining the problem and no time at all should be spent choosing the best solution. My theory is that a very well-understood problem which is subjected to a thorough and realistic analysis will have a solution flow so naturally that there will be no disagreement about which path to take.

In practice, poorly defined problems are subjected to faulty analysis and people sit around arguing about which option to choose! The next time you are in an argument about what choice to make, put the decision model (Figure 6.3) in front of your team and use the model to understand why you are arguing. Go back to the beginning: Does everyone understand the problem? Are the criteria useful? Have we scoped out enough options? Is our analysis correct?

You will probably discover exactly where your disagreement starts, which should help you to end it.

DEFINING THE PROBLEM/OPPORTUNITY

Proper problem definition or identification of an opportunity is the most important, and often one of the most neglected elements of a business case preparation. The problem should be formulated so that it allows for an appropriate, informed response consistent with corporate strategies and goals.

Before we begin, we need to distinguish a problem from an opportunity. In its simplest form, a problem means, "If I fail to act, negative consequences will flow to me" while an opportunity means, "If I fail to act, positive consequences won't flow to me." The bottom line is that if you don't solve a problem, you will definitely be in trouble! If you don't take advantage of an opportunity, you won't be optimizing, you won't be perfect, but you might be able to survive.

We tend to state the problem/opportunity in the context of symptoms or statements of fact, rather than well-formulated problem statements. For example, if our problem statement read, "We do not have a compressor in the shop," we have not identified a problem, we have stated a fact that is a symptom of some other problem. If it were to read, "We need to have a wheel-changing machine in the shop," we have stated an unqualified opinion, not a problem.

The real problem we are facing can be defined by referring to **impacts and consequences**. The problem should be defined as, "The inability to change wheels in the shop means that turnaround time in the wheel repair division is too slow, which is causing hardship for our customers."

Problem statements should expand the analytical horizon, so the analyst goes looking for solutions over the widest logical range. From the situation above, if they said the problem was, "We need a compressor," the analyst would search out different brands of compressors, which assumes that air tools are the best tools and wheel changing needs to be done.

On the other hand, if the problem said, "The inability to change wheels in the shop means that turnaround time in the wheel repair division is too slow, which is causing hardship for our customers," the analyst would look for ways to reduce hardship for customers, using the wheel division. The scoping of alternatives would include all types of wheel changing equipment, as well as outsourcing wheel changing to a vendor and outsourcing all maintenance to a vendor and closing our own division.

The problem statement should guide a decision maker to a full analysis of all logical alternative solutions.

The decision model (Figure 6.3) suggests that a significant amount of time should be spent on problem definition. This is because the problem statement establishes the framework for the remainder of the problem-solving process.

A well-formulated problem statement will focus the search for solutions on a set of reasonable options so that the best solution can be readily found. The same problem-solving process can be applied to complex corporate issues and to everyday personal situations.

Problem definition involves the following steps:

1. Identify your present position.
2. Identify why the present position is undesirable.
3. Identify the position you would like to be in (set an objective).
4. Identify why the new position is desirable.

Steps 1 and 2 are facts. Your present situation, the history of how you got into this situation and the impact that the problem has on operations, financial efficiency, customer satisfaction etc. are all pieces of background information that put the problem in context. This information does not define the problem, it simply defines the impact of the situation, and how we got here.

Most decision makers prefer all of the background information to be collected in a "preamble" to the problem statement. That way, the problem is simple, clear and unencumbered with facts from the past.

Steps 3 and 4 are opinion. Where we would like to be when the problem is solved, in the future, with uncertainty, is how the problem or opportunity is defined. Therefore, steps 3 and 4 become the problem statement.

A problem statement identifies, in future terms, the impact on the organization if the problem is solved. The compressor problem now becomes, "We need to improve the turn-around time in the wheel changing division to improve customer service, while reducing operating costs to improve financial returns."

The problem statement now defines results and outcomes, it alludes to the criteria to be used in the evaluation, which will be further developed in the next step of the analysis process and it promotes a search for solutions over a wide range of alternatives.

ON THIS TOPIC

A Real-World Example

My wife and I were flying Hawaiian Airlines out of Seattle on a recent vacation. We presented our tickets and the agent said, "We have a problem. It seems your reservation has been cancelled from this flight." I offered the agent some feedback on their reservation system (enthusiastically), and the agent responded by bumping us both to first class. We had a lovely trip to Hawaii.

I plan to fly Hawaiian Airlines again and I hope that its reservation system is still faulty because its "solution" is to do something beneficial for me.

Hawaiian Airlines has not solved their problem by reacting to customer complaints. It will only solve its problem when it discovers why the reservation system is not working.

www.hawaiianair.com

Four Levels of Problems and Opportunities

In order to focus on the problem, a decision maker starts by determining the **level** of the problem. Every problem or opportunity goes through four levels of analysis as described in Figure 6.4.

These levels don't refer to an organizational hierarchy but to the levels that a problem situation will go through.

FIGURE 6.4 Four Levels of Problems/Opportunities

Level	Analysis
Strategic	High-level analysis of the relationship of the situation to the realization of strategic goals
Project	Analysis of the major changes in the allocation of resources and organizational focus necessary to serve the strategic goals
Component	Analysis of the specific expenditure, design of the solution and identity of suppliers and brands of supplies
Operational	Analysis of maintenance and operation of initiatives

For example, when an organization is considering the development of a new revenue stream by opening a new product line, the decision will go through the four phases (see Figure 6.5):

FIGURE 6.5 Four Levels of Problems/Opportunities as to a New Revenue Stream

Level	Analysis
Strategic	How does a new division fit with the Mission and strategic goals?
Project	How will the division be defined by the types of products and services it carries?
Component	What are the names of the specific brands and the descriptions of specific services?
Operational	Where do we get materials and labour?

Imagine that a ski area wishes to expand its market and improve customer service by "developing a new attraction that is suitable for the market, and complementary to what is presently done." This is a strategic-level statement of opportunity.

At a strategic level, the ski area would scope out alternatives like water slides, a golf course, an ice skating rink, war games and go-kart racing. Then the analyst would apply the decision model (Figure 6.3) to rank the alternatives.

War games might be ruled out because of the social perspective among customers. Go-kart racing might be out because of the ski area's commitment to the natural environment, and blacktop and gasoline is not a good fit. Water slides, golf courses and ice skating rinks might be in because they all fit the demographic of the customer and the profile of the organization. In a real situation, there might be a large number of options still in the running because they meet the needs at a strategic level. The list can be pared down later with further analysis.

Now we can move to the project level and make the next choice by revising the problem statement to read: "We need to develop a new revenue stream that will yield a desirable rate of return while improving customer service levels in an expanding market and making the highest and best use of available land."

The project-level statement is more focused on the criteria that will be used to rank the remaining alternatives in order of preference. When the golf course, water slides and ice rink are compared using the criteria, we might have several conflicts about the order in which they should be placed. For example, a golf course might be the most attractive to our customer demographic, but least attractive for land use and capital investment. Water slides might be very attractive for land use, but their popularity is declining, and ice rinks might win on all counts.

If we assume the ice rink wins on all counts, we move to the component level of analysis where we revise the problem to read, "How should the ice rink be designed to maximize financial and customer service results?"

At this point, we are designing the rink. We need to choose between a community-centre type recreational rink, or a national level hockey arena with stands and concessions. Market demographics and financial evaluation of project returns will be used to rank the alternatives.

During the analysis of components, we move into the operating-level analysis frequently. During the development of the project we will deal with small business cases involving the question, "How can the maintenance and repair function work effectively, at minimum cost?" and when the project is complete, we will do ongoing operational cases involving replacement and maintenance of equipment.

One strategic-level business case analysis might result in several cases analyzing the possible projects, each project might result in several cases analyzing the components and each component might result in several cases analyzing the operational alternatives.

It is extremely important to determine the level of the decision you are facing. This is because if you are at an operating level, you need to focus the analysis there. You don't need to justify the strategic decision over again. It has already been made.

A problem that is properly defined increases the likelihood of a chosen solution being successful because the definition itself becomes a target — a focal point to channel your problem-solving activities.

The problem identification process enables us to direct our energies to produce efficient solutions, even if the solution is to determine that the problem is not worth solving and we should maintain the status quo or choose to do nothing. The process could also show that the problem comes from an area of our business that might be dropped entirely or abandoned. Abandoning a business function may be a reasonable solution to a problem if the activity does not support corporate strategies and goals.

Figure 6.6 illustrates the thought process used in solving the ski area's problems.

FIGURE 6.6 Four Levels of Problems/Opportunities for a Ski Area

Level	Analytical Question	Options
Strategic Analysis	"Should we develop a new attraction that is suitable for the market, and complementary to what is presently done?"	~~War Games~~ **Ice Rink** **Water slides** **Golf Course** ~~Go Kart Track~~
Project Analysis	From the options that survive strategic evaluation, the problem becomes, "We need to develop a new revenue stream that will yield a desirable rate of return while improving customer service levels in an expanding market and making the highest and best use of available land."	**Ice rink** ~~Water slides~~ ~~Golf course~~
Component Analysis	For the option that survives project evaluation, the problem becomes, "How should the ice rink be designed to maximize financial and customer service results?"	**Ice rink that is suitable for community use as a hockey arena, as well as an NHL summer training camp.** ~~Ice rink that is suitable for figure skating clinics and competitions.~~
Operations Analysis	For the design that comes from the component analysis, the problem becomes, "How can the maintenance and repair function work effectively, at minimum cost?"	**Purchase our own ice cleaning equipment and hire employees to run it** ~~Outsource ice cleaning to a company in the area who is willing and has the equipment to do the job.~~

As an element of sound management, problem-solving activities are valuable for the following reasons:

- They challenge thought processes and force creative thinking.
- They encourage us to examine situations from different perspectives, frequently causing new and better methods to be employed.
- They usually act as a catalyst for personal learning by the people involved.
- They quite often carry the seeds for new opportunities.

ON THIS TOPIC

A Real-World Example

This is an old story that needs to be retold.

In 1917, the White Truck Company built a milk truck. When they were finished they attempted to take the truck out of the building, only to discover that it was $1\frac{1}{2}$ inches too high.

Management discussed various ways to raise the door.

A person sweeping the floor came by and suggested they let the air out of the tires. They did that and got the truck outside.

This story has several morals. One is that management will tend to deal with problems where they see sparks. The fact that the roof of the truck hits the overhead door of the building is a minor issue when it comes to problem solving.

The second moral is that height begins at the floor. To get the result you want at the end of a process, you need to be willing to challenge every step along the way. Maybe your problem can be solved from something that occurs much sooner in the process.

The third and most important moral is to listen to floor sweepers! Sometimes the perspective of another person is needed to solve problems and you will be surprised when you start to listen to everyone in a process.

IDENTIFYING PROJECT GOALS

A complete problem statement contains a target for accomplishment, i.e. the deliverables that will accrue to the organization when the problem is solved.

Once the problem is defined and the underlying causes investigated, goals that describe specific end-results to be achieved must be identified. Goal identification should address the short-term purpose of the immediate issues being considered as well as the long-range goals of the company.

An expenditure proposal must identify and state clearly the goals that will provide specific measurable outcomes. The goals should address both the immediate short-term purpose and the long-range goals of the expenditure. In general, goals should pass the SMART test:

- **Specific**
- **Measurable**
- **Authority to Act**
- **Realistic**
- **Time Limited**

Experience has shown that most projects can be identified as one of seven types, because they are defined by the goals they are trying to achieve. Expenditures are made to accomplish one or more of the following goals:

1. Expand to meet an increase in customer demand.
   Add on to existing capacity by doing more of what we presently do.
2. Introduce a new division or revenue stream.
   Add to total revenues by diversifying our business to include new products or services that generate revenues.

3. Maintain current technical performance.
   Spend to protect our current level of operation as to quality and quantity.
4. Decrease or potentially decrease future capital and/or operating costs.
   Alter the process to reduce the amount required to operate the process. Become more efficient so that costs can be reduced.
5. Change processes, procedures or programs for technical improvement.
   Spend to improve the quality or accuracy of products and services with the expectation that customer satisfaction will be improved.
6. Introduce a new process, procedure or program to improve quality of customer service or solve an operating problem.
   Spend to enhance the level of customer service, the quality of service and/or the responsiveness of service with the hope that present customers will be retained and new customers will be found.
7. Change processes, procedures or programs to satisfy non-financial factors such as public perception, environmental issues, employee morale etc.
   Spend to achieve social or environmental gains. These are sometimes referred to as "sustainability" issues.

Strategies for Defining Goals

Each of the seven types of projects can then be further classified by the strategy being used to achieve the goal. When goals are being set, it is useful to consider the type of situation being faced. All organizations face four kinds of goals and four levels of risk.

Seek: Search for new, different opportunities or possible achievements that would make a contribution to the organization.

Do something brand new that we have never done before.

Avoid: Identify potential pitfalls and problems (either as a result of past experience, present concerns or future considerations), which can be avoided if proper priorities are established.

Protect what we are presently doing by making operations safe and reliable.

Build: Develop and capitalize on existing strengths in the organization or its operations so they can be exploited to the fullest extent possible.

Repeat a success by doing more of something that we know is working well.

Restore: Return things to a desired level or previous mode of operations after some unexpected departure or deviation from that desired status.

Get the old service level back from something that is not operating like it used to.

The risks of a "seek" project are that we have no direct experience with this project, therefore everything is uncertain. An "avoid" objective deals with the uncertainty of whether the event that is being avoided will occur. The "build" objective assumes that doing more of something successful will yield more success (bigger is not always better). The "restore" strategy assumes that what you had before is still desirable today.

We will use goal type 1 as an example. There are four ways to expand to meet customer demand: You can seek out something brand new, e.g., some new way to meet your customer. You can increase your present output by spending more on maintenance to avoid downtime. You can build on a past success by expanding what you already do. Finally, you can increase the service level of some old assets. The same four options would hold for any one of the seven types of projects.

The relevance of this analysis is that each of the four strategies for defining goals has a different type of risk attached to it. An organization's risk tolerance will impact how far it will go to attempt to solve a problem.

While the problem statement is being developed, give some consideration to what is being delivered and what project risks there are. (A more detailed analysis of risk elements will be dealt with in a later chapter on the decision model.)

CHAPTER SUMMARY

This chapter introduced a systematic problem-solving model that helps create projects that help organizations realize their short- and long-range goals. In addition, the chapter dealt with creating a problem statement that offers guidance to the remainder of the decision-making model.

The problem/opportunity statement is the most important element of the decision model. It sets the stage for where you will look for a solution. Therefore, great care must be taken to ensure that the right problem/opportunity is being dealt with.

Perhaps the best way to summarize the findings of his chapter is to use a "Problem Statement Checklist" (Figure 6.7). I use this checklist extensively with clients when we are trying to make sure that the analysis of a situation is beginning on the right footing.

On the left side of the checklist, there are a variety of characteristics of problem/opportunity statements. On the right side, there are comments about what a decision maker expects to see in the business case to deal with the characteristics of the problem statement. The checklist is useful because it provides the problem solver with a "heads up" about what is expected in the business case.

FIGURE 6.7 Problem Statement Checklist

Characteristics of the problem statement	What is the decision maker expecting to see in the business case?
Is the situation best described as a problem?	If I fail to act, there will be a negative impact.
Is the situation best described as an opportunity?	If I fail to act, I will not take advantage of a positive impact.
Is the problem/opportunity statement future oriented?	We cannot change the past. The statement must address what will happen next.

What type of problem/opportunity is this case trying to deal with?

New business, new revenues, new process	What are the values of financial and non-financial benefits and what are the project risks?
Ongoing project from previous years	Is this project still on scope, on budget and are risks not materializing?
Customer driven service quality or load growth	Is this the most effective means of meeting demand?
Regulatory or legal compliance	Is this the most cost-effective means of compliance?

The primary strategy of the case is to:

Seek (new business practice)	What is the fit with existing systems, and is their success uncertain?
Avoid (spend to avoid a bad outcome)	What is the probability the outcome will be avoided?
Build (enhance existing process)	Will doing more of the same reap the same benefits?
Restore (put the process back in good condition)	Will doing what we did yesterday apply to tomorrow?

Other issues around the case:

Does the statement lend itself to accurate measurement of success?	Can you find hard evidence that the project worked?
Does solving this problem require the co-operation of another division?	Who are they and what is expected of them?
Do you have the authority to solve the problem?	Should you pass this idea on to someone who does have the authority to act on the issue?

If you apply the checklist to your proposed problem/opportunity statement, you will find that you are clearer about the next steps you should take so you can prepare a convincing argument about adopting a solution to the issue.

CLOSING REMARKS

This chapter begins a four-part discussion of problem solving. We introduced the model to be used and we introduced some very important concepts about defining the problem or opportunity we are facing.

Chapters 7, 8 and 9 will walk you through the remainder of the decision-making model.

Remember that the primary purpose of this model is to **S**creen **A**dded **V**alue **I**nitiatives, or rather, to choose to do the things that will have the greatest positive impact on realizing the strategic goals developed in the first five chapters.

TERMS INTRODUCED IN THE CHAPTER

Decision making Choosing between alternative courses of action to take in the future.

Opportunity If you fail to act, positive consequences will not follow.

Problem If you fail to act, negative consequences will follow.

Problem/opportunity checklist A systematic method of matching the characteristics of a situation with the expectations of a decision-maker.

Strategies for defining goals There are four strategies for defining project goals: Seek, Avoid, Build, Restore.

The five C's of casing	A good case is consistent, complete, concise, not contrived and uses common sense.
***Total Impact* business case**	Conducting an analysis of a situation using financial, social and environmental impacts.
4 Levels of problems/ opportunities	Problems can be related to issues that range from strategic to operational.
7 types of problems/ opportunities	Virtually all problems/opportunities fall into seven broad categories.

QUESTIONS FOR CLASS DISCUSSION

1. Describe the difference between a problem and an opportunity.
2. Explain what each of the "five C's" of business casing mean.
3. Explain how the "process and culture of realizing goals" are two elements that need to be in place for goals to be achieved.
4. Using a scenario from your personal experience, discuss how you might deal with goals that conflict with each other in a decision-making situation. (How could you deal with a goal to have low costs and a goal to have high quality at the same time?)
5. Explain why, in the problem-solving model, the largest investment of time is in the development of the problem statement.
6. Using an example from your personal experience, differentiate the four levels of problem/opportunity found in Figure 6.4.
7. Explain why "seek, avoid, build and restore" are listed in descending order of risk.

A CASE FOR STRATEGIC PLANNING: MALCOLM AND RUBY'S NEXT STEP

Ruby is facing a major issue. While her current manufacturing process is working quite well in producing a quality product that is meeting the demand of the western Canadian marketplace, she has just received an inquiry about cost and availability of product that would meet the demand needs of the North American market.

Ruby estimates that for the next three years she will have to increase capacity 100-fold to fill the market with her product. After the three years, she would need 20 times her present capacity to maintain that market.

She has done some preliminary research and found that skilled labour for the assembly process is scarce, but that the people are available and they could be trained within three months. She also found that the Binford Tool Company has a line of robotic assembly machines that are quite expensive but with huge capacity. Malcolm has suggested that she look at contracting out the capacity she needs for the three years to other assembly companies. Then she would only have to increase her capacity 20-fold over the next three years.

Ruby put all her options on the table, those mentioned above and many more that she came up with, and she was totally confused. "All of these alternatives look like they would work. How am I supposed to choose just one?"

REQUIRED:

Develop a problem/opportunity statement for Ruby and then prepare a presentation for Ruby on how she might use the decision-making model to help find the best solution. You don't need to solve the problem; we will do that in the coming chapters. For now, you need to make Ruby a believer in using a systematic decision-making model.

CHAPTER ENDING CASE: A CASE ABOUT SOLVING PROBLEMS

You are the manager of a city work crew that is scheduled to begin the replacement of a water line under the main road in a new development in your city at 8:00 a.m. Sunday. This repair is essential to the integrity of the system as there has been a measurable increase in pipe wear because of ground shifting.

The replacement will involve closing the main access road to the development for about four hours. The local merchants, city council and the Chamber of Commerce were notified of the closure six months ago.

The development is regarded as a monument to municipal planning. It has an optimal mix of residential and commercial properties, and municipal services were constructed using state of the art technology. The development has received national recognition among architects and municipal planners.

The $65,000 repair involves a crew of 12 people as well as the necessary equipment. The $65,000 includes a $15,000 overtime premium paid to the crew, and an $8,500 charge for equipment rentals.

At 7:30 a.m. Sunday, just as the crew is about to start work, you get a call from the president of the Chamber of Commerce. Three months ago, the Chamber of Commerce asked the premier to come to the community centre today to preside over an awards ceremony and host a luncheon. The local municipal planners are to receive a major national award for their efforts in the development. At first the premier declined because of other commitments, so the event was cancelled. About one month ago, the Chamber of Commerce was advised that his schedule had changed, and he would be able to attend. The Chamber accepted, began the arrangements and offered limousine transport from the Vancouver airport for the premier and his entourage.

It seems the Chamber of Commerce forgot about your announced road closure and they want you to postpone your scheduled repairs. The next available time to do the repair is six months from now. The engineer says that the probability of a line failure because of ground shift wear is increasing daily. If a failure occurs, the water supply would be interrupted for 12 days and the repair costs would exceed $500,000.

It is pouring rain outside and the intersection is about two miles from the community centre. The premier is bringing a delegation of 27 people for the ceremony. They are scheduled to arrive at 10:00 a.m. and leave at 1:30 p.m. You have also been advised that the other access to the development from the industrial site is closed for repairs by the department of highways. It would take three days to make the road through the industrial site passable.

What do you do?

CHAPTER 7

Decision Criteria and Scoping the Options

All truth goes through three stages.
First, it is ridiculed. Then, it is violently opposed.
Finally, it is accepted as self-evident.

LEARNING OBJECTIVES

After reading this chapter, engaging in class discussion and doing the exercises at the end of the chapter, you will be able to:

1. Identify and define relevant criteria that will help in evaluating courses of action.
2. Demonstrate the linkage between decision criteria and strategic as well as project goals.
3. Establish measurement concepts for decision criteria, including the five strategic "accounts:" financial, sustainability, stewardship, safety and service to the customer.
4. Develop monetary and non-monetary values for decision criteria.
5. Incorporate an analysis of risk into project evaluation.
6. Define the boundaries for a search of reasonable alternative solutions to the problem/opportunity.

YOUR RESPONSIBILITY

To get the most from Chapter 7, you need to raise your awareness of the range of issues facing managers today and to recognize that those issues help define the criteria that will be used in problem solving.

Find a manager in any organization and ask if his or her job is more complicated than it was ten years ago, not because of technology, but because a greater number of issues must be factored into decisions.

When the manager tells you about the environment, global politics, free trade, changing social values, 9/11 etc, ask him or her how these issues find their way into the decision process. You might be surprised by the number of people who agree that these new issues are important, but don't know how to deal with them.

INTRODUCTION TO CHAPTER 7

From the problem-solving model, Figure 7.1, we have moved the highlight to "criteria and alternatives." In this chapter, we will be taking the problems/opportunities defined in Chapter 6 and advancing them through the model by developing a set of decision criteria that reflect strategic goals, collecting information that will help do a non-financial evaluation (financial evaluation will be done in Chapter 8), and prepare for an evaluation process that will enable alternatives to be ranked in order of desirability (which will be done in Chapter 9).

FIGURE 7.1 The Problem-Solving Model

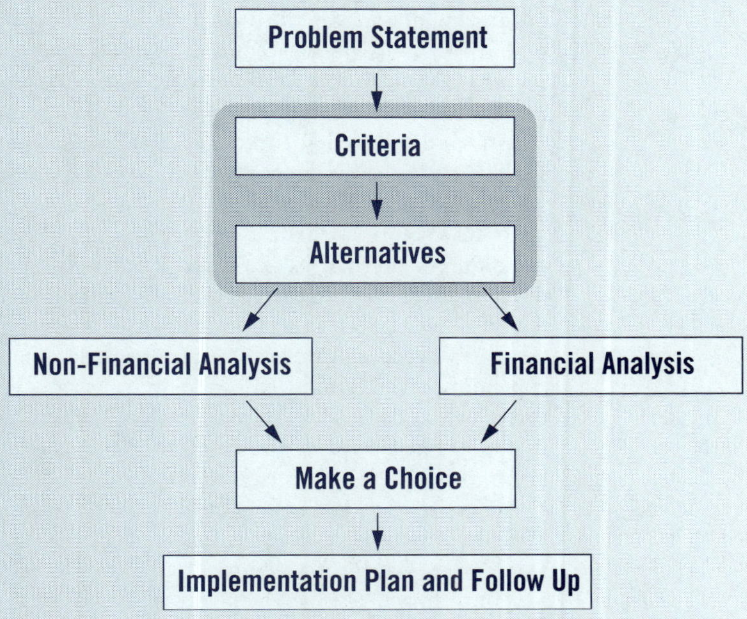

Once we have criteria, alternatives and non-financial analysis done, and we have covered the financial issues in Chapter 8, we can finish the process of choosing between alternative courses of action that will optimize strategic gains, in Chapter 9.

ESTABLISHING DECISION CRITERIA

A decision criterion is a "driver" for choosing between alternative courses of action to solve a problem or take advantage of an opportunity. What drives the selection of an alternative is the one that best fits with the criteria. Sometimes this is simple. If I am trying to decide what kind of dog to get for a pet and my most important criterion is that it must weigh less than three pounds, then deciding to get a Chihuahua and deciding not to get a Saint Bernard is a simple application of "best fit" to a decision driver. If my sole criterion instead was "pleasant personality," I would need more sophisticated methods of testing "best fit" with the criteria. Of course, in real life we would be using more than one criterion to make a choice. Some best fits will be easy, some difficult and some will need to be traded off against each other.

Well-established criteria help the decision process because managers look for solutions that maximize returns in the context of the criteria. Poorly-formed criteria will lead to less than optimal solutions. If, for example, we were dealing with the problem, "I need to buy an automobile to get to work" and we set the decision criterion as fuel economy alone, we will search for small cars as a solution to the problem. If we set the criterion as maximum carrying capacity alone, we will look for large cars. Our perfect car might have: reasonable fuel economy, low capital cost, good performance, low maintenance costs, high reliability, suitable carrying capacity, safe brakes and tires, a seat that suits the driver and a colour that we find appealing. Multiple criteria make decision making more complex.

To evaluate the alternatives of a project, you need to investigate tradeoffs. A simple situation would be choosing the lowest cost alternative if a set of alternatives were similar in every regard except cost. But a problem is rarely so easily solved. Projects that suit reliability, safety, environmental or customer service criteria might well fail in financial evaluation or economic development areas. We need to expand the scope of decision criteria so that a decision maker can fully understand the trade-offs to be made.

Using the *Total Impact* Evaluation Framework, you can collect information that will allow decision makers to make informed value judgments on what something must be "worth" to justify a particular alternative. Often the accounts will conflict with each other (for example: optimizing financial performance versus minimizing environmental impact).

The five *Total Impact* accounts: *financial efficiency and effectiveness, sustainability of the economic environment, stewardship of the natural environment, safety of employees and the public and service to the customer* represent the broad framework for a set of decision criteria that will maximize stakeholder returns. To allow decision makers to make informed tradeoff decisions, each of the five accounts needs to be expanded by identifying sub-items that are relevant to each account, then using the sub-items to help define the different impacts that each alternative solution will have on the sub-item. The sub-items are the criteria we will use to put different alternatives in a priority order. The alternative that creates the best positive outcome in relation to each of the sub-accounts (criteria) will be the most desirable solution to a problem.

The five accounts are used as a framework to go shopping for the potential impacts of an expenditure. You don't need to find impacts from each of the five accounts for your expenditure, but you do need to examine each of the five accounts to see if there is a possible impact that might help to place a value on the benefits of your project. For the sake of clarity, we will begin to call these accounts "criteria" for the remainder of this chapter.

We are trying to take the blinders off by prompting you to look farther afield for project benefits. Simply evaluating the financial consequences of an expenditure does not tell the whole story. Use the *Total Impact* framework to help you discover a wider range of benefits for your project. This will help you sell your idea to decision makers.

Each of the five broad criteria can be further broken down into sub-criteria that serve as examples of potential project benefits.

The remainder of this section expands on the various sub-items within the five main criteria for project and initiative evaluation. These sub-items provide detailed criteria against which alternative solutions could be evaluated. In other words, instead of referring to financial efficiency as a criterion for decision making, it is more informative to refer to new revenue streams or cost reductions as the criteria for the decision.

Note that the five broad "criteria" and the many sub-criteria under each do not suggest that this is a complete list of criteria that should be considered for your project, but only a "shopping list" of potential criteria. In your project situation, you will likely discover unique criteria that relate to your unique situation.

Financial Efficiency and Effectiveness

This criterion documents the "cash-flow" impacts on the organization and stakeholder groups that result from project alternatives. These impacts are captured by the financial reporting system and are mostly internal to the organization since the benefits will be felt by stockholders and financial investors.

Usually, items of financial impact are the easiest to quantify because organizations already have financial reporting systems that can be harvested for the information you need to determine the financial impact of an alternative. Thus, when you are considering the purchase of a new asset to solve a problem or take advantage of an opportunity, the vendor will provide lots of financial information to help in the selling process. Now it is your job to figure out if they are telling the truth!

The complete financial evaluation system is being covered in Chapter 8. For now, we are introducing financial impacts to begin the thought process.

Some examples of items that directly affect financial performance are shown below in Figure 7.2.

FIGURE 7.2 The Financial Criteria

Sub-Criteria	Measurement Concept
Financial returns to stockholders	Return on equity, return on assets, profit margin etc. These are aggregate, or high-level measures of financial success.
Operating cost savings	Productivity improvements such as reduced processing costs, (materials and labour) sickness, injury and absence, maintenance costs and support/overhead costs.
Salvage value of equipment	The sale of existing assets (buildings, land). These benefits flow at the end of the life cycle of the project.
Reduced acquisition costs of assets, goods or services	Lower costs of acquiring capacity through asset purchases. These benefits refer to being able to improve capacity through the purchase of more efficient capital assets that cost less to buy relative to the capacity achieved.
Asset value savings	Workspace savings (reduced office space), increased equipment use (more capacity from existing machines) and asset life extensions (prolonging the service life of producing assets).

ON THIS TOPIC

A Real-World Example

It is very common for organizations to set financial targets and then ask management to develop projects that meet or exceed the targets.

In 1990, Chevron Canada set a goal called "15 in 95," meaning that they wanted to achieve a 15% return on assets used, by the year 1995. The catchy phrase "15 in 95" became a driving force for projects to achieve efficiency gains or new revenues, all in support of the "15 in 95" goal.

www.chevron.ca

Social and Stakeholder Criteria

The remaining criteria have financial impacts that are not internal to the organization. The financial impacts are felt by stakeholder groups. In addition, the stakeholder groups have a variety of non-financial impacts that come from projects and initiatives. Some of the internal stakeholders, i.e. employees and customers, will benefit from the four remaining criteria. Society at large will also benefit from the four remaining criteria.

Social criteria are broadly collected under the concept of "sustainability." In this context, sustainability refers to the investments that organizations must make in the social system to satisfy the needs of the stakeholders in the social system so that those stakeholders will allow the organization to continue operations. The bottom line is that no matter how profitable you are, if you pollute, if you operate unethically or illegally or if you damage the social system, your licence to operate will be challenged. Organizations recognize that a comprehensive plan is needed so the necessary resources can be allocated to ensure that operations can continue into the future.

You might ask why some of the social benefits are relevant to an analysis of a decision. They are relevant for several reasons:

- If two alternatives' financial costs and benefits are identical, then the alternative that best suits the social system should be chosen out of a sense of social responsibility.
- If two alternatives have no financial benefits, only financial costs, then the non-financial impacts will be used to rank the alternatives.
- If a project requires the approval of a government before the project can be put into place, then the social impacts of the project will be used to rank alternatives.

Thus, the following impacts will be useful in capturing the *Total Impact* of a project.

Sustainability of the Economic Environment

Organizations are recognizing that the economic system is a network of partnerships, and, though you may be competing with others in your industry, all organizations need to prosper for the economic system to flourish.

Organizations impact the community in which they live in two ways. They create jobs that stimulate the economy and they create spin-off businesses that support the organization. These benefits can be measured as follows in Figure 7.3:

FIGURE 7.3 The Sustainability Criteria

Sub-Criteria	Measurement Concept
New Employment	The primary quantified measure for economic development is the number of person-years of employment that is created and its duration. Provide estimates of the number or percentage of currently unemployed persons who will find employment as a result of the project, particularly regionally. Indicate what types of employment will be created, for example highly versus low skilled.
Economic Activity Benefits	Identify the new business created by your initiative, specifically business that did not exist in the region before our project was in place. The primary benefit of stimulated business is the increase in the flow of funds in the economic system.

ON THIS TOPIC — *A Real-World Example*

Economists suggest that the net tax benefit of a job, i.e. the contribution that job makes to the tax system, is $17,140. Therefore, if the cost of creating a new job is less than $17,140, there will be a net gain in the economic system.

When you expand operations or begin a new business in a region, the jobs you create have value to the community. In addition, the economic stimulation you create might attract other new businesses to serve the customers you are attracting. If you open a new mega grocery store in a new community, you will soon be surrounded by gas stations, fast food restaurants and video stores, all trying to serve your customers.

Stewardship of the Natural Environment

The environmental criterion documents a wide range of potential impacts that project alternatives could have on the natural environment. It is important to consider the "end" impacts of a particular situation. For example, the end result of effective environmental management is to cause an improvement in:

- wildlife health
- aquatic health
- vegetation health.

It is most desirable to measure the effect on the end impacts. If you can capture a measure of change caused by your project in these end impact areas, then that measure should be used.

In many cases, the limitations on our ability to capture end impact measures might require the use of "means" measures rather than "ends" measures. For example, if our project has an impact on aquatic health as an end result, we could find accurate measures of effluent emissions that will be reduced by our project as a "means" of improving aquatic health.

Examples of "means" measures are found in Figure 7.4.

FIGURE 7.4 The Environmental Criteria

Sub Criteria	Measurement Concept
Air emissions	Parts per million of airborne contaminants.
Water emissions	Parts per million of waterborne contaminants.
Contaminated soil	Parts per million of solid contaminants.
Recycled materials	Quantity and proportion of recycled materials to other forms of waste.

Regardless of the "means" measure you choose, your analysis should demonstrate a clear link between the change in the measurement caused by your project and the effect on the end result.

The ultimate end result is to improve the quality of life for plants, fish, animals and humans. A very popular measure of the end result benefit of environmental stewardship is equating a particular substance, say sulphur dioxide, with the direct healthcare costs of dealing with that pollutant as it impacts humans. The economic value of the healthcare costs avoided then becomes the economic justification for investing to reduce the presence of that pollutant in the environment.

ON THIS TOPIC

A Real-World Example

Over the last 30 years, pressure has been brought to the automobile industry to reduce emissions from autos. The pressure came in the form of legislation that forced emission reductions.

The response from the industry was to design more fuel-efficient cars and pass the cost on to the consumer, who was apparently willing to pay the price.

The importance and value of conservation can be seen in the advertising for the new Jaguar. This top-end car is being promoted as a luxury car, which we expect, but also because of its aluminum construction, making it lighter and more fuel efficient. The advertising goes to the extent of estimating the fuel saved during the life of the car and estimating the impact on the natural environment and healthcare system of that fuel not being consumed.

Jaguar assumes that its customer is very sophisticated and well versed in environmental issues.

www.jaguar.ca

Safety of Employees and the Public (Social Impacts)

It is important to note that safety means more than physical injury. As stewards of an organization, whether profit- or service-oriented, society as a whole expects that management will conduct operations so that negative impacts on quality of life will be minimized and positive impacts will be maximized. Those impacts must be analyzed for employees, direct customers and members of society at large.

"Safekeeping" the quality of our lives therefore means that projects must be analyzed in terms of their impact on a broad range of social safety issues.

In the recent past, the power of social stakeholders has become quite significant. Many organizations have created "corporate affairs" departments whose sole responsibility is to monitor social perspectives and then ensure that those social perspectives are effectively included in the organization's planning and decision-making processes.

Items to consider under the social criteria could include the following areas in Figure 7.5:

FIGURE 7.5 The Social Impact Criteria

Sub-Criteria	Measurement Concept
Aesthetics **Areas of cultural, historical or archaeological significance** **Quality of life** **Equitable treatment of the public**	Usually measured with a public opinion survey that captures the perception of stakeholders regarding the value they place on having the issues present in their social environment. Most frequently, the measures centre around crime reduction, access to community services like schools and hospitals, the quality of the transportation system, access to day care and seniors' homes. While it is the job of government to manage these things, it is the job of organizations in the system to support and finance them.
Recreation	Count the change in the number of users of recreation facilities and other services. The assumption is that increased recreation improves health, which reduces healthcare costs. Among youth, increased recreation reduces youth crime and the related victim costs.
Public and worker safety	Accident rates both on the job and in the community at large.
The organization being a progressive employer	Employee turnover, absenteeism, and other morale and employment equity measures.

This list only scratches the surface of potential social criteria. The issues are constantly changing and normally they are specific to a region or an industry.

ON THIS TOPIC — *A Real-World Example*

All levels of government are producing business cases to justify their investments in the social system. Governments need business cases because increasing pressure from taxpayers to improve service, along with reduced financial resources, is causing managers to try and get more bang for their bucks.

Here are three of the many Web sites that are available to help quantify social benefits:
Leisure Information Network, http://www.lin.ca/htdocs/index.cfm
The Benefits Web site, http://www.lin.ca/htdocs/benefits.htm
International Center for Crime Prevention, http://www.crime-prevention-intl.org/

Customer Service Impacts

It has been proposed that the ultimate measure of customer satisfaction can be found on the income statement. If the customer is not satisfied, he or she will not buy from you! I agree, the identity of the customer is quite simple: the customer is the one who transfers cash from his or her account to yours.

Finding out that your customers are not happy by looking at the income statement is far too late. If you want to effectively manage the outcome, which is more sales, you need to manage all the dimensions that contribute to the outcome.

Analyzing customer service is important because it causes people to think in broader terms about how to satisfy customers. This in turn causes managers to take a more proactive stance in managing customer expectations.

Customer satisfaction is more than the customer being happy with the product or service and perceiving that he or she has received good value. Customer service can also involve how potential customers are treated, how friends of customers are treated, how customers see your organization as a member of the community and how customers are impacted in other ways when they consume your product or service.

Some dimensions of the customer service criteria follow in Figure 7.6.

FIGURE 7.6 The Customer Service Criteria

Sub-Criteria	Measurement Concept
Quality of products or services	Customer satisfaction survey Number of repeat customers % Market share
Cash-flow implications	Either positive or negative cash-flow implications for customers in the form of prices and costs that are incurred through their use of your products or services.
Market or one-time impacts to customers' land or property	Cost or benefit impacts on real estate values or other assets owned by the customer.
Changes to the quality of non-core service areas such as providing technical assistance or advice, or providing general information	Measures of attitude, friendliness, responsiveness and professionalism as collected in a customer opinion survey.

ON THIS TOPIC

A Real-World Example

Remember the mission statement from Coca Cola introduced in Chapter 2?

To sell more of our superior products, through the customer, to the consumer, at a profit

Coca Cola recognizes that its customer, the buyer, is not necessarily the consumer. By separating the "customer" into two dimensions, Coke is clearer about how it meets customer needs. (coca-cola.com)

Risk, Often the Most Powerful Criterion

In addition to the five broad criteria for locating project benefits, there is one overriding criterion that impacts all decisions. That criterion is risk. Risk is loosely defined as "the likelihood that a consequence you don't want will happen to you." If you're like me, you don't want a piano to fall on your head. Also, if you're like me, you recognize that the likelihood of that happening is so remote that you don't worry about it, you don't plan for it, you don't expect it.

If you're like most organizations, you don't want to suffer losses, and you don't want to be ill prepared for unforeseen success, (risk works both ways). And if you're like most organizations, you worry about losses, you plan for losses and you expect losses. That's just good risk management.

Too often, we experience superior performance from an investment decision when the decision was made without adequate analysis. Luck, while a desired condition, can't be relied on. Similarly, we have made excellent decisions that have had bad outcomes. While conditions may have changed to cause the outcome to deteriorate, it is still in our best interest to learn from the decision-making process.

The most important thing we have learned is that comprehensively analyzing the risks in a project will improve the decision process and increase the likelihood that the optimal solution will be realized.

In a problem-solving process, risk must be addressed twice. First, in analyzing alternatives, we must recognize that each alternative has inherent risks because alternatives represent a change in future conditions. Given the unpredictability of the future, the alternatives may or may not deliver as predicted. We might accept a solution based on assumed deliverables without analyzing risk, and we might reject the alternative after the risk has been analyzed.

We assess the risk again as a final vetting of the project after the optimal solution has been found. In that context, we are dealing with the risk of a total project failure.

First, we will deal with the risks of assumptions made in analyzing alternatives.

Dealing with Risks in the Analysis Phase

In any project proposal, a primary consideration is the cost of the project, against which future benefits may be evaluated to determine the appropriate benefit/cost ratio. This ratio does not always need to be a financial benefit/cost ratio (as explained in Chapter 8). The relationship of costs to levels of service, safety, environmental stewardship, customer satisfaction and employee morale can be captured in non-financial terms. Usually, however, the benefits are captured in non-financial terms and the costs are reflected using financial terms. We can establish how many dollars we are investing in safety or customer satisfaction and then use that information to help in the ranking process.

Every alternative has risks. Our job is to identify as many risks as we can, deal with their impact on the decision and make a choice with full knowledge of the uncertainty involved. It is often useful to analyze options with "most likely, optimistic and pessimistic" scenarios.

Some of the risks that should be considered are:

- timing of the project/cash flow sequence,
- project completion risk,
- assumption error,
- estimate error,
- obsolescence,
- risks related to operational efficiency, maintenance frequency and system reliability.

Analyzing alternatives should address issues such as these:

- What are the risks and where is the major uncertainty in the project?
- How sensitive is the expected benefit/cost ratio or net present value to a change in assumption for important variables such as in-service date, projected benefits or costs?
- How much of the project cost would be lost if something major went wrong?

It may not be possible to adequately identify and quantify risk. However, being aware that risks exist and being able to quantify some of them will provide a balanced justification for the expenditure. Items such as liability insurance, builder's insurance, performance bonds and equipment warranties are examples of risk management tools that may help to decrease the impact of risks in an expenditure decision.

Dealing with Risks from a Total Project View

The final vetting of a project, prior to submission, should include an objective analysis of the inherent risks. Given that a project is a prediction of an outcome that has consequences in the future, and given that the future is not entirely predictable, this vetting is extremely useful for both the project initiator and the decision maker. The decision maker will take on a project with full knowledge of potential downsides, and the initiator will develop action plans for mitigating the effect of risks should they materialize.

The procedure for a risk analysis is to take every single event and assumption in the project and ask the following questions:

- What could go wrong?
- What could go more right than expected? (too much success is risky)
- What is the likelihood of this event occurring?
- How will the effect be felt?
- What can be done to mitigate the effect?
- What system will I use to tell me when the risk event has occurred?
- What is the earliest possible time I can notice that things are not going as planned?
- What corrective action needs to be taken after the event has occurred?
- What risks are associated with staying with the status quo or the do nothing alternative?
- Am I comfortable enough with the probability and cost of risk to allow the project to proceed?

There are two views of risk analysis, a micro view that deals with project-specific risk and a macro view that deals with risks coming from the environment.

THE MICRO VIEW OF RISKS

Project-specific risks are the risks associated with project events, such as:

- technical fit with existing systems,
- projected costs and benefits,
- supplier delivery and quality control,
- meeting the installation timeline.

Project-specific risks are generally regarded as predictable and controllable by managers. If the effects of these risks are understood, the manager can either mitigate the risk by choosing another alternative, or mitigate the effect of the risk by having an action plan in place to deal with the event.

Some of the risk events in the micro view might be caused by environmental forces that are not controllable but are predictable. A manager should be able to predict the event and have a plan in place for dealing with the event.

THE MACRO VIEW OF RISKS

The macro view deals with environmental risks that are outside the project scope. These risks might be predictable but are largely uncontrollable by the manager. Examples of these risks are:

- technical obsolescence,
- economic forces, (recession and inflation),
- legislative changes in areas such as environmental compliance and human rights,
- population growth and preferences.

Though these events are largely uncontrollable, a manager can still mitigate the effect of the risk by developing a system that enables the event to be recognized early on and having an action plan in place to deal with the consequences.

The basic principle of a risk assessment is the need to have a thorough knowledge of the likelihood and costs of risk events. This will allow a decision maker to evaluate the tradeoff between this project and some other project with different risks.

In the final analysis the choice of an alternative comes from a balancing of trade-offs. The *Total Impact* criteria are useful in this regard because they prompt the manager to consider all the impacts — social and financial — of a project.

Making a choice should be so obvious that it takes virtually no time at all. What takes the time and effort is putting yourself in the position where you are able to make a choice. We can easily choose to buy the Ferrari on the condition that all involved parties to the decision process, including the banker, have agreed that ego gratification is a good criterion, and that financial considerations are not as important.

If we have been diligent in formulating a problem statement, establishing the criteria, searching for alternatives and evaluating alternatives, a choice should flow naturally from the process.

USING CRITERIA TO RANK ALTERNATIVES

At this point, you should have several criteria to help select the best solution to a problem. The criteria define the dimensions of the analysis that alternatives will be subjected to. For example, if you need to buy a car, before you go shopping, you might say "I'm looking for a six-passenger station wagon for under $10,000." Clearly, your criteria will offer some focus while you go shopping for solutions to your problem. No sense going to the Ferrari dealership!

You will also find that criteria need to be weighted as to their relative significance in the decision process. "Because there are six people in my family, the car must have six passenger spaces, and while a station wagon is preferred, a large car would be ok, and I could borrow up to $15,000 if absolutely necessary. The six spaces criterion is non-negotiable."

The same logic holds in business decisions. Before you go shopping for alternative solutions to a problem, rank your criteria in descending order of importance, and put values on how the criteria will be measured, either in financial or non-financial terms.

Ranking criteria in order will certainly help the decision process, because what is most important as a criterion should be what is most important in ranking alternatives. In most cases, criteria will be traded off against each other while the search for the best solution goes on.

You might find a criterion that is so powerful it stands alone. I call these "show stoppers." Imagine that you have five criteria to use in ranking your alternative choice of which automobile to purchase: low cost, good fuel economy, low maintenance, large trunk, appealing colour. All these criteria have ranges within which the criteria can be met and tradeoffs can occur. Implied in your analysis is one hidden criterion: you must have a driver's licence to use the car. When your licence is suspended for some legal reason, the analysis of alternatives stops. The "show stopper" is a single criterion that, if unmet, will cause all the alternatives to fail.

We use criteria to choose among alternatives. Now that we have some criteria, let's find the alternatives.

IDENTIFYING ALTERNATIVES

The quality of the ultimate solution depends on the range of the search for alternative courses of action. In ideal circumstances, we wish to search a sufficiently broad range of options so that we can be sure that the optimal solution is contained in the set. At the same time, we do not wish to search such a broad range that we have included illogical alternatives. We want to spend time efficiently, not waste time analyzing alternatives that cannot be used.

Identifying alternative courses of action involves the following steps:

- Use the problem statement to set the guidelines for where the search for a solution will take place.
- Use the decision criteria to locate alternatives that might prove to be the optimal solution.
- Search for a limited number of alternatives. The manager employs various methods of scoping to find a few selected alternatives relevant to the goals of the problem statement and the choice criteria.
- Put a boundary on the scope of the search by rejecting obviously unsuitable alternatives, i.e. the ones that are not related to the problem or will not fit the decision criteria.
- Don't be afraid to challenge or shift existing rules, perceptions and assumptions.

Conceptually, identifying alternatives is a parallel rather than sequential process. In any expenditure decision, the manager considers several potentially acceptable alternatives at the same time. As new information is collected and evaluated against the alternatives, the alternatives that do not contribute to achieving the specified objectives are rejected immediately. Acceptable alternatives are kept in the manager's active file until he or she is ready to evaluate them.

The range of alternatives to be examined will depend on your level in the problem identification process. At the strategy level, we challenge existing rules and assumptions by scoping alternatives from a very broad set. At the project level, we narrow the set to deal with options that meet the accepted strategy. At the component level, we find options that satisfy the project, and at the operating level, we deal with specific items such as maintenance and operating costs.

In all organizations there are many problem areas where service quality must be evaluated in light of an environmental or economic effect. The search for alternatives should be comprehensive enough that an enlightened tradeoff can be made.

Identifying alternatives is normally conducted with limited time and money. Regardless of how much time and money are spent in pursuit of additional information, the search seldom obtains all the information related to a particular alternative course of action. In other words, the time and effort required to obtain additional information should be considered in relation to the value of the information.

All problem situations have a variety of alternative approaches:

- **Abandonment** Eliminate the problem by abandoning the process that is the cause.

  We do not need to replace equipment that breaks down if the equipment is not making a valuable contribution to corporate goals. Nor do we need to maintain a department or function if the contribution is not favourable. Abandonment is a key issue in maximizing organizational effectiveness. Processes that can be abandoned often represent sizable investment in capital and operating resources that can be put to better use elsewhere.

- **Redevelop** Eliminate the problem by employing a new process or changing an old process.

  Once we have located the cause of a problem, we can permanently alter the process so that the problem does not occur again. A recurring problem has not been solved. We have simply developed a response to a symptom. The solution is optimal when the symptom does not occur again. This usually involves a change in the amount of capital or operating expenditure.

- **Rehabilitate** Eliminate the problem by replacing the process with a similar process.

  Replacement puts us back in the position we were in before the problem came to light. The concept of restoring ourselves to the position we had in the past assumes that the past is desirable for the future. In other words, no logical improvements could be realized with a different asset or process. Sometimes an equipment breakdown is an opportunity to replace with an improvement.

- **Do nothing** Stay with the status quo.

  Any proposed change in a process should be compared against the status quo situation. A good alternative is one that provides higher benefits than simply continuing with what we have. Staying with the status quo is different than doing nothing. It means we will continue to maintain and manage the existing system. Doing nothing implies that we will let the process naturally deteriorate. In some cases, it is logical to choose to do nothing and simply let the asset expire.

There are risks involved in not acting on a problem. Sometimes the risks of inaction may be straightforward and have potentially adverse effects, for example, public safety, reliability or regulatory compliance. In other areas, however, the risks of inaction are less obvious. The cost of doing nothing may result in foregone opportunities in lost revenue, reduced efficiency, or loss of customer goodwill. Foregone opportunities are quantifiable risks that can be evaluated with economic and financial analysis.

In general, a well-scoped list of options will facilitate a logical and well-balanced analysis of the possible solutions to a problem.

Once we are satisfied that the complete set of logical solutions has been found, it's time to match the alternatives to the criteria and put the alternatives in order of attractiveness.

CHAPTER SUMMARY

This chapter was about building a framework for making a decision. The foundation of the framework is the set of decision criteria to be applied to a set of reasonable alternatives, which might solve the problem/opportunity.

This chapter teaches two critical lessons:

1. Care must be taken to ensure that the set of criteria are complete and that the criteria have measures so that alternatives can be ranked.
2. The scoping of alternatives must be broad enough to contain the best possible solution.

Problem solving can be easy if you do it wrong, but you won't be finding the best solution!

CLOSING REMARKS

We are almost ready to make a choice, except for one major element: financial evaluation.

The financial evaluation is often the most complex part of decision analysis. That's why it deserves a chapter of its own.

At this point, you should understand that a complete *Total Impact* analysis of a situation requires a detailed understanding of all the potential elements of the situation. Only then can you be assured that moving towards strategic goals is possible and is happening.

TERMS INTRODUCED IN THE CHAPTER

Abandon, redevelop, rehabilitate, do nothing Four potential actions that could be taken in the face of a problem/opportunity.

Alternatives A range of potential solutions to a problem/opportunity.

Criteria A set of drivers that will enable the selection of one alternative as the best solution.

Customer service criteria A decision driver that refers to the customers' perception of how they are treated while they do business with an organization.

Financial effectiveness	Maintaining quality and other social dimensions while being financially efficient.
Financial efficiency	Conducting operations at the lowest possible cost.
Risk	The likelihood that a consequence that you don't want will happen to you.
Safety and social criteria	A decision driver that refers to the impact of operations on social elements as they relate to employees and members of the public.
Scoping	Searching out a reasonable set of alternatives for consideration in the decision process.
Stewardship of the natural environment	A decision driver that refers to the impact of operations on the physical environment.
Sustainability criteria	A decision driver that refers to the role the organization plays in the economic system.
Using criteria to rank alternatives	The process of matching alternatives to the decision criteria by determining which alternative has the best fit to the criteria.

QUESTIONS FOR CLASS DISCUSSION

1. Identify a set of criteria one might use for an auto purchase decision.
2. Identify a set of criteria one might use for choosing a college or university.
3. What do you see as the major differences in the criteria cited in questions 1 and 2?
4. For each of the five *Total Impact* criteria, develop a criterion and a measurement concept and relate them to the decision to construct a hospital in your community.
5. Offer an example of a "show stopper" criterion that might be found in a decision to automate a process that is currently labour-intensive.
6. Describe a situation where customer service goes beyond the purchase and use of a product or service.
7. Describe how the concept of sustainability of the economic system might apply to the forest products industry.
8. Define the risks you faced for a situation from your personal experience.
9. Describe what is meant by putting a boundary on the scope of alternatives.
10. Assume you have a machine that is fairly inefficient. Using the four alternative approaches to solving a problem, identify four general alternative courses of action that could be taken

A CASE FOR STRATEGIC PLANNING: MALCOLM AND RUBY'S NEXT STEP

REQUIRED:

Using the scenario regarding expanding capacity as presented in Chapter 6, develop a set of decision criteria and a list of alternative solutions that Ruby should consider.

To refresh your memory, the Chapter 6 scenario has been reproduced below:

> *Ruby is facing a major issue. While her current manufacturing process is working quite well in producing a quality product that is meeting the demand of the western Canadian marketplace, she has just received an inquiry about cost and availability of product that would meet the demand needs of the North American market.*

Ruby estimates that for the next three years she will have to increase capacity 100-fold to fill the market with her product. After the three years, she would need 20 times her present capacity to maintain that market.

She has done some preliminary research and found that skilled labour for the assembly process is scarce, but that the people are available and they could be trained within three months. She also found that the Binford Tool Company has a line of robotic assembly machines that are quite expensive but with huge capacity. Malcolm has suggested that she look at contracting out the capacity she needs for the three years to other assembly companies. Then she would only have to increase her capacity 20-fold over the next three years.

Ruby put all her options on the table, those mentioned above and many more that she came up with, and she was totally confused. "All of these alternatives look like they would work. How am I supposed to choose just one?"

CHAPTER ENDING CASE: A CASE ABOUT DECISION CRITERIA

Over the last 10 years, your city has enjoyed a growth rate of over 10% while the average growth rate for cities in Canada is less than 2%. The primary reason for this growth is that city council has embarked on a huge campaign to attract new high-tech industry to the area. The plan is for the city to become Canada's technology capital.

Ten years ago, the city rezoned a 300-hectare parcel of agricultural land for light industrial use, created commercial building lots and offered tax relief to prospective buyers. Within three years, the industrial park was fully sold and industry began building and moving in. Council was ecstatic with the result. In fact, 32,000 new jobs were created and 20,000 new residences were constructed in the residential area of town.

Five years ago, when the site was half-developed, complaints began rolling in about the excessive travel time from home to work. It seems council neglected to plan for the additional traffic caused by the development. Now, five years later, with the site fully developed, protesters attend every council meeting demanding that something be done. Commuters are spending about two hours to commute 10 kilometres and commercial vehicles are complaining about lost revenue.

There is presently a two-lane road connecting the development with the residential community. And there is a bridge on the route crossing the river. The bridge was constructed in 1947 and engineers report that it could be widened to two lanes each way for about 70% of the cost of constructing a new bridge.

REQUIRED:

Generate a set of criteria that city managers should use to guide their decision process and then generate a list of alternative courses of action they should consider.

CHAPTER 8

Financial Evaluation

"Confidence" is the feeling a person has before he or she fully understands the situation.

LEARNING OBJECTIVES

After reading this chapter, engaging in class discussion and doing the exercises at the end of the chapter, you will be able to:

1. Conduct a thorough financial evaluation of alternative solutions to a problem/opportunity using discounted cash flow analysis.
2. Use Net Present Value, Benefit to Cost Ratio, Internal Rate of Return and Cash Payback period to rank alternatives in order of financial attractiveness.
3. Understand the implications of making cash flow predictions into the future.
4. Separate the financial analysis into two parts: the financial impacts on your organization and the financial impact on society at large.
5. Use financial evaluation to value social and sustainability investments where the financial benefits cannot be calculated.
6. Conduct a "Critical Value" and "Marginal Value" analysis to help in prioritizing expenditures.
7. Use the spreadsheet, provided as a supplement to Chapters 8 and 9, to prepare a comprehensive financial evaluation of project alternatives.

YOUR RESPONSIBILITY

To get the most from Chapter 8, you need to strengthen your understanding of how money fits into the mix of criteria that govern decisions. Things have changed recently. It used to be that financial issues were the most powerful and often the only criterion used to make choices.

This chapter requires use of a supplemental spreadsheet found on the Fane Online Learning Centre at www.mcgrawhill.ca/college/fane. Instructions for downloading and using the spreadsheet can also be found on the Online Learning Centre, under the heading: PROJECT EVALUATION SOFTWARE USER'S GUIDE FOR USE WITH "TOTAL IMPACT ANALYZER."™

The advent of sustainability and social responsibility has caused organizations to mix money with other issues. It hasn't been easy because most information systems are based on the accounting system. Therefore, the most comfortable measure of results is money. Now we are asking organizations to measure results in other than monetary terms.

Find some annual reports. Notice that only a portion of the report deals with financial results. Notice how the organization plans to measure the results in other strategic areas.

INTRODUCTION TO CHAPTER 8

Referring again to the decision-making model, Figure 8.1 indicates that the highlight has moved to the financial evaluation portion of the model.

FIGURE 8.1 The Decision-Making Model

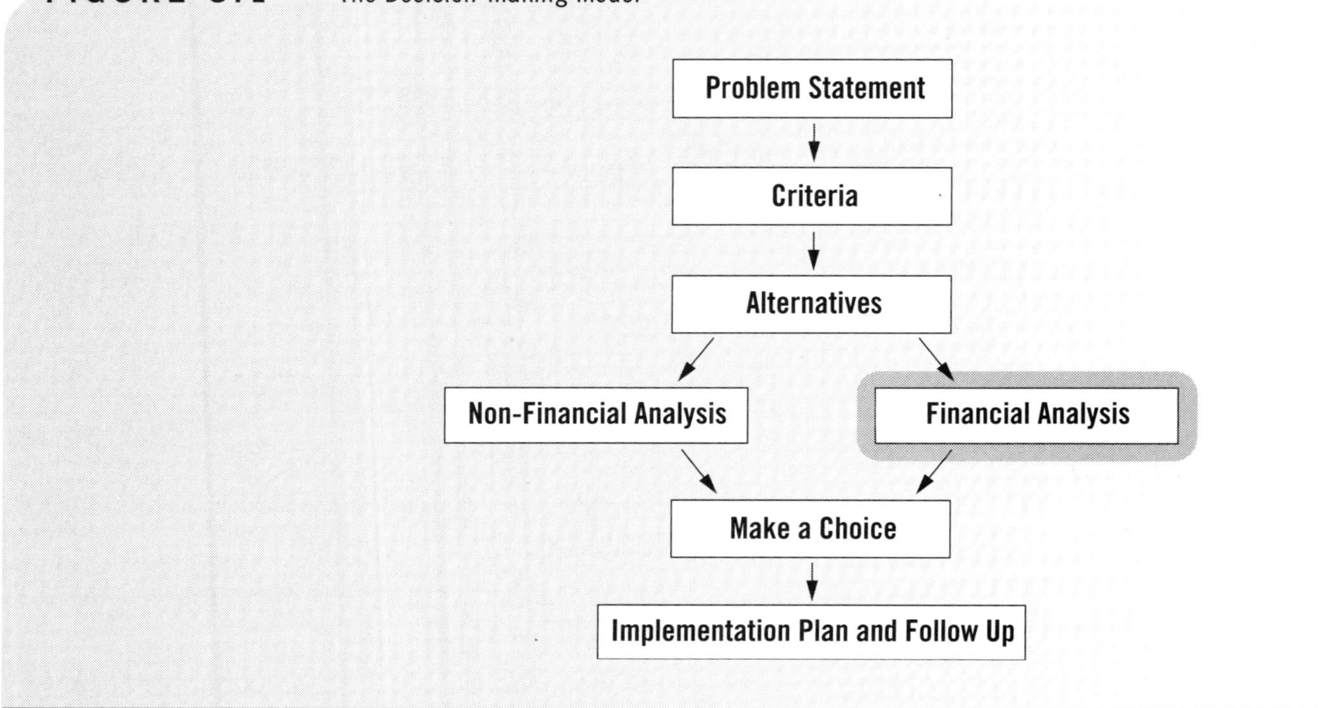

Financial analysis deserves special consideration for two reasons. First, it is often regarded as the most complex part of the evaluation process and second, financial efficiency and effectiveness are very powerful strategic goals. Though social evaluation may take a variety of forms, financial evaluation is normally conducted using discounted cash flow analysis.

It is very important to note that financial and social evaluation go hand in hand. Projects are not approved on financial or social considerations alone. One may take precedence over the other, depending on the situation, but no social project should ever be approved without considering the financial dimensions, and no financial project should be approved without considering the social dimensions.

Once we have concluded our study of financial issues, we will be able to merge the two evaluation systems to make our choice of the optimal solution, in Chapter 9.

REASONS FOR FINANCIAL EVALUATION

The purpose of this chapter is to enhance your understanding of financial evaluation so that you can:

- initiate and perform financial evaluations to support the analysis of decision alternatives,
- understand the implications on the business decision of cash flow estimates into the future,
- develop a sufficient understanding of financial analysis to be able to incorporate financial considerations in the business case.

A financial evaluation is only one of the tools used to prioritize projects. While we have accepted projects with nominal financial returns in exchange for some strategically driven initiatives in *Total Impact* analysis, there is one common feature that binds all projects regardless of the measures of benefits. All projects have an identifiable cost in the form of the resources given up to initiate the project. Though financial evaluation might not be the key driver for choices in all projects, it is clear the financial impacts are felt by all projects.

There are two objectives of financial evaluation:

- To array the long-term financial implications of proposed expenditures so that investment decisions can be prioritized.
- To quantify the expected results of the proposed expenditure so that the quality of a decision can be measured.

Financial analysis is a system that is used to capture the financial effects of a decision. Other systems, such as improved public image, are used to capture the non-financial effects. The techniques used to array or rank the financial impacts of investment decisions should be part of a manager's daily routine in business decision making.

Financial evaluation is the comparison of investment costs to financial benefits received.

INVESTMENT COSTS DEFINED

A cost is defined as a resource used to achieve an objective. An investment cost is not just the invoice price paid for an asset. The investment is the total package of resources committed to the project for the life of the project. This includes the original invoice price, operating and maintenance costs, the cost of changing other elements of the business to meet the needs of this new asset and the opportunity costs of not having those resources available for other projects.

In general terms, any cost could represent:

- an increase or potential increase in capacity,
- a decrease or potential decrease in operating costs,
- a change in processes or procedures for technical improvement alone,
- a change in processes or procedures to satisfy non-quantitative factors.

There are five key points associated with this definition of investment costs:

1. **Investment costs are not just capital.**

   The cost of items such as employee development programs, staff increases and advertising can be subjected to financial evaluation techniques.

2. **Investments represent a change in future conditions.**

   Marginal costs and marginal benefits (marginal meaning the added costs or benefits that will accrue in the future) are the product of an estimate of future conditions. Historical financial information is used to build a model for prediction, but **all future costs and benefits are estimates** that have some uncertainty.

3. **Investments relate to corporate objectives and business unit strategies.**

   The key issue in the investment decision is compliance with corporate goals and strategies. A business case must therefore link financial and operating issues to planning goals.

4. **Investments deal in a world of uncertainty.**

   Any prediction of future conditions is uncertain. Inherent in the financial evaluation model is the risk of attempting to quantify the future.

5. **Investment benefits and costs are assumed to be quantifiable.**

   Financial evaluation will help identify the real financial costs and benefits associated with a decision. In projects involving added revenues or cost savings, the relationship between financial inputs and outputs is very clear. When a project delivers intangible returns, every effort should be made to apply logical financial values to those intangible accounts where those logical values would enhance the quality of a financial evaluation.

Before we can effectively deal with these issues in a financial evaluation, we need to discuss the most critical element of the decision model. All financial decisions, whether they are in a business or on a personal level, involve comparing what is to be achieved financially to what could be achieved by using your money doing something else. This concept is called "opportunity cost."

Opportunity cost means that if you do something, you can't do something else. If you go to school, you can't work full time. The opportunity cost of going to school is therefore the wages you are giving up.

In financial decisions, we don't always have something specific to compare against. We don't say that if I buy this specific asset it means I won't be able to buy some other specific asset. We usually say that if I spend on this project, I won't have funds available to spend on any other projects.

We capture this broad comparison by using a "Cost of Capital."

COST OF CAPITAL DEFINED

When investment decisions are made and appropriate funds committed, there are capital costs associated with these decisions. "Cost of capital" (also called "hurdle rate") is more appropriately thought of as an opportunity cost of capital. Capital refers to money invested to get an outcome. Therefore, opportunity cost of capital refers to all the things you can't do because your resources are tied up in this investment.

It is like a hurdles race in the Olympics: you cannot win unless you clear the hurdles. In our hurdle race, we measure the height by which you clear the hurdle, not just the fact that you cleared it. Therefore, when your project meets the hurdle rate, you have not activated a trigger that assures project approval. It is entirely possible, in the competition for funds, that some other project not only beats the hurdle rate, but also beats the rate of return from your project. Given that projects will be compared to each other, the projects that beat the hurdle by the highest amount will be preferred from a financial point of view.

Most public organizations have adopted an internal opportunity cost of capital of 10% because it is thought, from a long-term economic view, that financial projects need to earn 10% in order to remain financially viable and cost effective.

In industry, the opportunity cost of capital refers to the cost of acquiring the funds needed to finance an investment decision, plus a risk adjustment premium that reflects the uncertainty faced in the business environment. For your project to be financially attractive, it must beat the minimum required rate of return.

The investment hurdle rate calculation used by industry is:

- **The prime lending rate** (the rate for rented money)
- plus a premium for **general economic risk** (inflation)
    - The uncertainty of recession, inflation, and global economic affairs
- plus a premium for **economic risk faced in this industry**
    - The uncertainty of technological change, competitor reaction and customer demand changes
- plus a premium for **risk faced in dealing with assets of this type**
    - A measure of the asset specific risk that relates to obsolescence, technical change, and the function of the asset itself

In total, the cost of capital (hurdle rate) is the minimum desired rate of return for projects of this type in this economic environment. For example, a dairy farmer evaluating the acquisition of a new milking machine would have a smaller hurdle rate than a computer manufacturer evaluating a new machine that manufactures micro chips, because there are few risks in the dairy business in comparison with the computer business. The hurdle rate is set as corporate policy and is different in each industry.

Public organizations take advantage of government debt financing, with interest rates that are usually below those available to the private sector. Consequently, the cost of borrowing is lower, but the hurdle rate will still reflect adjustments for risk premiums.

ON THIS TOPIC

A Real-World Example

City governments and provincial ministries normally use a hurdle rate of 10%.

Businesses use a much higher rate. Scott Paper, for example, uses 30%.

The rate used in business is higher than in the public sector because business faces competitive forces that are not normally faced by governments. The hurdle rate needs to be higher so that there is a greater margin of safety against risk in private sector decisions.

Now that we have a hurdle rate in place, or a standard of comparison from a financial point of view, we can begin our analysis of alternatives by looking at the cash flow implications of each alternative.

The financial impacts of a solution to a problem are captured with an analysis of cash flows. Amortization of capital equipment and other accounting estimates is not relevant to this analysis. We are making a financial decision, not an accounting decision. The merit of a project is measured only by the cash flow impacts of the project over the entire life of the project.

CASH FLOW ANALYSES

TIME VALUE OF MONEY

Investment decisions normally impact more than the current accounting period. Benefits and costs represent a stream of cash flows that will take place over a series of accounting periods. We must consider the financial value of a decision in light of the stream of benefits and costs as they relate to the time value of money.

The streams of benefits and costs need to be modified so they can be compared at a single point in time. This comparison is termed "Discounted Cash Flow."

Discounted Cash Flow

The objective is to compare cash streams at a single point in time with reference to the established hurdle rate. There are two financial concepts that should be reviewed, simple interest and compound interest. The formulas are presented below.

Simple interest formula = $P \times i \times n$
Compound interest formula = $P \times (1+i)^n$
Where:
P = the sum of money we are considering at the present time
i = the interest rate or discount rate under consideration
n = the number of years considered

Simple Interest Example
An investment is made and the proceeds from interest are withdrawn at the end of each year.
When considering an investment of $1,000 made at an interest rate of 12% for 5 years, the simple interest return on the investment is:

Simple Interest = $P \times i \times n$
Simple Interest = $1000 \times .12 \times 5$
Simple Interest = $600

(The simple interest formula assumes that the interest return on the $1,000 is not reinvested.)
This means that at the end of five years, the initial investment will be intact at $1,000 and you will have withdrawn interest income of $600. The problem is that the $1,000 will be worth relatively less in five years time because of the change in the purchasing power of the dollar.

To keep pace with economic growth, interest needs to be reinvested so that interest earns on interest. The process is called "compounding."

Compound Interest Example
Most solutions to problems involving investments of organizational resources are not cash investments in a bank that pay interest. Our investments earn financial returns that are automatically reinvested in the organization through profits and operating savings. Therefore, we cannot withdraw the returns from an investment the same way you could withdraw cash from a bank. In our situation, an investment is made and the proceeds are left in the investment. Interest is therefore earned on interest.

Consider this time that the annual return on our $1,000 investment is reinvested. The value at the end of five years, where "S" is the compound sum, is calculated as follows.

$S = P \times (1+i)^n$
$S = 1000(1+.12)^5$
$S = 1000 \times 1.76234$
S = $1762.34

When we look at this example we see that we have "earned" $762.34 compared with $600 in the simple interest example. The difference of $162.34 represents the value of leaving the interest in the investment to earn interest on itself.

Present Value Example
To conduct an analysis of cash flow into the future, we need to take a mirror image of "compounding" so that we can see how much value there is today in the prospect of receiving cash some time in the future. For example, if I were to promise to give you $1.00 one year from now, and if we use a 10% cost of capital, instead of giving you a dollar one year from now I could offer to give you $.909 today. You would regard the two values as equal because if you invested the $.909 in something returning 10%, the $.909 would accumulate to the dollar one year from now.

The formula to find present value is the "opposite" of the compound interest formula. An investment of $1,000 at 12% will be worth $1,762.34 in five years. Put another way, if you want to have $1,762.34 on hand at the end of five years, you could invest $1,000 today at 12% and the compound interest would accumulate over five years.

Most business investments are not a lump sum investment with a lump sum benefit. Rather, they are an investment in today's dollars that will yield a stream of recurring benefits over a long planning horizon. If an investment decision saves $100 in costs per month, then it will save $1,200 per year, $2,400 over two years and $6,000 over five years.

In terms of the time value of money, the $100 saved in month number one is more valuable than the $100 saved at the end of five years. Logically, we should be calculating the present value of the cash flows in each of the years, using the formula above. Fortunately, pocket calculators and present value tables eliminate the need to do the cumbersome mathematics.

A series of tables are presented in the following figures for discussion.

FIGURE 8.2 Present Value Table, 10% Hurdle Rate

Present value of a dollar to be received in the future at a 10% hurdle rate

Year 1	2	3	4	5	6	7	8	9	10
0.909	0.826	0.751	0.683	0.621	0.564	0.513	0.467	0.424	0.386
Year 11	12	13	14	15	16	17	18	19	20
0.350	0.319	0.290	0.263	0.239	0.218	0.198	0.180	0.164	0.149

FIGURE 8.3 Present Value Table, 30% Hurdle Rate

Present value of a dollar to be received in the future at a 30% hurdle rate

Year 1	2	3	4	5	6	7	8	9	10
0.769	0.592	0.455	0.350	0.269	0.207	0.159	0.123	0.094	0.073
Year 11	12	13	14	15	16	17	18	19	20
0.056	0.043	0.033	0.025	0.020	0.015	0.012	0.009	0.007	0.005

FIGURE 8.4 Compound Amount Table, 10% Hurdle Rate

Compound of a dollar left in an investment at a 10% hurdle rate

Year 1	2	3	4	5	6	7	8	9	10
1.100	1.210	1.331	1.464	1.611	1.772	1.949	2.144	2.358	2.594
Year 11	12	13	14	15	16	17	18	19	20
2.853	3.138	3.452	3.797	4.177	4.595	5.054	5.560	6.116	6.727

FIGURE 8.5 Compound Amount Table, 30% Hurdle Rate

Compound of a dollar left in an investment at a 30% hurdle rate

Year 1	2	3	4	5	6	7	8	9	10
1.30	1.69	2.19	2.85	3.71	4.82	6.27	8.15	10.60	13.78
Year 11	**12**	**13**	**14**	**15**	**16**	**17**	**18**	**19**	**20**
17.92	23.29	30.28	39.37	51.18	66.54	86.50	112.45	146.19	190.05

For the purpose of comparing the public sector to the private sector, Figures 8.2 and 8.4 refer to the public sector hurdle rate of 10% and Figures 8.3 and 8.5 refer to the private sector rate of 30%.

Figures 8.2 and 8.3 show the present value of dollars to be received in the future. One dollar to be received in 20 years in a 10% world is the same as $.149 to be received today. One dollar to be received in 20 years in the 30% world is the same as $.005 today.

Figures 8.4 and 8.5, "Compound Amounts," shows how money accumulates over time, using the cost of capital as the investment rate. In a 10% world, one dollar will accumulate to $6.727 in 20 years, and in a 30% world one dollar will accumulate to $190.05 in 20 years. In other words, if your public service organization uses a cost of capital of 10%, then your $1.00 invested in a project will grow to $6.272 over 20 years. If your commercial organization needs a 30% hurdle rate because of business risk, your project will provide enormous returns if it is successful.

The major lesson to be learned here is that there is no point in projecting cash flows over very long horizons because the dollar values become insignificant, especially in the business world of 30%.

This knowledge is also useful in making decisions. For example, if you are uncertain about a cash flow in year 20, and you are trying to determine if the salvage value of a piece of equipment will be $10,000 or $11,000, you can use present value to help resolve the dispute. Observing from the table, you are not having a $1,000 argument, you are having a $149 argument. So why not just split it and move on!

This logic is important to financial evaluation because as dollars are predicted farther into the future, their present value becomes smaller, which means that as we become less able to predict cash flows farther into the future, those predictions are actually having a smaller impact on our financial evaluation. This explains why business is looking for short-term returns to minimize its risks, and why the public sector is willing to plan infrastructure over longer-range planning horizons.

As you can see, the discount rate has a major impact on the financial analysis. The discount rate or "Opportunity Cost of Capital" incorporates the financial risks of a project in three ways:

1. The streams of benefits in the form of either savings or revenues are not entirely predictable.
2. The value of money changes in terms of inflationary purchasing power.
3. There is some uncertainty about the changing "rental rate" for funds.

The further into the future an expenditure is projected the more unlikely it is that we are able to predict what will happen. Therefore, when a project earns more than the hurdle rate, we have some confidence that our financial risks will be covered.

If we were uncertain about the future cost of capital because of changing economic conditions, we should engage in sensitivity analysis. This concept looks at discounted benefit and cost streams for a variety of discount rates, providing the decision maker with a range of values rather than a single figure to examine.

We are ready to use a financial evaluation model. As a first step, we need to describe the cash flows used in the analysis.

CASH FLOW ESTIMATES

The information used in business decision making is not gathered in accordance with generally accepted accounting principles. Accounting procedures provide for the measurement of total business activity, while we are concerned with the measurement of activity that comes only from specific investments. Investments need cash outflows and they provide cash inflows. Therefore, in ranking investment alternatives, we need only look at the cash flows associated with the various options.

Keep in mind that "sunk costs" (i.e. those relating to an investment that have already been made) are not relevant to the decision at hand.

TYPES OF CASH FLOWS

Cash outflows (expenditures made to start the project and keep it going for its whole life):

- Initial investment: Any reasonable cash flow to bring a project on-site and make it usable.
- Recurring maintenance costs: Routine payments made to maintain the project in the state that was predicted in the initial estimates.
- Recurring operating costs and negative benefits: A cash flow measure of the marginal operating costs coming from this project. Note that it would be considered a cash outflow if the project generated negative benefits, such as reduced revenues.
- Periodic improvement costs: Periodic payments made to improve the performance of the project, or to enhance its usefulness in any way. This may include replacement of major components that wear out from time to time.

Cash inflows (financial benefits received from the project for its whole life):

- Incremental Revenues: The cash flow revenues that are directly attributable to this project.
- Incremental Savings: The direct operating cost savings in labour, materials or overhead that are attributable to this project.
- Proceeds on Disposal: The cash flow coming from the salvage value of this project at some time in the future. This also includes the salvage that came from disposing of an asset to make way for this project.

We deal only with cash inflows and outflows that are directly attributable to the decision at hand. Every business decision must stand alone and succeed or fail on its own merit.

FINANCIAL EVALUATION TECHNIQUES

Having established a cost of capital (hurdle rate) and having estimated cash inflows and outflows over the life of the investment, financial ranking is possible. The difficult part of business case preparation is in estimating relevant cash flows with some credibility. We are particularly curious about cash flows 20 years into the future. Obviously, we are more confident making predictions about things that will happen one year from now than we are making predictions about things that will happen 20 years from now.

The mathematics of the financial evaluation model compensates for the uncertainty of future cash flow predictions by making the dollars of less value in present terms.

The following example (Figure 8.6) demonstrates financial evaluation using a 10% opportunity cost of capital.

The investment in question requires $400,000 to be invested immediately. This initial investment is not discounted because it happens today, and is therefore in today's dollars.

During the life of this investment, $150,000 in financial benefits are returned each year for the five years of the project. Using the 10% discount factors, $150,000 to be received one year from now is the same as $136,350 to be received today, and so on through each of the five years of the project.

FIGURE 8.6 Financial Analysis Techniques

	PRESENT VALUE dollars	FACTOR	ANNUAL CASH INFLOWS					
			0	1	2	3	4	5
INITIAL INVESTMENT	400,000	1.000	(400,000)					
Present value of annual cash flows	136,350	.909		150,000				
	123,900	.826			150,000			
	112,650	.751				150,000		
	102,450	.683					150,000	
	93,150	.621						150,000
TOTAL BENEFITS	**568,500**	(sum of the present values of cash inflows)						
NET PRESENT VALUE	**$168,500**	(difference between the present value of inflows and the initial investment)						

Once the financial cash flows have been plotted over time, a variety of evaluation techniques are used which are described below.

BENEFIT/COST RATIO = $568,500/$400,000 = ... 1.42
PAYBACK PERIOD IS $400,000/$150,000 =..... 2.67 YEARS
INTERNAL RATE OF RETURN IS 25.41%

Net Present Value (NPV)

The Net Present Value of an expenditure is determined by subtracting the sum of the discounted costs from the discounted benefits. In formula terms:

Net Present Value = Sum of Discounted Benefits − Sum of Discounted Costs

For example, the $400,000 investment will generate $568,500 in present value benefits over the life of the project. Therefore, the $168,500 NPV is the amount by which this investment exceeds some other 10% investment in dollar terms. We will make $168,500 more than we would have made if we went with some other 10% investment. This is a measure of how much we cleared the hurdle in dollar terms.

The net present value is also referred to as "margin of safety." Given that it's the distance by which we cleared the hurdle, it is therefore the amount by which my estimates of cash flows could be wrong while net present value would still be positive.

Benefit/Cost Ratio

- The ratio between the sum of the discounted benefits and the sum of the discounted costs. If the Benefit/Cost ratio is greater than 1, then the project is viable from the financial point of view.

- This simple variation of Net Present Value helps in ranking a series of investment projects that are being reviewed. To rank a large number of investment projects, we would rank those with the highest Benefit/Cost ratio first.

For example, the $568,500 return exceeds the initial investment of $400,000 in the ratio 1.42 to 1 (568500/400000=1.42)

Therefore, every dollar invested in this project is returning $1.42 in benefits. This is a measure of the amount by which we cleared the hurdle in ratio terms.

Payback or Payout

- The concept of payback or payout does not require using discounted cash flow information. Payback is an unsophisticated ranking method that measures the speed with which investment costs might be recovered. The method is relatively accurate when the payback period is short.
- We are less certain of predictions as they are made farther into the future. Therefore, an investment that generates sufficient cash benefits to pay for itself early in its life is less risky than one that takes longer to pay for itself.

Using the previous example, the cash payback would be:

Initial investment/annual benefits = $400,000/$150,000 = 2.67 years.
Therefore, this investment recovers its cash outlay in approximately 2 years 8 months.

Our margin of safety is found in the fact that the project has an estimated five-year life. Therefore, if our cash payback is less than the life of the project, we can afford to live with approximations of cash flows.

Internal Rate of Return

- The internal rate of return is the true rate of interest earned by the investment.

A $400,000 investment that earns $150,000 per year for five years yields a 25.41% rate of return. When we compare this to the hurdle rate of 10%, we are performing well.

LIMITATIONS OF FINANCIAL EVALUATION TECHNIQUES

All financial evaluation methods have strengths and weaknesses. The key is to recognize the limitations, and to make decisions based on a series of evaluation techniques rather than to rely on only one.

When using financial evaluation methods, consider these questions:

- Does the method indicate the intrinsic attractiveness of the project?
- Does the method permit selection of the best alternative?
- Does the method correctly rank projects in order of relative attractiveness?
- Are there significant cash flow constraints that the test ignores?

Specific Limitations

Net Present Value (NPV)

- Some projects may fail because of an inappropriate hurdle rate.
- Large capital investment may have large NPVs even though the rate of return is not high.
- Managers may reject projects that meet the corporate hurdle rate, but don't meet the rate of return presently earned by the business unit.
- Managers may accept the first project that beats the hurdle rate without looking farther for a project that maximizes returns.

Benefit/Cost Ratio

- Might favour small short-term projects where long-term projects could be better for the organization.

Cash Payback

- Ignores the time value of money.
- Does not relate an investment to projected economic returns.

Internal Rate of Return

- Ignores project size. For example, a 25% return on a $1.00 investment looks better than a 20% return on a $1,000,000 investment.

Comparing Alternatives

All three of the discounted cash flow methods may be used to rank alternatives. However, the user of a financial evaluation must be aware of what the methods indicate.

Net present value is the conceptually superior method. However, we must be aware of the significance of the assumptions made with respect to the hurdle rate, the integrity of future cash flows, and the risks inherent in the model.

The benefit cost ratio has the advantage of enabling comparison of projects of different sizes and cash payback illustrates the amount of time that you are at risk. The internal rate of return lets you test the integrity of the discount rate.

Sound decision making is a function of the integration of financial studies with marketing, engineering, personnel and all other relevant analytical situations affecting a business decision. A proper comparison of alternatives involves analyzing a broad cross-section of issues.

CRITICAL VALUE ANALYSIS

An alternative approach to the valuation of benefits is to use the total investment in the project to derive a unit value calculation. For example, if you are considering investing $100,000 in improving a non-core business service such as the avoidance of an accident, and there are 10,000 customers in the region, you have therefore valued the accident at $10 per customer.

Critical value analysis is a method of evaluation that is useful when the benefits or costs of a project are non-financial in nature. In the past, attempts have been made to unitize and to express financially the social impacts of a project. There has been considerable success in unitizing social elements, but limited success in expressing those same elements financially. For example, it is possible to estimate the number of recreational visits a park will have, the number of jobs created by a new business activity or the number of fish that will be born in a salmon spawning ground. These unitized values and methods of capturing performance changes are quite acceptable. We have difficulty, though, when the values are translated into economic terms such as: a recreational visit is worth $5.00, a new job is worth $25,000 or a fish is worth $10.00.

A frequently used statistic in the safety area is the value of human life. Some organizations have valued the benefit of not losing a human life at $3,000,000. Some have assumed that this means that they have found the "market" value for human life. The reality is that they would be willing to invest up to $3,000,000 in a project that would be an addition to an existing project or process, which would save the life of a human with absolute certainty. If the cost of the project was $4,000,000, they might consider dropping the project or process that is the source of the risk of loss of life. As an analogy, you will invest amounts of money to maintain the brakes and tires on your automobile in exchange for reducing the risk of a failure. When your spending becomes too high to maintain your desired level of safety, you will replace the car or quit driving entirely. You won't spend $3,000,000 on tires because you don't have absolute certainty that the tires will blow and you will die in the process. You therefore decide to spend what you think is an appropriate amount to mitigate the risks.

We have an obligation to serve the five accounts of *Total Impact* evaluation as well as the related sub-accounts. In order to serve these accounts we are willing to spend money. We are not willing to spend an unlimited amount of money. To satisfy accountability, we need to spend money with some sense of priority, dealing with the most urgent social elements first and choosing projects that will generate the highest returns first.

The one thing that is consistent with all projects is that they have a financial cost, regardless of whether the benefits are financial or non-financial. We may not be able to place a value on the benefit of saving a fish or a human life, but we can impute a value by matching the unitized measure of benefits against the financial measure of costs.

The "critical value" is defined as the value of the non-financial impacts of a project that will cause the benefits to be equivalent to the costs. In other words, if net present value is zero, the benefit/cost ratio would be one.

For example, if the present value of the cost of a project is $50,000, and the project involves preventing 50,000 worker injuries over the project life, then the implicit critical value is $1.00 per injury avoided. If a competing project with the same costs saved only one injury, its critical value would be $50,000 per injury. There is no policy that states that $1.00 is okay and $50,000 is not, but as a decision maker, you would be motivated to look quite differently at the second project.

THE USEFULNESS OF "CRITICAL VALUES"

It has been successfully argued that the social attractiveness of a project cannot be captured in financial terms where the units of impact are given a financial value before the analysis begins. For example, we cannot say that a healthy aquatic environment is worth $50.00 per litre of water because the financial value has no logical reference point. We know the cost of a loaf of bread in financial terms but its value to our nutritional needs cannot be measured. At some point, however, bread will become too expensive and we will seek out alternative sources of nutrition.

All investments are subjected to a tradeoff decision, e.g., bread for rice, safety for efficiency or speed for accuracy. We are being asked to consider tradeoffs among the five *Total Impact* accounts and all of the sub-accounts. This does not imply that to have benefits in one account, we must have costs in some other account. It does imply that in order to commit to this project with these benefits in these accounts, we may have to reject some other project and lose the benefits contained in that project.

As we gain more experience in the use of critical values, the projects from the field will begin to provide our system with evidence to show the logical amounts to invest in social benefit accounts. Future projects will build a database of example expenditures that will form the information base for future expenditures.

ON THIS TOPIC

A Real-World Example

The British Columbia Ministry of Parks and Recreation has calculated a critical value of $5.00 per visitor day in provincial parks. This critical value has become a standard of comparison for the development of new parks.

If the total cost is divided among the projected visitors and that unit cost is more than $5.00, managers are motivated to reduce costs or find a way to make the park more attractive so that more visitors share the economic cost.

MARGINAL VALUE ANALYSIS

As a final measure of the quality of benefits, we should attempt to identify the marginal benefits that flow from marginal dollars. We might be able to attract 90% of the benefits by spending 50% of the dollars. This is useful knowledge in the presence of scarce resources because a decision maker would want to spend effectively in those projects where the highest marginal gain can be achieved for the fewest dollars.

Marginal value analysis enables a decision-maker to deal with an initiative in logical pieces so that scarce resources can be committed to the most lucrative projects across all five of the *Total Impact* accounts. For example, if a $100,000 investment results in an increase of 50,000 people using a recreational property, and a $150,000 investment increases that use to 60,000 people, the first investment yields a critical value per visitor of $100,000/50,000 or $2.00 per person, while the incremental investment yields a critical value of $50,000/10,000, or $5.00 per person. If you had determined that it is acceptable to spend $3.00 per person on recreation development, you might have calculated $150,000/60,000 = $2.50, and accepted the total project. The marginal analysis reveals that the first $100,000 yields acceptable returns and should be accepted, while the next $50,000 yields unacceptable returns and should be rejected.

CHAPTER SUMMARY

There is a wide variety of methods for evaluating expenditure alternatives. Some rely on monetary values and financial evaluation; some rely on qualitative analysis and intrinsic evaluation. The primary consideration in an evaluation system is that when the system is universally applied, the outcome is the same in each case. In other words, every time the system is used, the projects should be ranked in the same descending order of attractiveness.

The analysis and evaluation of alternatives to an expenditure initiative must be:

- balanced/objective,
- realistic/attainable,
- easily understood,
- appropriate for the situation.

We also discovered that financial evaluation can be fairly complicated. We hope that the spreadsheet provided as a supplement to this chapter will make financial valuation much easier. (See appendix to Chapter 8).

CLOSING REMARKS

At this point, we have discovered a useful decision model, we have developed an understanding of the non-financial elements of a decision, (Chapter 7) and we have a good understanding of the financial evaluation system (Chapter 8).

The next step is to make a choice. If our non-financial and financial evaluation has been accurate and relevant, making a choice will be easy. If our evaluation systems are flawed, making a choice may be impossible.

Chapter 9 will deal with making choices and developing action plans so that we can follow through on our choices.

TERMS INTRODUCED IN THE CHAPTER

Benefit/cost ratio The relationship, as a ratio, between the sum of all benefits received and all costs invested.

Capital The monetary resources used to finance alternatives.

Cash flow Dollars going out and dollars coming in as a direct result of a particular alternative.

Compound interest The principal of an investment is left intact and the interest earned each year is left in the investment so that interest earns on interest.

Cost of capital Also called opportunity cost of capital and hurdle rate, it is the value of resources committed to an alternative in comparison to what else could be done with those resources.

Critical value analysis Dividing the cost of an alternative among the social benefits received to determine the investment being made per unit of social returns.

Financial evaluation Determining the relationship between financial benefits and costs of each alternative in a decision-making process.

Internal rate of return The true rate of interest earned by an alternative. This rate is then compared to the hurdle rate.

Investment cost Any resource, long-term capital or short-term operating, that is given up in order to finance the adoption of an alternative.

Marginal costs and revenues The future changes to cost and revenues that will come with adoption of an alternative.

Marginal value analysis Dividing the alternative into investment chunks to determine if it is more cost effective to receive perhaps 90% of the benefits with only 60% of the spending.

Net present value The difference between what is spent today versus the value of money to be received in the future in dollar terms.

Payback The amount of time it takes to recover the initial investment through the benefit of cash flows.

Present value The value in today's dollars of money to be received in the future.

Simple interest The principal of an investment is left intact and the interest earned each year is cashed in and consumed.

Uncertainty Making cash flow predictions in the future.

QUESTIONS FOR CLASS DISCUSSION

1. What is meant by "have sufficient understanding of financial analysis to be able to incorporate financial evaluation into your business case"?
2. Cost of capital is more appropriately thought of as "opportunity cost of capital." Explain why this is true.
3. Describe a situation in your personal or business life that involves "opportunity costs."

4. Cost of capital is also called "hurdle rate." Assuming the hurdle rate is 30% in your company, how would you describe the "hurdle rate" to someone who has just joined your company and is looking to you to explain this piece of company policy?
5. Why, when evaluating an alternative solution to a problem/opportunity, is it only necessary to look at the marginal cash flows?
6. What is meant by the term "margin of safety" as it applies to Net Present Value?
7. How is the benefit/cost ratio different than NPV regarding how each deals with large versus small projects?
8. Why is having a short payback period a good thing?

A CASE FOR STRATEGIC PLANNING: MALCOLM AND RUBY'S NEXT STEP

Ruby is thinking about buying the Binford 3000 assembly machine. She was impressed by its quality and it meets her capacity requirements for the next three years. After three years, the machine would have to be discarded with no salvage value.

The Binford 3000 will cost $475,000 to purchase, consume $55,000 per year in overhead costs and cost $10,000 in annual maintenance. On the benefits side, it will generate $265,000 in added profit on sales, and it will save $22,000 per year in labour.

She is also looking at the Acme 4000, which has identical capacity and quality to the Binford 3000. While it is more expensive to operate, it will have a salvage value at the end of three years.

The Acme 4000 will cost $550,000 to purchase, consume $60,000 per year in overhead costs and cost $10,000 in annual maintenance. On the benefits side, it will generate $265,000 in added profit on sales. In three years, at the end of its useful life, the Acme 4000 can be sold for $75,000. The mayor of the city also called and asked Ruby to please buy the Acme machine. It seems that if Acme gets this order from Ruby, Acme will locate its new sales office in the city, which will generate $20,000 in property taxes.

REQUIRED:

Using the financial evaluation tab on the spreadsheet provided with this chapter, determine, from a financial point of view, whether or not either of these alternatives would pass financial evaluation. Then go to the next step in the decision-making process.

This chapter ending case requires the spreadsheet provided as a supplement to Chapters 8 and 9. To access the spreadsheet, please visit the Fane Online Learning Centre at www.mcgrawhill.ca/college/fane. Instructions for downloading and using the spreadsheet can also be found on the Online Learning Centre, under the heading: PROJECT EVALUATION SOFTWARE USER'S GUIDE FOR USE WITH "TOTAL IMPACT ANALYZER"™.

CHAPTER ENDING CASE: COMPUTER MAINTENANCE

The computer maintenance department is proposing the purchase of a piece of diagnostic equipment that will enable technicians to isolate a particular problem and initiate repairs to the computer.

For the previous five years, the computer maintenance division paid a contractor an average of $15,000 per year to conduct the diagnosis and repairs. The contractor also did the repairs because, since the computer needs to be partially disassembled to do the diagnosis, it made sense to continue with the repair. The manager of computer maintenance assumes that the $15,000 payment will continue for the foreseeable future unless the machine is purchased, in which case the payment to the contractor would be avoided.

The piece of diagnostic equipment would enable mechanics within the computer maintenance department to more readily determine the cause of mechanical failure. This would ensure that the appropriate repairs are completed quickly. The manager estimates that there will be productivity gains of $10,000 per year with this piece of equipment. because computers will not have to be transported from the shop to the contractor.

The equipment will cost $75,000 plus $3,000 in installation costs. At the beginning of the third year of operation, the equipment will require an overhaul valued at $10,000. A second $10,000 overhaul will be needed in the sixth year of the equipment's life, and a further $10,000 overhaul will take place in the twelfth year. The equipment is estimated to have a twenty-year life span and no salvage value.

During year one, approximately $5,000 will be spent in direct training costs. The equipment requires $1,000 in annual maintenance and $2,500 in annual administration.

Apart from the financial aspects of this decision, the manager has identified significant benefits in customer service, job turnaround time and employee morale.

This piece of diagnostic equipment is only useful for Microsoft compatible computers. The manager has said that he does not think that in the foreseeable future the computer division will change from its current commitment to Microsoft compatible computers

REQUIRED (USE ONLY THE FINANCIAL EVALUATION TAB ON THE SPREADSHEET):

Assuming a corporate cost of capital of 10%, develop a financial analysis of this situation by plotting cash flows over the life of the project.

Make a decision about whether or not you would proceed with this purchase, and identify the most important factor you used to support your decision.

This chapter ending case requires the spreadsheet provided as a supplement to Chapters 8 and 9. To access the spreadsheet, please visit the Fane Online Learning Centre at www.mcgrawhill.ca/college/fane. Instructions for downloading and using the spreadsheet can also be found on the Online Learning Centre, under the heading: PROJECT EVALUATION SOFTWARE USER'S GUIDE FOR USE WITH "TOTAL IMPACT ANALYZER"™.

CHAPTER 9

Making a Choice and Presenting the Business Case

A conclusion is sometimes the place where you got tired of thinking.

LEARNING OBJECTIVES

After reading this chapter, engaging in class discussion and doing the exercises at the end of the chapter, you will be able to:

1. Conduct an evaluation of the financial and non-financial elements of alternative solutions to a problem/opportunity.
2. Understand the importance of relevant and accurate data to be used in an analysis.
3. Choose a course of action that maximizes several criteria that link to strategic goals by using an evaluation matrix.
4. Develop a step by step implementation plan for the chosen course of action including resource requirements, responsibility and benchmark results.
5. Develop a control system for implementing the chosen course of action and monitoring its progress throughout its life.
6. Make an effective presentation to decision makers that will enable them to understand what will be delivered with the chosen solution and agree that the chosen solution is the best possible solution.

YOUR RESPONSIBILITY

To get the most from Chapter 9, you need to carefully observe someone solving a problem. Watch a friend make a choice of which restaurant to go to. Watch people where you work make choices to do something, or even to not do something.

You need to observe the process people use to make choices. Sometimes the process is random (a toss of a coin) or complex (a committee at work) and sometimes people try to be sophisticated, but their analysis falls apart and they make a random choice instead.

This chapter requires use of a supplemental spreadsheet found on the Fane Online Learning Centre at www.mcgrawhill.ca/college/fane. Instructions for downloading and using the spreadsheet can also be found on the Online Learning Centre, under the heading: PROJECT EVALUATION SOFTWARE USER'S GUIDE FOR USE WITH "TOTAL IMPACT ANALYZER"™.

If you watch carefully, you will see how mistakes are made. People rely on luck or gut feel or they are influenced by their peers. They should be relying on a scientific model that will ensure they make the right choice.

INTRODUCTION TO CHAPTER 9

The next step in business case preparation is to identify and select the recommended course of action for implementation (Figure 9.1).

Selecting the best alternative requires identifying the alternative that comes closest to accomplishing the objectives of the expenditure initiative. Selection must wait until all attractive alternatives have been evaluated. Conceivably, many of the alternatives will not be particularly desirable after a systematic evaluation has been carried out. The choice will therefore be narrowed down to just a few "best" alternatives.

FIGURE 9.1 The Problem-Solving Model

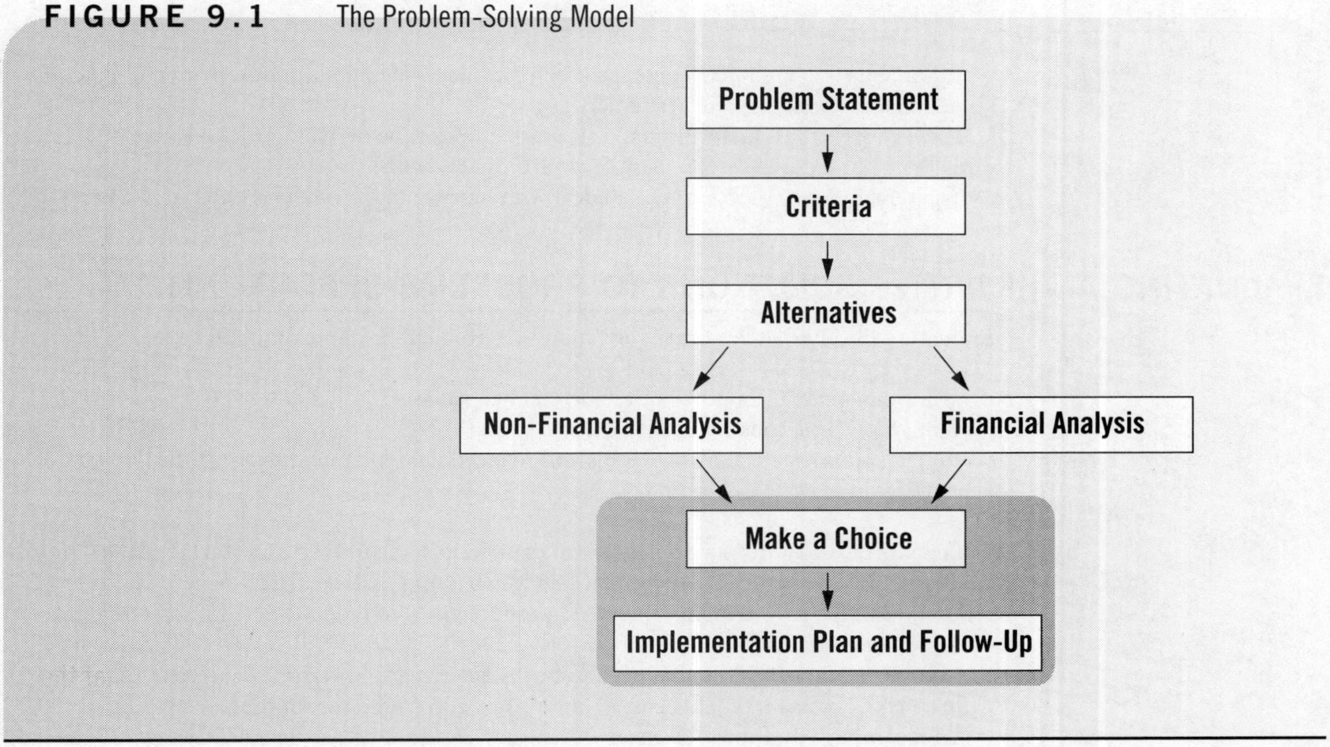

Other things being equal, the best alternative to choose will be the one with the following characteristics:

- an acceptable level of risk,
- the largest benefits (financial and/or non-financial),
- the lowest costs,
- the best benefit/cost ratio.

The choice of best alternative should be immediate and unanimous. If not, go back to the beginning of the model.

FIGURE 9.2 Make A Choice Checklist

	Yes/No
Do we share an understanding of the strategic plan?	
Do we mutually understand the problem we are facing?	
Do we agree on the type and relevance of decision criteria?	
Are we all satisfied that the range of alternatives was broad enough?	
Do we agree that the qualitative data was relevant and accurate?	
Do we agree that the quantitative data was relevant and accurate?	
Do we agree that the evaluation system effectively dealt with the information?	
Are we free from issues involving something other than this problem situation? (Hidden agendas?)	

Arguments about choices come from bad problem statements, poor criteria and inadequate scoping or incomplete evaluation.

If the choice is not forthcoming, do a quick audit of the decision process to see where the difficulty is. In Figure 9.2, you identify your difficulty when you answer "NO."

The remainder of this chapter will deal with how we make sure every answer is "yes."

EVALUATING ALTERNATIVE SOLUTIONS TO PROBLEMS/OPPORTUNITIES

Evaluating the alternative courses of action to a problem or opportunity involves:

- identifying benefits, opportunities and residual values,
- identifying costs, constraints and risks,
- applying appropriate analytical tools and management judgment to select the data that will be useful in making a choice.

Benefits resulting from a decision must contribute to achieving corporate strategies and goals and must be identified and quantified as much as possible. Direct benefits, such as reduced resource requirements, increased productivity and reduced downtime, should be expressed in dollar terms.

Another group of factors that need to be considered are "externalities." These may be defined as the costs or benefits passed on to society from the corporation's activities.

To accomplish multiple objectives, a manager should consider financial and non-financial measures of benefits and costs simultaneously. It is important to note that the traditional perspective that qualitative information is always opinion, and quantitative information is always financial, is not true. There are many quantitative statistics that capture non-financial performance, and many financial statistics or projections that reflect opinions.

Our primary purpose in evaluating alternatives is to deal with issues of intrinsic attractiveness (usually non-financial measures), issues of hard returns in benefits and costs (usually financial measures) and to effectively balance and trade off these issues in locating the best solution to a problem.

The *Total Impact* approach is useful in this regard. By segregating the five broad criteria and by uniformly applying analysis tools within each of the criteria, a decision maker will be able to prioritize expenditures within each criterion and then prioritize expenditures between criteria.

For example, at the strategic level we need to be able to compare good environmental projects with good customer service or social projects. This is not to say that we put the environment ahead of safety, rather, that a decision maker needs to know the tradeoffs that are being made with all decisions. Then, at the project level, we need to be able to rank, in order of attractiveness, all the projects that will provide a higher level of environmental stewardship.

The business case approach provides managers with the framework to seek out opportunities. It allows the manager to go beyond "It's in my budget" and ask, "How can I better contribute to the strategies and goals?" Scarcity of resources compels us to seek innovative ways to increase productive capacity and/or reduce consumption of resources. A well-prepared business case and its accompanying financial evaluation will improve the quality of the decision-making process and help managers and decision makers to recognize opportunities as quickly as possible.

THE EVALUATION PROCESS

Once we are satisfied with our set of alternatives, we should carry out a systematic evaluation of each one. As much as possible, all alternative courses of action should be considered and evaluated. Otherwise, the evaluation may suggest an alternative as optimum when actually it is only the best among the alternatives considered, not necessarily the best of all possible ones. We should also put a process in place to quickly eliminate alternatives with unacceptably high risks and/or low payoffs ("show stopper" criteria, Chapter 7).

The evaluation of alternative courses of action is a three-stage process:

1. Data Collection
2. Analysis
3. Evaluation

1. DATA COLLECTION

Before an evaluation can begin, a manager needs relevant, necessary and sufficient information about the impacts of proposed solutions. The search for information should be carefully governed so that he or she is not inundated with volumes of irrelevant data, or presented with sparse inaccurate data. Before beginning a search for information, a manager should identify the attributes of relevant and necessary information and the amount that would be sufficient to establish a clear opinion of the solution being analyzed.

Data collection can begin as soon as the problems and goals are sufficiently defined to indicate the types of data needed to develop the business case.

There are three types of data:

- **Quantitative** data based on observations that describe organizational, procedural, physical and operational relationships and flows.
- **Qualitative** data based on observations that describe these same relationships and flows.
- Data based on the **opinions, intuition and personal judgment** of experts.

Quantitative data are most amenable to scientific analysis. Qualitative data do not usually permit as rigorous an analytic manipulation nor as definite a conclusion. However, a combination of quantitative and qualitative data provides the best mix for problem solving.

Frequently, we can minimize the effort of collecting data by reviewing the relevant published literature for data that already exist. Whatever data are not readily available from the literature may be obtained through internal sources; otherwise, substitutes for data must be improvised through assumptions and estimates.

As data are collected, they should be carefully referenced so that original documents can be retrieved if needed. We should also make a clear distinction between factual data, estimates and assumptions. The reliability of the conclusions drawn from data is no better than the reliability of the data themselves.

Because information is imperfect, it is not economic to attempt to collect all the data that might be pertinent to an optimum solution and make all of the analyses and evaluations of all the alternatives that may conceivably yield useful results. As well, the uneconomic collection of detailed, accurate data and the use of refined analysis should be avoided when rough approximations will do the job effectively.

The basic data required for an economic and financial analysis are the timing and the amount of cash flows. These come from an understanding of the present situation and projection of future situations. Besides the current minimum acceptable rate of return (Hurdle Rate) and today's cost commitments, we need knowledge about future opportunities, risks, resources and operational constraints. (This was discussed in detail in Chapter 8.)

The basic data required for a *Total Impact* analysis might be quite different. Many social elements of projects, such as aesthetic impacts and the value of customer service or recreation opportunities for the general public, cannot be captured with financial data. However, these issues might be captured with quantitative measures of the numbers of people affected or a public opinion survey.

The final consideration in data collection is accuracy. We should be as accurate and objective as possible, given economic constraints. It is a natural tendency of decision makers to test the quality of information before management action is taken. This process of "tapping the gauge" is the final filter of an analysis before a choice is made. You might tap the fuel gauge in your car when it reads empty just to be sure the gauge is accurate before you take action. Projections of benefits in a problem situation are gauges of deliverables tied to your solution. Most decision makers will check the credibility of the data before they proceed.

2. ANALYSIS

Analysis of the relative attractiveness of the alternatives can begin when relevant quantitative and qualitative data have been collected. Analysis involves using tools that rank alternative solutions to the problem in descending order of attractiveness, according to the decision criteria set out earlier.

To analyze the data about automobiles we might like to purchase, we could rank the options in descending order of fuel economy using published statistics, descending order of cost using the invoice prices, descending order of carrying capacity using supplier statistics and descending order of "ego gratification," using an opinion survey. The optimal solution could be found right now if the same vehicle is at the top of all of the lists. The chances of that are slim at best.

Statistical, economic and financial tools can be applied to quantify the benefits and costs of each alternative within each of the five accounts of *Total Impact* analysis. The financial account lends itself to monetary measures, while the non-financial accounts lend themselves to non-monetary quantitative and judgmental measures. Regardless of the type of measure used, a consistently applied evaluation of the benefits and costs will enable us to select the best alternative to be implemented.

Before ranking begins, the quality of the information to be used in the evaluation needs to be tested. Good information should be used in the analysis; bad information should be discarded. The quality of data should be analyzed in three areas.

1. Identify all major assumptions used in the collection of data.

- Time frame:
  - **Physical life** (projected operating life)
  - **Technological life** (equipment obsolescence)
  - **Product useful life** (economic obsolescence)
- Cost data:
  - Sum of dollars associated with the total project cycle, from the business case preparation to post-implementation evaluation
- Benefits/savings data:
  - Increase in revenues and/or decrease in costs over the life of the project
  - Increase in efficiency/productivity

2. Identify operating and non-financial impacts:

- Employees with appropriate skill sets may be unavailable when required
- Availability of technology and support systems

- Environmental impact
- Compliance with legislated/regulatory requirements.

3. Risks:
- Identify any risks that could affect the expenditure initiative.

3. EVALUATION

The quality of the evaluation process depends on the availability and collection of relevant data relating to the expenditure as well as the application of appropriate analytical tools. A logical method of ranking the attractiveness of alternatives should be employed for each of the *Total Impact* accounts. If the world were highly organized for project evaluation, there would be financial measures that could capture all elements of project benefits and costs. If this were the case, then a simple benefit/cost calculation could be used to rank alternatives. Presently, we do not have financial measures that can capture the full effect of a project. However, if everything else is equal in terms of social impact, then the project with the most desirable financial consequences should be chosen. The consequences might be the highest benefit/cost ratio or the lowest capital investment.

In most cases, projects have varying levels of financial and other stakeholder impacts. It is up to the project initiator to convince the reader that the financial investment of a project is worth the financial and other stakeholder returns.

The evaluation system used for non-financial impacts will be different for each situation. For example, there is no standard practice for evaluating the impact of a suggested solution on customer perception or employee perception. The nature of the impact will lead to a logical system of evaluation. A customer opinion survey could be used to capture the impact of perception changes, or employee turnover rates could be used to measure employee satisfaction. In any case, the system used to evaluate the alternatives must be objective and fair.

In the case of financial evaluation, there is a standard procedure. Adopting this procedure will ensure consistency in evaluating the financial consequences of a solution to a problem. If we all measure costs and benefits the same way, and draw the same conclusions from comparing costs to benefits, then we will be able to effectively compare one project to another.

FINANCIAL EVALUATION

Chapter 8 dealt with the mechanics of the financial evaluation process in the calculation of Net Present Value, Benefit to Cost Ratio, Payback Period and Internal Rate of Return.

From that analysis, you should have a picture of the "Internal Tangible" financial impact of an alternative as well as the "Total Impact" financial impact of an alternative, if appropriate.

To refresh memories, the internal tangible financial impact measured the cash flows, in and out, of an alternative where those cash flows occurred directly into the hands of the organization. Thus, the internal tangible analysis is the "bottom line" impact on the organization itself.

Including the cash flow, the *Total Impact* financial evaluation involved impacts on society at large in the analysis to determine the financial results that would accrue to the organization as well as society at large. Note that the social impact is measured in cash flows. For example, if you design a safer automobile, fewer injuries will occur and society will save money in healthcare costs and litigation. If you build a teen recreation centre and the result is less crime and vandalism, then the cash benefits come from fewer victim costs and fewer policing costs. If you safeguard your hazardous material against an environmental spill, there will be fewer clean-up costs borne by society.

In many, but not all, alternatives, there might be a financial impact on society at large. Some projects will be evaluated only on the internal impacts if a direct cash impact on customers and society can't be found. It is true, however, that all alternatives will have some internal financial impact that must be considered in the analysis.

Ideally, you are seeing that this analysis is quite narrow. There is more to the health of people, the reduction of crime and the safety of fish than can be measured with money.

ON THIS TOPIC

A Real-World Example

The opening page of the Volvo Cars Web site reads:

> *For 75 years, the design of every Volvo has been guided by our concern for the safety and well-being of people. Over time, this commitment grew into three core Volvo values: safety, quality and environmental care.*

This isn't just for advertising. When you go deeper into the Web site, you will see a host of measures that Volvo uses to make sure their three principles are being met.

www.volvocars.us

Like many other organizations, Volvo realizes that choosing between alternatives to engage in realizing corporate goals will require more than financial evaluation. It needs to discover the alternatives that are the safest, the highest quality and that offer the best environmental care.

This leads us to the non-financial evaluation of alternatives.

NON-FINANCIAL EVALUATION

Some business cases need to be advanced even though they do not have benefits that can be measured in financial terms. Cases involving environmental stewardship, worker and public safety, serving a community with infrastructure such as parks and lifestyle benefits and cases involving public perception levels might have some financial impacts, but their true impact could only be measured using some other measurement scale.

It has been mentioned previously that there is no "established procedure" for non-financial evaluation other than counting the number of people impacted by an alternative, collecting opinions from people about the importance of the impact, counting the number of fish saved or counting any dimension of social impact. (Review Chapter 7 on social criteria and sub-criteria to see the range of what can be measured in non-financial terms.)

Even when alternatives have no financial benefits of any form, they still have one financial dimension in common: they all have a financial cost. Pleasing people or saving fish will require resources to be spent by an organization. There will also be alternative ways to please people or save fish and each of these alternatives will have a different cost, and perhaps a different level or number of people pleased.

One method that helps rank non-financial alternatives in order of preference is using financial costs to drive the rankings. This is called "Critical Values" analysis. It involves figuring out what is being spent per person or per fish, then asking decision makers if that amount of investment is logical.

Critical values were introduced briefly in Chapter 8. Now let's go a step further.

From a pure business sense, if you were about to spend $10.00 to serve a customer, determining whether or not that is logical is easy. If that customer brings you more than $10.00 in profit in the future, the investment is worthwhile.

In many cases, though, we spend money pleasing people who aren't customers. We do this out of a sense of social responsibility.

What price, then, should we pay to save a bird? Imagine that you are proposing that the organization spend $5.00 per person to save birds that live in the region. You make your presentation to the decision makers and they ask, "What kind of bird?" Why is this relevant? If the bird is a crow, the decision makers might not spend the $5.00, but if it is the second-to-last spotted owl, they might spend $50,000 (the last spotted owl would be too late). Critical values analysis doesn't calculate what should be spent, it calculates what will be spent, so that decision makers can judge the appropriate level of spending.

It is important to note that critical values are only useful as an evaluation tool if the financial evaluation of a project shows negative results. Critical values analysis is a method of apportioning a negative net present value among beneficiaries to determine the level of investment made for each of the beneficiaries.

Using the second tab (non-financial values) of the *Total Impact* spreadsheet that you downloaded from the Online Learning Centre (www.macgrawhill.ca/college/fane), work through the following scenario.

Imagine that the park in the neighbourhood has a present value of financial costs of negative $712,800, which comes from the financial spreadsheet, assuming a $500,000 construction cost and $25,000 per year in maintenance for an estimated 20-year life of the project.

As there are no financial benefits, the present value of the costs of the park must be matched to the users of the park.

When you open the "Non-Financial Values" tab, the following screen appears:

FIGURE 9.3 Non-Financial Analysis Input Screen

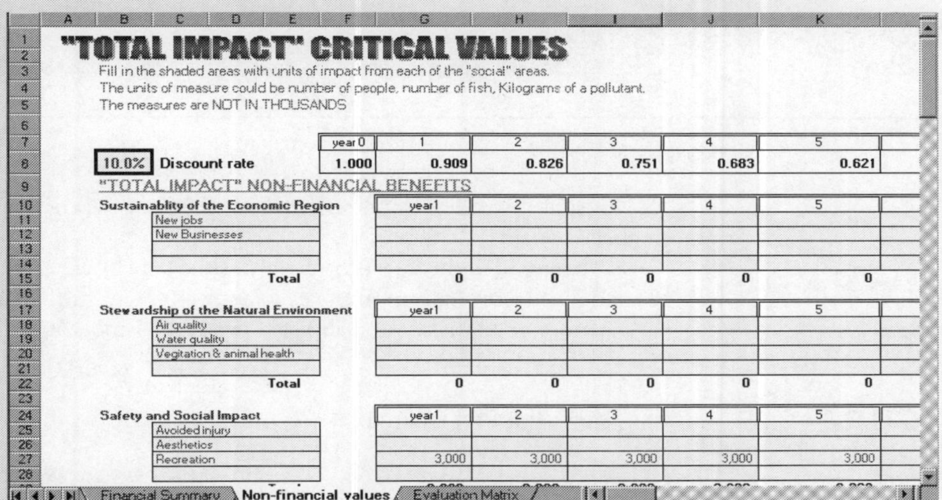

In our example, we estimate there will be 3,000 park visits per year for each of the 20 years of the life of the project. The benefits are broken into categories that match the *Total Impact* benefit accounts. Note that the entries **are not in thousands of units**. As explained on the spreadsheet, the benefits could be visitor days, or units of pollution in the air, or number of people living in the region. In fact, the benefits could be any unit of measure coming from the broad criteria introduced in Chapter 7. The spreadsheet can collect any measure of impact in any category of benefits, as long as the measures are not financial

At the bottom of the spreadsheet, you will find the results of the analysis. After the financial costs in the financial spreadsheet, and the non-financial benefits at the top of the non-financial spreadsheet, you will find the analysis screen, if you page down to the bottom of the screen.

FIGURE 9.4 Critical Values Analysis

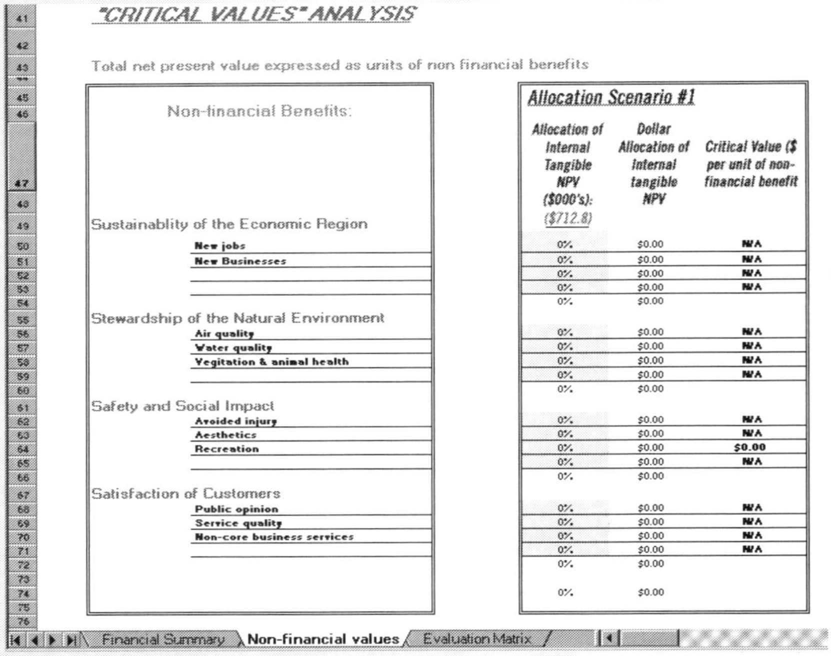

This screen is asking you to decide how the financial costs will be shared among the non-financial benefits of the project.

As we have identified park visits only as the benefit of the project, a zero will appear in the recreation account. This prompts us to apply 100% of the benefits to the recreation account. When we do that, the value invested per park visit becomes:

FIGURE 9.5 The Value Of A Park Visit

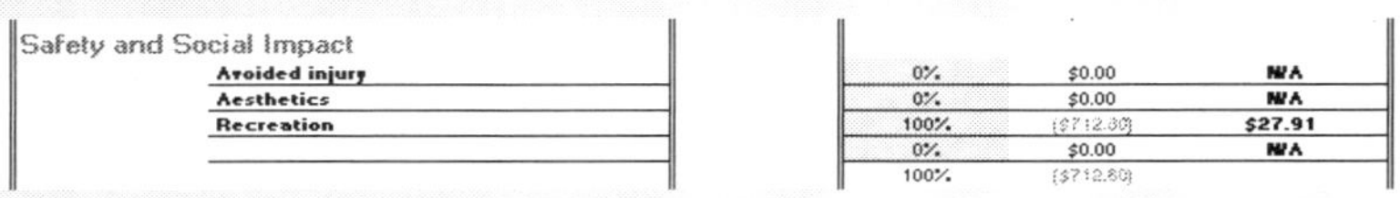

This means that we are investing $27.91 in each park visit per person. The financial value would then be matched against some qualitative judgment. Does it make sense to pay that much per park visit?

As we create more social benefits in each of the accounts, we can split the benefits among the accounts, thus reducing the unit costs. Remember, though, that this analysis is only necessary for cases with limited financial benefits. If there were financial benefits, they would be reported and evaluated in the financial analysis in the first tab.

Sometimes a business case has more than one social impact. For example, if our project also creates five new jobs in the region, we split the investment between the two "Social" accounts. The investment made per job is $8,366.20 and the investment per park visit is $13.95.

FIGURE 9.6 Shared Benefits

Row	Item		Share	Amount	Unit value
49	Sustainablity of the Economic Region				
50		New jobs	50%	($356.40)	**$8,366.20**
51		New Businesses	0%	$0.00	N/A
52			0%	$0.00	N/A
53			0%	$0.00	N/A
54			50%	($356.40)	
55	Stewardship of the Natural Environment				
56		Air quality	0%	$0.00	N/A
57		Water quality	0%	$0.00	N/A
58		Vegitation & animal health	0%	$0.00	N/A
59			0%	$0.00	N/A
60			0%	$0.00	
61	Safety and Social Impact				
62		Avoided injury	0%	$0.00	N/A
63		Aesthetics	0%	$0.00	N/A
64		Recreation	50%	($356.40)	**$13.95**
65			0%	$0.00	N/A
66			50%	($356.40)	

The more social benefits are defined for projects, the more those benefits will be shared among the social accounts. The best project will be the one that minimizes the unit cost and maximizes the social benefits, i.e. if $13.95 is judged to be too much, you could find a way to reduce the costs of the park or increase park use.

The concept of critical values says that we would compare the investment made in a social return to a judgment about appropriate investments to make that are in the best interest of the public.

ON THIS TOPIC

A Real-World Example

The city of Abbottsford, B.C. has two swimming pools. Swimming pools traditionally lose money, so they need to be subsidized by taxpayers.

A critical values analysis was done on both pools. One had a critical value (subsidy) of about $1.50 per swimmer, the other had a rate of subsidy over $7.00.

When presented with this information, city council was able to deal with some alternatives. It could close the pool, or it could increase the pool's attractiveness to the community by investing in improvements so that more people would use the pool, thus bringing the subsidy rate down.

http://www.city.abbotsford.bc.ca/default.htm

THE "EVALUATION MATRIX" SPREADSHEET

The third tab on the spreadsheet presents a tool that might be useful in ranking and selecting alternative solutions to a problem.

The tool enables the decision maker to rank alternatives against the criteria that meet the requirements of the strategic plan.

There are four steps in the process of using the matrix. It is important to note that these steps are parallel, rather than sequential. The first time you use the matrix, go through the steps in sequence, but be prepared to modify preceding steps as discoveries are made in the evaluation process.

STEP 1 ESTABLISH DECISION CRITERIA

- Using the strategic plan, set out the criteria that the problem is addressing.

STEP 2 APPLY WEIGHTING FACTORS

- The weighting factor is a percentage scale. The total of financial and non-financial impacts cannot exceed 100%, therefore, the first job is to distribute the scale between financial and non-financial issues. If your project has a heavy financial impact and a minor social impact, you might assign 90% to financial and 10% to non-financial. The financial issues would then share the 90%.

STEP 3 RANK THE ALTERNATIVES AGAINST EACH CRITERION

- Give your best option the highest value on the five-point scale and your worst the lowest, and position intermediate alternatives somewhere in the scale.

STEP 4 CALCULATE THE WEIGHTED SCORES

- Using the values from the criteria and the values for each alternative, calculate the weighted values. The best alternative will have the highest weighted value.

A tab on the Excel spreadsheet will do the calculations for you electronically.

The result of this analysis is that the alternative that best meets the most important criteria will be given the highest numerical value.

FIGURE 9.7 Evaluation Matrix

Evaluation Matrix

DECISION CRITERIA	WEIGHTING FACTOR	RAW SCORES Rank alternatives on a scale of 1–5			WEIGHTED SCORES		
		OPTION 1	OPTION 2	OPTION 3	OPTION 1	OPTION 2	OPTION 3
FINANCIAL IMPACTS							
Internal financial returns							
New revenue sources	20%	5	3	1	1.0	0.6	0.2
Cost reduction	30%	3	1	5	0.9	0.3	1.5
External financial returns					0.0	0.0	0.0
FINANCIAL SUB-TOTAL	50%	8	4	6	1.9	0.9	1.7
NON-FINANCIAL IMPACTS							
Sustainability of the economic system					0.0	0.0	0.0
Stewardship of the environment	50%	2	5	1	1.0	2.5	0.5
Safety of employees and public					0.0	0.0	0.0
Satisfaction of customers					0.0	0.0	0.0
NON-FINANCIAL SUB-TOTAL	50%	2	5	1	1.0	2.5	0.5
GRAND TOTAL	100%	10	9	7	2.9	3.4	2.2

INTEGRATING THE EVALUATION WITH YOUR BUSINESS CASE

The spreadsheets are only tools to support the business case. The case itself will be a combination of quantitative analysis provided by the spreadsheets and qualitative analysis provided by the text of the case.

It is hoped that by providing templates for the quantitative analysis, sophisticated comparisons of project alternatives can be included that will enhance the quality of the decision process. The spreadsheets are designed to make this process easier.

ON THIS TOPIC

A Real-World Example

The British Columbia Buildings Corporation, the Crown Corporation that owns all the physical buildings used by the government of B.C., has adopted a business case analysis framework as corporate policy.

The framework uses the evaluation matrix to help the initiator of projects do their ranking of alternatives.

Part of the corporate policy is that senior management state the weighting factors that will be used for each criterion to evaluate alternatives.

www.bcbc.bc.ca

IMPLEMENTATION PLAN AND CONTROL SYSTEMS

Controlling projects and initiatives is an absolutely critical element of being effective in a management situation. The public outcry about lack of control in government spending, and the outcry of stockholders in the private sector when expenditures are not as effective as they would like is evidence of the importance stakeholders place on being accountable for managing the complete investment.

There are two focus areas in developing control systems to manage expenditures. The first is to control the scope, time and money spent while a project or initiative is being constructed or developed, and the second is to control the operation of the project or initiative for the life of the project while costs are incurred and benefits are earned. In other words, we control the investment and then we control the results.

In the project development and construction phase, we are controlling the investment. When the project begins its service life, we focus on results. Therefore, we need to measure the performance of the project **as it is built** and then measure performance **after it is built**. At first, we focus our attention on controlling the project as it is built.

Implementation Plan

Projects do not succeed by selecting the best alternative and spending the money. A project can only be called a success when the implementation has proceeded, the project has created the anticipated benefits and a measure of the benefits has been received. To get to the benefits, you need to have a successful implementation. An implementation would be considered successful if the project is on scope, on time and on or under budget.

The logic of an implementation plan is quite simple. We set an expectation of what will be done, we do it, and then we compare what we said we would do with what we actually did.

The implementation plan deals with two elements:

1. What has to happen to be successful?
2. How will you know if you have achieved the benefits?

The first element identifies the construction aspects of the project that must take place before benefits can be realized and the second element takes place while the benefits are realized. Risk assessment is ongoing during the complete life span of the project.

Step 1 Build the Project

Once the best alternative has been selected and approved, appropriate action must be taken to ensure that the expenditure initiative will be constructed as planned.

The construction phase should identify project management responsibilities:
Assign individual(s) to:

- be in charge of the overall project,
- plan the project schedule,
- determine resource requirements,
- ensure that the project is completed on time/within budget.

Timetable
Develop a timetable to cover all phases of the project that includes:

- project duration,
- area of responsibilities,
- key project events,
- deliverables and due dates.

Resource Impacts
The impact of a project on resources is normally managed through the budgetary process. Traditionally, budgets are forecasts of the financial issues of a business into the future. Budgets are used to stimulate financial planning, and to provide a benchmark for performance measurement by comparing budgeted expenditures and results to actual expenditures and results.

Financial budgeting involves the creation of two types of budgets:

1. CAPITAL BUDGETS

   Long-term investment analyses using Net Present Value and Payback are for planning and controlling long-term fixed assets for continued operations. The capital planning process focuses on maximizing returns from these types of expenditures.

2. OPERATING BUDGETS

   An operating budget is a network of detailed budgets used to plan, control and evaluate the effectiveness of the various operations of the organization. The operating budget is a reflection of the short-term resources needed to get the job done.

Effective project management also requires the creation of a third, non-financial budget.

3. NON-FINANCIAL BUDGET

   A non-financial budget is a statement of the human and other resources needed to get the job done, such as enthusiasm, dedication, leadership and morale, as well as any other resources required.

The following template (Figure 9.8) is useful for organizing project implementation issues.

Step 2 Control the Results

Control also takes place at two levels. The first level is to control the expenditures and the second level is to control the results. It is necessary to understand what is meant by "Control."

Normally, we believe a process is in control if it is meeting our expectations. Therefore, we set expectations first, and then compare the results to the expectations. The expectations have been set in the budget. The control aspect will come from comparing the budget to the actual expenditures at the construction level, and to compare expected performance results to actual performance results at the ongoing level.

We must be careful of any assumption that is built into the analysis. If we assume that the budget is perfect and we then find performance that is different than the budget, we might take action to put ourselves back on budget. This is fine if the budget is perfect. But if the budget has flaws, we will be forcing operations to comply with the flaws.

FIGURE 9.8 Action Plan Template

Problem to be solved				
Solution to be implemented				
"Total Project" result	**When the project has been implemented, what are the primary results that will be delivered?**			
	Beginning date		**Ending date**	

Summary of Activities and Tasks				
Activity	**Resources**	**Responsibility**	**Timeline**	**Results and outcomes**

The difference between a budgeted amount and an actual amount is called a variance. It is the variance that causes a management reaction. Variances are a powerful management tool to use to control a process.

NOTE: The term "budget" refers to total project expectations in all measured criteria. Therefore, we will budget financial expectations as well as expectations from all the *Total Impact* criteria.

Variances as a Management Tool

Variances are an integral part of financial and operating performance appraisal. They are intended to motivate compliance with operating standards and to motivate efficient use of assets.

A carefully managed program can yield the desired results. A poorly developed program can cause negative behaviour, and advocate the inefficient use of resources.

Therefore, we must ensure that these areas are considered:

- The variance fairly reflects a manager's control area.
- The variance isolates relevant deviations from the plan.
- Management reaction is appropriate to the magnitude and severity of the variance.
- The act of isolating variances and taking corrective action causes desired changes in behaviour.

Variance Analyses, Management by Exception

When performance is evaluated, two factors are considered:

- Has there been a deviation from the plan? If so how large?
- Was the deviation controllable, and by whom?

Financial performance review is only one of the elements of business performance appraisal. Issues of reliability, safety, environmental compliance, customer service, and social issues also need to be examined.

Variance Theory

Variances are deviations from the plan. They are calculated by taking the value of what actually happened (actual) and comparing it with what was supposed to happen (planned). The difference is the variance. A variance analysis will generate observations like:

- Spending on materials and labour is $50,000 higher than expected.
- Customer demand is 15% less than expected.
- Customer satisfaction is 15% greater than expected.
- The emission of solid particulates into the airborne environment is 5% more than expected.
- The impact of job creation on the economic system is 7% more than expected.

Variances represent a value for other than expected performance. We are therefore cautioned not to regard the presence of a variance as bad performance, as it could simply be that the expectation or standard was out of line.

Variances do:
- identify the presence of a deviation from the plan,
- attach a value to the deviation from the plan,
- identify possible cause areas.

Variances do not:
- fix blame,
- suggest remedial action.

The fundamental purpose in isolating a variance is to prompt the manager to examine the cause of the deviation and to take remedial action.

Remedial action must be taken as quickly as possible and the variance review must point the manager in the right direction as accurately as possible. Remedial action may involve the following activities:

- Directing the process into an "in-control state," by forcing the process to meet the budget.
- Changing the budget, if the variance was caused by a permanent change in operating conditions, which causes the budget to be wrong.
- Ignoring the variance and taking no corrective action on the assumption that the variance was a temporary aberration that will not repeat itself.

When to Investigate Variances

Variances should be investigated when the cost of investigating and correcting the process is less than the cost of allowing the process to continue in its out-of-control state.

In pure economic terms, we do not wish to initiate $10,000 solutions to $5,000 problems. In non-economic terms, we may wish to initiate variance investigation in the following situations:

- A process appears to be heading for an out-of-control state.
- The variance is minimal but repeats itself constantly.
- The investigation may have a desired behavioural side effect.

In general terms, variance investigation should be subjected to benefit/cost analysis in economic and non-economic terms.

We will therefore seek out solutions to variances that occur in the construction or implementation phase of a project to be sure that the project is still on scope, on time and on budget, and we will seek out solutions to variances that occur while the project is underway, using a performance management system. (Performance management is discussed in detail in Chapters 10 to 12.)

MAKING EFFECTIVE PRESENTATIONS

The following offers some suggestions on report format and communication styles that you might find useful in preparing your presentation of your proposed alternative to decision makers.

We will follow simple rules of case presentation so that your decision maker will clearly understand the implications of your case and be able to make a fully informed judgment.

- Effective business communication uses objective language. We must persuade the reader that the information we are providing is accurate, deserving of consideration, relevant and important.
- What we say and how we say it should be driven by the needs of our reader.
- It is important to align your written and oral submissions with the information needs of the reader in a convincing manner.

Effective business presentations are developed using a logical process involving these three steps:

Planning

- Clearly establish the objectives and the style of the report to meet the reader's needs.

Using a Logic Model

- Overcome resistance to change by presenting a conclusion that is supported by objective facts and sound business rationale.

Proving the Conclusions

- Provide evidence for the source of information used in the analysis and evidence of the costs and benefits associated with the solution to a problem.

Planning Your Case Presentation

Now that you have found the best solution to a problem, it is time to communicate your findings to a decision maker. This is not easy since the decision maker likely does not share your values or your knowledge of operations. Therefore, you must carefully plan to communicate with someone who needs all the information in a complete and concise form.

- Set your objective:
  - What do you wish to accomplish as a result of your submission?
  - What must you convince the audience of to achieve your objective?
  - What conclusions will you guide your audience to reach?
- Identify the concerns you have of the audience and their:
  - Perspective, (Financial? Performance? Image?)
  - Prior knowledge
    - What do they know of your submission?
    - What do they not know?
  - Attitude
    - Indifference?
    - Acceptance?
    - Objection?
- Identify additional conclusions the audience must reach based on the audience analysis.
  - The style of a presentation should be influenced by the audience's personal agenda.
- Identify the proof that can be provided to support each conclusion the audience is required to reach.
- Order your conclusions and proofs in descending order of importance to your audience.
  - What will they want to hear first?
- Identify the appropriate language to use with the given audience.
  - Is your language personal?
  - Are you communicating in the active voice?
  - Are you using language that is simple and easy to understand?

A business case presentation must stand alone. Most of the time, an initiator of a case does not have an opportunity to follow the case through the decision process and verbally explain its content to each level of decision authority. A decision maker must be able to make an informed choice on the basis of what is written in the case.

Business Case Report Format

The act of decision making is a different process than reporting a decision. The business case document is a summary of your findings. It should not invite additional analysis from the reader.

A perfect business case will leave no questions in a reader's mind, and will allow a logical and informed decision to be made.

Your case could include the following headings and information:

A) PREAMBLE

Describe the "big" picture and how the expenditure relates to corporate strategic plans and objectives. Describe the nature, function and condition of the item in question. Identify any relevant operational assumptions.

B) PROBLEM DEFINITION

Clearly identify the problem being solved in terms that the reader will understand. Avoid focusing on symptoms; state your problem in "future impact" terms. For example, it is not a problem that we have made inefficient use of a resource in the past. Nor is it a problem that we presently make inefficient use of resources. The problem is that we are about to make inefficient use of resources in the future. We cannot correct symptoms from the past. We can correct conditions for the future.

C) RECOMMENDED SOLUTION

Identify the alternative chosen early in the report. It is important for the reader to have a clear understanding of the choice before the rationale. This enhances buy in by leading the reader to your conclusion rather than inviting more analysis. You have made a choice, now you are announcing that choice.

D) SELECTION CRITERIA

Offer a description of the criteria used to make the choice with particular reference to the five *Total Impact* criteria and the sub-criteria for each.

Most objections raised by decision makers in business cases come from the criteria used to make choices, not the choices themselves. Allow your reader to buy in to the criteria so that the choice selection becomes obvious.

E) ALTERNATIVES

Demonstrate to the reader that a sufficient number of good quality alternatives were considered. To sell the credibility of your choice, you must convince the reader that a broad cross-section of alternatives was analyzed and that the one chosen is the best of the set of possible alternatives. Your analysis should include the "do nothing" alternative.

F) ANALYSIS OF ALTERNATIVES

Non-financial issues

Offer a general description of the non-financial effects this acquisition will have on employees, customers and the community at large. This could be described in terms of added safety, reliability, quality of service and future technical and/or environmental advantages.

The purpose of non-financial analysis is to identify for the reader the operational effects as well as the societal effects of this expenditure. It might be useful to express these issues in the context of the consequences of not making this expenditure. The decision maker must be apprised of all relevant effects of an expenditure.

Financial issues

It is essential that expenditures be subjected to Benefit/Cost and Net Present Value analysis where appropriate. A pure benefit/cost analysis becomes difficult, if not impossible, when significant project benefits are non-financial. However, a cost analysis can be completed in all cases. The purpose of this analysis to convince the reader that this particular acquisition is the most cost-effective method of achieving the non-financial returns.

For investments involving financial returns, comparing the discounted cash flow streams from an investment will identify the economic returns the organization can expect over the life of an investment. We must express all relevant inflows and outflows in cash terms and perform a discounted cash flow analysis on the expenditure decision.

G) IMPLEMENTATION PLAN AND FOLLOW UP

Offer a detailed implementation plan, including project timelines and management responsibilities, as well as a description of the measurement tools that will be used to track progress and identify project benefits and costs.

H) RISK ASSESSMENT

A detailed description of all risk elements, including project specific risk and environmental risks, should be included.

When it is difficult to specifically identify risk values, you could include a summary statement of the most likely pessimistic and optimistic scenarios. It is imperative that the decision maker have the best possible information regarding the risk elements of your project.

Proving Your Conclusions

Quality decisions are supported by quality evidence. While the reader may not always refer to the evidence, it is far safer to have credible evidence on hand for reference than to let readers arrive at their own rationale for the conclusions. If an unsupported conclusion is reached, the reader tends to disallow the conclusion, even though it may have been the best possible answer to the problem.

It is not sufficient proof to simply say, "I believe this to be true" or "It is common knowledge that..."

Credible evidence will be presented as:

- example
- expert testimony
- analogies
- statistics
- personal experiences

The emphasis should be on quality over quantity. Too much evidence can be as confusing as too little.

It is also important in your analysis of alternatives to offer the reader a clear rationale for your choice of optimal solution. To enhance the reader's understanding of the situation, you should offer a clear rationale as to why the second choice alternative is not the optimal solution. It is natural for a decision maker to compare your choice with the next best alternative. Rather than leave this analysis up to the reader's assumptions and values, you should direct the reader through the process you used to rank your choices in the order presented.

Conclusions Regarding Presentations

- Business communications are concise, factual and to the point.
- An illogical or unsupported approach to communicating solutions to problems may result in deferred action, even though the chosen action best solves the problem.
- The most efficient communicators will tailor the presentation to the needs and perceptions of the audience.
- Good communications will actually improve the decision-making process.
- It may be advisable to have your document reviewed by a colleague prior to final submission. The author is often too close to the document to notice deficiencies in presentation style.
- Make a point of learning from every proposal you submit, the good ones and the bad ones.
- Make a point of using the financial analyst in your business unit or department. This person can make your job easier.

CHAPTER SUMMARY

There were three themes in this chapter: making a choice, controlling the project and making an effective presentation to get approval for your solution to a problem/opportunity.

Making a choice is easy if the analysis is complete and logical. Controlling the project is easy if expectations are reasonable and variances are reviewed frequently. Making a presentation is easy if a model is used that satisfies the logic of the listener.

It's all easy if you follow a model. It becomes difficult, confusing and frustrating when you depart from logic and start being random or relying on gut feelings or personal opinion.

CLOSING REMARKS

There is one last aspect of business casing that needs to be covered. It deals with performance measurement, i.e. showing evidence that the results we are looking for are actually occurring.

The concepts of performance measurement and performance management are covered in Section 3, Chapters 10 to 12.

Though performance measurement/management has a direct linkage to business cases, the concept also applies to strategic goals, operating departments and people. Therefore, we will be looking at one model of performance measurement/management that applies to all aspects of an organization.

TERMS INTRODUCED IN THE CHAPTER

Business case report format A systematic format for the business case presentation that ensures that all bases are covered and that a reader will fully understand the situation.

Capital budget An expression of the need for long-term financial investment in a project.

Choice Upon examining all available alternative solutions, one will provide the best mix of returns on decision criteria.

Control systems The assurance that a project is on scope, on time and on budget while it is being built, and during its entire productive life.

Data collection Finding relevant and accurate information to help the decision process.

Evaluation matrix A tool to rank alternatives according to all their criteria.

Evaluation system A method of evaluation that will be applied the same way to each alternative so that the evaluation is consistent and fair.

Externalities Issues relating to government and society at large that are external to operations.

Implementation plan The systematic set of steps we go through to construct a solution to a problem/opportunity.

Non-financial budget An expression of the need for long-term and short-term investment of people and other resources in a project.

Operating budget An expression of the need for short-term (annual) financial investment in a project.

Proving your conclusions Offering evidence that will satisfy the information needs of your decision maker.

Variances A departure from expected performance.

Weighting factors A method of expressing the relative importance of decision criteria as they apply to all alternatives being analyzed.

QUESTIONS FOR CLASS DISCUSSION

1. Under what conditions would "making a choice" become difficult in a decision process?
2. When proving your conclusions, why is it necessary to show evidence that satisfies the needs of your reader rather then you?
3. It is necessary to order your proof in descending order of importance to your audience. How would you decide what is important to your audience?
4. What function does the evaluation matrix perform in a decision-making process?
5. What do the weighting factors represent on the evaluation matrix?
6. What is the distinction between a capital and an operating budget?
7. What kind of data should be collected and reported in a decision system?
8. What does a variance represent?
9. What are the three things a manager can choose to do to resolve a variance?
10. What kinds of resources would be included in a non-financial budget?
11. What are the general areas of information that would be included in an implementation plan?

A CASE FOR STRATEGIC PLANNING: MALCOLM AND RUBY'S NEXT STEP

Ruby has decided to go with the Acme 4000 machine. The details are reproduced from Chapter 8:

> *The Acme 4000 will cost $550,000 to purchase, consume $60,000 per year in overhead costs, and cost $10,000 in annual maintenance. On the benefits side, it will generate $265,000 in added profit on sales. In three years, at the end of its useful life, the Acme 4000 can be sold for $75,000. The mayor of the city also called and asked Ruby to please buy the Acme machine. It seems that if Acme gets this order from Ruby, Acme will locate its new sales office in the city, which will generate $20,000 in property taxes.*

Ruby approached Malcolm with the idea, and, while Malcolm understands the need for the machine, he told Ruby that their financial resources are exhausted. In fact, he had just got a call from the bank saying that no new monies would be lent to them and there was some discussion at the bank about calling their loan unless the bank saw some cash flows soon!

Ruby sees this investment as critical to her strategy of retaining control of the business while meeting customer demand. She is reluctant to approach private lenders because they will want an ownership share of the business.

Ruby has arranged a meeting with the bank manager, the mayor of the city and Malcolm.

REQUIRED:

Using whatever tool you deem necessary, prepare an oral presentation for this audience that will be a convincing argument for loaning the money to Ruby.

CHAPTER ENDING CASE: A CASE ABOUT MAKING YOUR POINT

Able fertilizer company has been evaluating three alternative solutions to a production problem regarding processing raw materials into fertilizer. The existing situation needs to be resolved because operating costs are 15% higher than the competition, and the higher costs are eroding company profits.

When the analysis began, Able discovered that its existing machine does not comply with environmental regulations. It would be allowed to continue using the machine if it chooses to do so, but any change to the process will require compliance with the new regulations.

Three new machines are being examined:

1. The model 100 meets the minimum environmental standard, is the cheapest to buy, meets 70% of the quality standard and 80% of profit expectations.
2. The model 200 is only 10% more costly, but meets 80% of the quality standard, 90% of the profit expectations and exceeds environmental requirements by 10%.
3. The model 300 costs 50% more than the model 100, meets 100% of the quality standard and exceeds environmental requirements by 30%, but, due to higher operating costs, meets only 75% of the profit expectations.

Each of the three machines will produce enough product to meet demand. The production manager says that any of the three could be installed and the existing human resources would have few problems adapting to the new process, except in the case of the model 300. The production manager estimates that production would be below expectations for the first three months.

The marketing manager says that customers appear to be somewhat indifferent to product quality, but are more interested in packaging and price.

The finance manager reminded everyone that because the old machine had eroded profits, financial resources were severely strained and any new investment in equipment would have to be financed with an owner's investment of capital. No internal financial resources are available.

REQUIRED:

Based on the information given, use the evaluation matrix to make a choice of the optimal solution. Then, using the business case report format, prepare an oral presentation to be made to a decision-making team.

SUMMARY OF PART 2

Chapters 6 to 9 of this book dealt with a decision-making model that reflected the strategic plan, by promoting decisions using the SAVI acronym.

Screening Added Value Initiatives

For plans to become reality, action must be taken on the plans. Creating value-added projects is a very important step in realizing strategic goals. Not only will these projects make a contribution to progress, they will also provide an opportunity for people in the organization to communicate with each other by clearly defining the elements of a project and the expected results from the project. This does a great deal to improve everyone's understanding of the changes the organization is making.

The next section of the book will deal with measuring and managing performance.

We have a plan (Section 1) and we have some action items (Section 2). Now we need to build a system that shows evidence that progress is being made.

Part 3

MEASURING PROGRESS TOWARDS GOALS

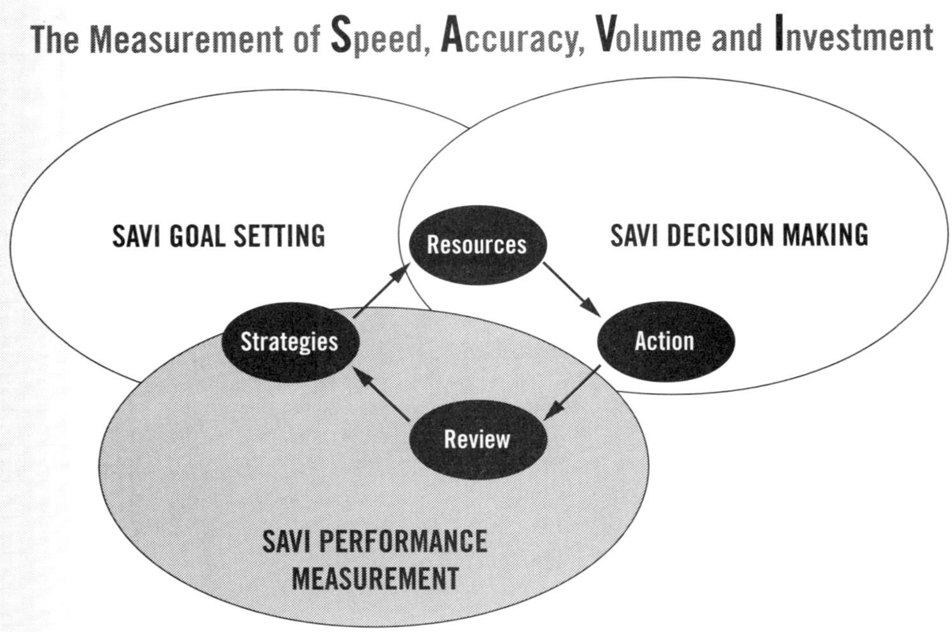

INTRODUCTION TO CHAPTERS 10 to 12

Performance measurement is the most neglected and yet critically important element of the management cycle. The organizations I have encountered that have not embraced performance measurement have cited "fear of what will be done with the information" as their reason for not even attempting to put forward some performance measurement ideas.

The principal reason for measuring performance is to close the loop on the strategic management process. Having identified what it is that needs to be accomplished, and having made some decisions to initiate actions to try to do what needs to be accomplished, it is now time to build a system that will report whether or not those accomplishments are happening.

The SAVI management model introduced earlier will be used again to locate the function of performance measurement in the management process.

Note from the model that the results of measurement will be fed back into the goal-setting process so that appropriate management action can be taken.

Performance measurement is the last step in the SAVI management model cycle.

The Management Model

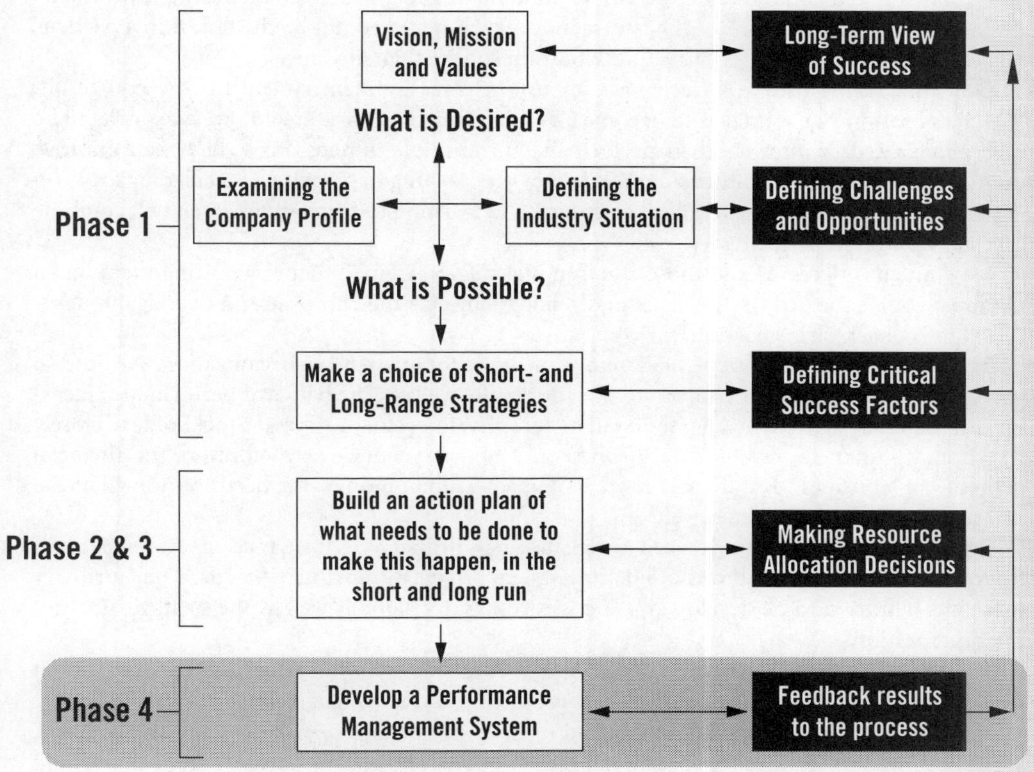

Most organizations have failed to use a scientific method of measuring performance and reporting results to the management system, but they still use their unsophisticated methods to form opinions about how the organization is doing. A frequently asked question, "So, how's business?" solicits a wide range of responses:

- Not good, our customers appear to be unhappy
- Pretty good, except the employees are not motivated
- Very good, sales are up and we are beating the competition
- Excellent, we made more money last year than ever before

Comments like these become the fuel for the decisions that will be made around changing performance. You expose the weaknesses of these comments when you ask, "How do you know that?" If the response to the question is, "I just have a feeling," or "I heard it from some senior manager," or "I asked a customer," then you are forming an opinion based on very weak evidence.

If, on the other hand, the responses are, "62% of last month's sales were returned by customers," "Employee productivity is 18% below industry average," "Sales are up 12% for us and down 16% for the industry" and "Our profits are up 14% and stockholders' return on investment is now 23%, 17% above industry averages," then you have some good measures of performance.

They are good measures, but they are not complete. Whether they are public or private, organizations are not simple systems that can be measured in one dimension. Certainly the penultimate measure of success in a business is profit, and the penultimate measure in a public organization might be customer satisfaction, but to achieve those end results, there are hundreds of tasks to be performed, all of which need to be measured.

A simple analogy is found in the analysis of a performance of an Olympic downhill ski racer. On the day of the race, there is one measure, time. There are no points for costumes or artistic impression as there are in figure skating, no judgments or opinions, just time, measured by a clock that is tested and proven to be fair. Commentators make the race interesting by measuring speed in various sections of the course, but the winner need not be the fastest in a particular section as long as he or she gets to the bottom sooner than anyone else.

Downhill racing uses a perfect one-dimensional measurement system for the end result. Now let's examine what it takes to become an Olympic racer. Ten-year-old racers aspiring to be Olympians need to improve their performance in multiple dimensions so they can improve their performance in one dimension. While they are learning to be perfect racers, they focus on a variety of small issues like learning to crouch and learning to turn, all of which will combine to make up overall performance.

How much progress would those children make if you trained them by putting them on an Olympic course, turned on the clock and made them take the run over and over again, never offering feedback or instructions?

The performance measurement system is the same for any kind of organization. We need to measure both the results of efforts and the efforts themselves. The basics of performance measurement already entrenched in the system for private sector business. Stockholders closely monitor the financial results of a business and management closely monitors the financial activities of a business. But there is more to a business than money: the needs of non-financial stakeholders have to be met as well.

Public sector organizations need to create their primary performance measures because there is no traditional financial evaluation system trying to maximize profits. Their primary measures will need to be developed using Mission and Vision, as well as the strategic goals of the organization.

If a police department wishes to "protect and serve," the taxpayers who fund the department must see measurable results that show that protecting and serving is going on.

In Section 1, we developed clear expectations, corporate and operating goals. In Section 2, we built projects, solved problems, capitalized on opportunities and started actions that would help us realize our goals. In these last three chapters of the book, we are going to deal with transforming plans into reality.

Now, in Section 3, we will do two things: we will learn how to **measure** progress and we will learn how to **motivate** progress.

Measuring progress is a scientific model of capturing change in desirable performance areas.

Motivating progress is about performance management, enabling people, our most valued and least understood asset, to embrace measurement so they can use it to help them improve. It is an art form rather than a science because people's feelings and behaviours are involved.

The bottom line is that you can have the best plan in the world, but it's not going anywhere unless you understand how to make your people want to do it.

CHAPTER 10

Performance Measurement And Performance Management

Things could be worse: Suppose your errors were counted and recorded every day like a baseball player's.

LEARNING OBJECTIVES

After reading this chapter, engaging in class discussion and doing the exercises at the end of the chapter, you will be able to:

1. Understand the linkage between performance management and the realization of strategic goals.
2. Understand the levels of performance management as they relate to people, operations, projects, divisions and the organization in total.
3. Understand the distinction and relationship between performance management and performance measurement.
4. Understand a basic performance measurement system that measures activity as well as results.
5. Identify and apply the characteristics that define a good performance measure.

YOUR RESPONSIBILITY

To get the most from Chapter 10, you need to observe the many ways that measurement goes on around you and, at the same time, observe what people do in response to those measures.

What happens when you get a bad grade on an exam? How do you react? What happens when you get criticized at work or get criticized by your partner in a relationship or your mother-in-law? Why is the range of reactions so wide?

Measurement is a very delicate subject. It causes all kinds of fear among performers and it often causes hard feelings among people, especially when performance is linked to rewards.

Be aware of measurement, when it works and when it doesn't. It is hoped that the next three chapters will shed some light on the subject.

INTRODUCTION TO CHAPTER 10

This chapter offers a rationale for measurement in an organization, it offers an example of a simple measurement system and it begins a discussion on performance management. The management cycle (Figure 10.1) points to where performance measurement takes place.

FIGURE 10.1 The Management Cycle

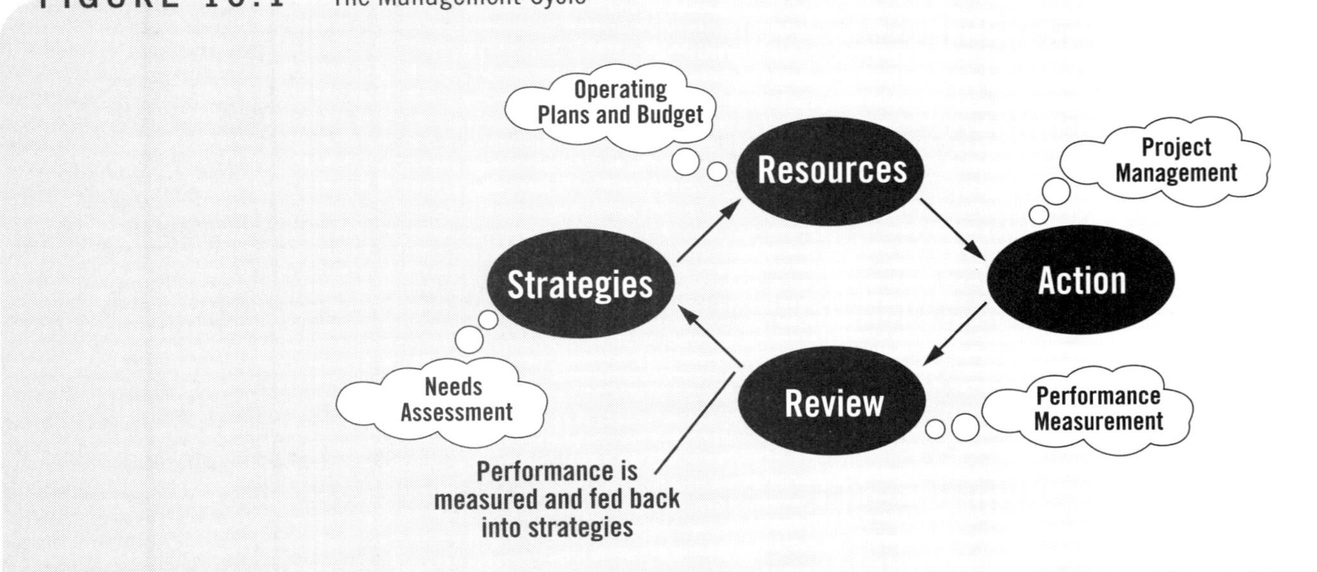

For an organization to know that change is happening and happening in a direction it wants, the organization needs to measure change and link it to goals.

Seems so simple.

The concept is simple. The process of doing it is not.

LINKING PERFORMANCE MEASUREMENT TO STRATEGIC PLANS

WHY IS MEASUREMENT NECESSARY?

1. To show progress towards achieving strategic goals

Most organizations have discovered several areas where improvement is **possible** and change is **desirable**. The strategic path for an organization includes initiatives that call for change and improvement in the context of corporate strategic goals.

The corporate goals represent the broad areas of operations where improvement is both possible and desirable. The purpose of performance measurement is to identify and report the financial and non-financial effects of all aspects of the organization so those aspects can be managed to best meet the needs of the organization.

Each objective calls for a significant change in the business processes used, and each of the new business processes calls for a change in the culture of the team and the style of management to be used.

A strategic plan addresses visions and values, concepts and philosophies. Turning a strategic plan into a plan of action requires the concise definition of activities in terms of results and outcomes that can be measured and tracked to see performance gains. Strategic plans normally call for some measure of change in an organization, and it is assumed that the change will be positive.

Those who write strategic plans are now waiting for evidence to show that the plans are being realized.

The primary role of performance measurement at the initial high level will be to provide summary evidence about progress that will satisfy senior management's need to evaluate the effectiveness of the strategic planning initiatives.

It is important to note that this high-level performance measurement system must be supported by operating-level measures that capture not only the core activities of strategic teams who are focusing on strategic goals, but also the ongoing activities of operating departments throughout the organization.

ON THIS TOPIC

A Real-World Example

On the Black & Decker Web site, www.bdk.com, the following vision statement and 2002 highlights were published.

Vision Statement
Black & Decker's objective is to establish itself as the preeminent global manufacturer and marketer of power tools and accessories, hardware and home improvement products, and technology-based fastening systems.

2002 Highlights

- Outstanding Financial Performance:
  - 28% increase in recurring earnings per share
  - 3% increase in sales despite weak economic conditions
  - Record-level free cash flow of $360 million
- Outstanding Operational Performance:
  - More than $100 million of Six Sigma savings
  - Continued improvement in working capital management
  - Solid progress in restructuring to reduce cost base

Notice that most of the highlights contain measures that are financial and two of the highlights contain no measures.

Further in the site, there is a section on corporate affairs and environmental strategies with some measures of social issues.

The bottom line is that the highlights don't seem to report progress towards achieving their vision!

2. To show evidence for the performance gaps in areas where strategic outcomes are not being met

Performance gaps prompt management reaction. Before a reaction is implemented, management must be sure that the measure used to identify the gap is a performance measure that is worthy of a management reaction.

Sometimes we measure things that cannot be corrected. Sometimes we measure things that are not performance related.

3. To show evidence that allows superior performance to be recognized and rewarded

When a performance gap is positive (showing better than expected performance), there needs to be a system that recognizes and rewards superior performance. This will help ensure that the performance continues, and it will help motivate others to achieve high performance levels.

We must be particularly careful in the design of the "motivating" system. Sometimes our best intentions are interpreted differently by our performers and we actually get worse results! (This issue will be discussed further in Chapter 12)

4. To show evidence that lets poor performance be recognized and corrected

When a performance gap is negative, showing worse than expected results, there needs to be a system that isolates the cause and corrects the problem. This will ensure that the bad performance stops and is replaced by the performance that is desired.

Systems that capture and report bad performance are also "motivating systems." Unfortunately, people are sometimes motivated to avoid getting caught rather than to improve performance.

RELATING "PERFORMANCE MANAGEMENT" TO "PERFORMANCE MEASUREMENT"

Many authors have gone to great lengths to distinguish between performance management and performance measurement by suggesting that measurement is the simple act of capturing accurate measures of performance, and management is the process of using the information provided by the measures to develop action plans for dealing with performance.

I believe that there is a very limited distinction between the two processes. In fact, the processes are integrated and fully dependent on each other. You can't manage anything that is not measured, and there is no point in measuring something that can't be managed.

I prefer to view performance management and performance measurement as simultaneous tasks occurring at various levels of the organization.

To relate this to a strategic plan, management embraces Vision, Mission, Values and Strategic Goals (Section 1). Now management expects that performance will be "managed" to achieve these goals, and "measurement" is one of the tools to be used.

Measures of progress will be done by capturing relevant information about specific programs, activities and business practices.

Performance measurement will take place at all levels, and from all views, of the organization.

- Directors will monitor high-level satisfaction, economic and strategic benefit measures.
- Management will monitor the productivity and effectiveness of resources deployed in achieving strategic outcomes by developing measures of projects and initiatives.
- Operating personnel will constantly track and control the efficiency of resource use by measuring specific tasks and events.

Performance management also embraces the idea that the organizational culture must be capable of viewing the measurement of performance as a constructive and positive management tool that will improve the likelihood, and increase the value of, performance gains.

Developing a culture is an essential ingredient. The best measurement system possible will not function if those being measured view the system as a tool to be used for punishment. Unfortunately, most efforts to date have done just that by using performance information to make a case against someone or some business process. There are many examples of situations where a person has been fired over evidence gathered about his or her performance when the person did not know the evidence was being gathered, and did not know that what was being measured was critical to the job. It seems that someone went looking for a reason and then created the evidence to support the reason.

If we are to develop meaningful measures of performance, we need to capture all relevant dimensions of performance and we need to communicate those dimensions to performers so they understand what is expected of them.

The following diagram depicts the various levels of the SAVI model as it relates to measuring performance and keeping all of the levels of management as well as several dimensions of performance in balance.

AN OVERVIEW OF PERFORMANCE MANAGEMENT

Directors empower management to direct activities towards achieving strategic results. This feeds into the change management system, and the results of the accomplishments are reported back through the performance measurement system. Figure 10.2 depicts the relationship and integration of high-level performance management through to operating performance management.

FIGURE 10.2 Levels of Performance Management

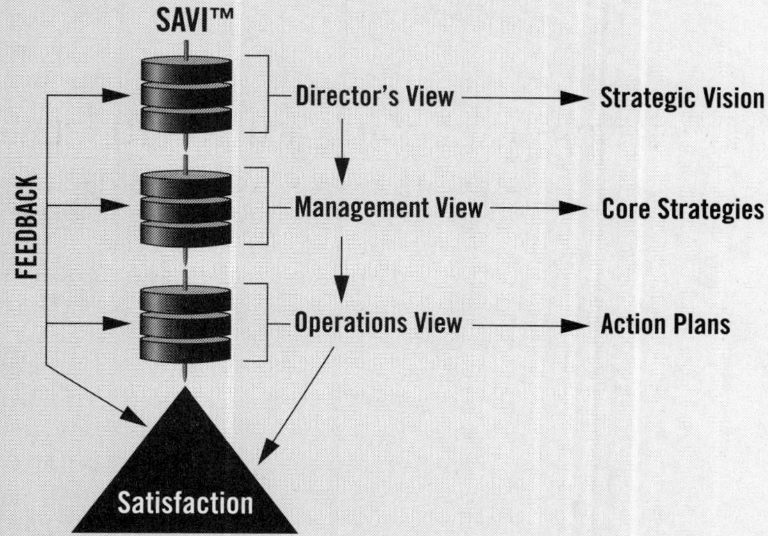

The visual image of the spinning "tops" is important. Each level of the organization has a variety of issues to manage, all requiring effort and concentration and all must work in balance with the other issues. Directors are trying to balance high-level strategic goals, middle management is making sure that the right programs are in place to serve stakeholders and operating personnel are focused on the various operating dimensions of the organization.

All these views combined will support stakeholder satisfaction, which, at the end of the day, is the ultimate result we are looking for. Therefore, if any one of the dimensions of a "spinning top" gets out of balance, the model will fall, which will harm satisfaction.

High-level measures relating to directors and senior management need to be developed at the same time as operating level measures because operating information feeds the performance measurement system. The performance measurement system is simply a more detailed view of the levels of performance management where business activities are pinpointed with performance measures that capture controllable and active performance.

The **performance management** view of an organization is a top-down view. Senior management adopts strategic goals and empowers and directs middle management to adopt operating goals. Middle management then empowers and directs operating personnel, who do the actions required, all in the framework of achieving strategic goals.

An Overview of Performance Measurement

Performance measurement takes a bottom-up view. Performance measurement is the business of feeding information about results back up the line so that progress can be measured.

The following diagram (Figure 10.3) depicts the translation of performance management concepts into performance measurement statistics.

Notice that the diagram is reversed, which indicates that **satisfaction**, the supporting concept, requires diligently managing a multitude of performance issues, all kept in a precarious balance

Satisfying stakeholders is a precarious task since many of the stakeholder demands on an organization operate at cross purposes to each other. For example, the organization must achieve environmental and safety outcomes at a high level while maintaining financial outcomes. This is why it is necessary to constantly monitor and manage the results expected from each stakeholder group.

FIGURE 10.3 An Overview of Performance Measurement

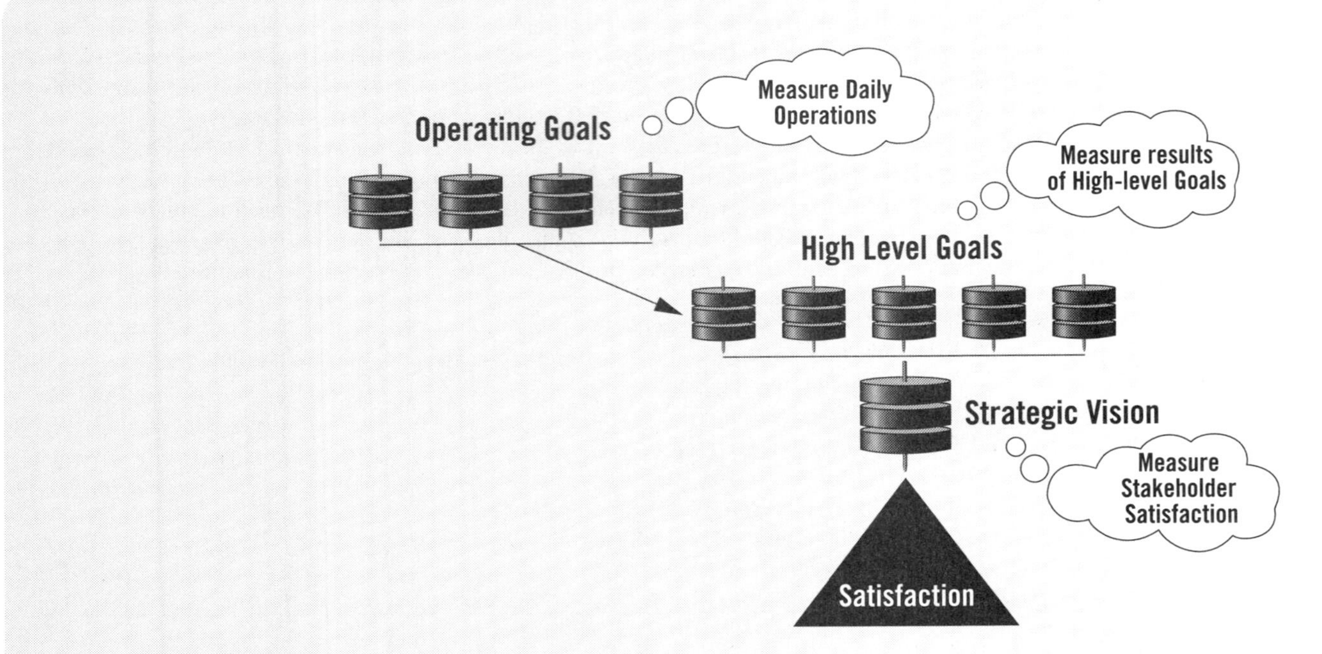

BUILDING A MEASUREMENT SYSTEM

The first effort in performance measurement is to develop measures of results and outcomes coming from the high-level strategic goals. The information will be useful to senior management and directors in judging the effectiveness of strategic planning initiatives.

Once the high-level strategic goals have broad measures, we can translate the strategic goal into an operating goal and develop more specific measures to match the operating goals. So we can become more specific in the development of measures, we need to think of measurement as having two principal dimensions.

1. **We need to measure activity.**

   Hours spent, materials consumed, overhead used

2. **We need to measure results and outcomes.**

   Things built, customers satisfied, money made

Work is not what you see people doing: that is activity. Work is what you see when the activity is finished. Some people are very active, attending meetings, sending memos, consuming resources and spending time…accomplishing very little. The core principle here is that measurement systems focus on the results of activities, not the activities themselves. When going to work, people should have in mind that they intend to accomplish something, and though activity is necessary to accomplish anything, the primary focus should be on the result of the activity.

A good measurement system focuses on what is accomplished as the primary measure. It is important to measure activity, but only if that activity adds value to results and outcomes. Too often we fall into the **activity trap**, meaning that we measure the effort expended in doing a job without measuring the results of doing the job, and we assume that because a large amount of effort has been expended, there must be good performance. Students constantly complain about results of exams by going to the professor and complaining that they are unhappy with the result because they spent hours preparing for the exam, and they still failed. What they are missing is that they spent **hours doing the wrong thing**. It is even more frustrating when they prepare for the next exam by doing even more hours of the wrong thing.

The desired result of study is knowledge, not consumed time. The truth is that the result you are looking for might be accomplished by doing fewer hours of the right thing. To summarize, what you are doing is an activity measure, what you get when you are done is a performance measure. It is necessary to measure both. After all, you could get the exam result you are looking for by cheating, but that would not be the desired activity.

At the end of the day, the most important result of management in any organization is the satisfaction of all stakeholder groups. We tend to spend too much time measuring satisfaction and too little time measuring the events that cause satisfaction. We need to measure things that are controllable and that actively contribute to satisfaction so that managers can pinpoint what needs to be done to correct a problem, or what can be done to maximize a success.

ON THIS TOPIC

A Real-World Example

Dell Computers (http://www.dell.com/ca) reports the following Mission Statement:

Dell's mission is to be the most successful computer company in the world at delivering the best customer experience in markets we serve. In doing so, Dell will meet customer expectations of:

- Highest quality
- Leading technology
- Competitive pricing
- Individual and company accountability
- Best-in-class service and support
- Flexible customization capability
- Superior corporate citizenship
- Financial stability

How will Dell know it is getting there? Dell will need to define every measurement concept in the mission, "Highest, leading, competitive" etc. and build measures that show progress being made in these areas.

Dell will also need to be very careful to separate activity from results so that it can know what it is doing and it can know how successful it is.

HOW DOES THIS RELATE TO SAVI?

Although there is one group of internal stakeholders and one group of external stakeholders (which are then broken down into many sub-groups), there are four very different views of what is important to stakeholders, or what needs to be measured to ensure they continue to be satisfied.

The Director's View

- From a director's point of view, in the process of preparing strategic goals, the **stakeholders**, including owners, investors, creditors, customers and the public at large will be satisfied when they can see that **Added Value** is coming to them from their **Investments** in the organization.
- Directors need high-level summary measures that show progress towards achieving strategic goals.

The Management View

- In response to needs identified by boards of directors, management will create systems that advocate developing and maintaining business practices that help to realize strategic goals by **Screening Added Value Initiatives**.

- Management needs detailed measures that show the results of specific projects and initiatives and how they are contributing to strategic goals.

The Operating View

- Operating divisions will develop information systems that track progress towards strategic goals by monitoring the Speed, Accuracy, Volume and Investment of the daily activities of the organization.
- At the operating level, performers need measures of tasks and accomplishments in every activity of a project or initiative which show how those accomplishments contribute to the success of the project. This in turn contributes to the realization of the strategic goal.

The Project View

- A set of measures will be developed for specific projects aimed at performance improvement where those measures link to the operating, divisional and corporate results in achieving strategic goals.

This logic is the foundation of the performance measurement framework.

So far, the organization has set strategic goals using the SAVI Goal-Setting Tool, and has initiated projects and initiatives to achieve strategic goals using the SAVI Decision-Making Tool. Now it is time to use the final SAVI tool to set performance measures at the input and output levels for each element of the business that supports the strategic goals.

The following diagram depicts the relationship of "Input Measures" and "Output Measures" to realizing the strategic goals (Figure 10.4).

FIGURE 10.4 Input and Output Measures

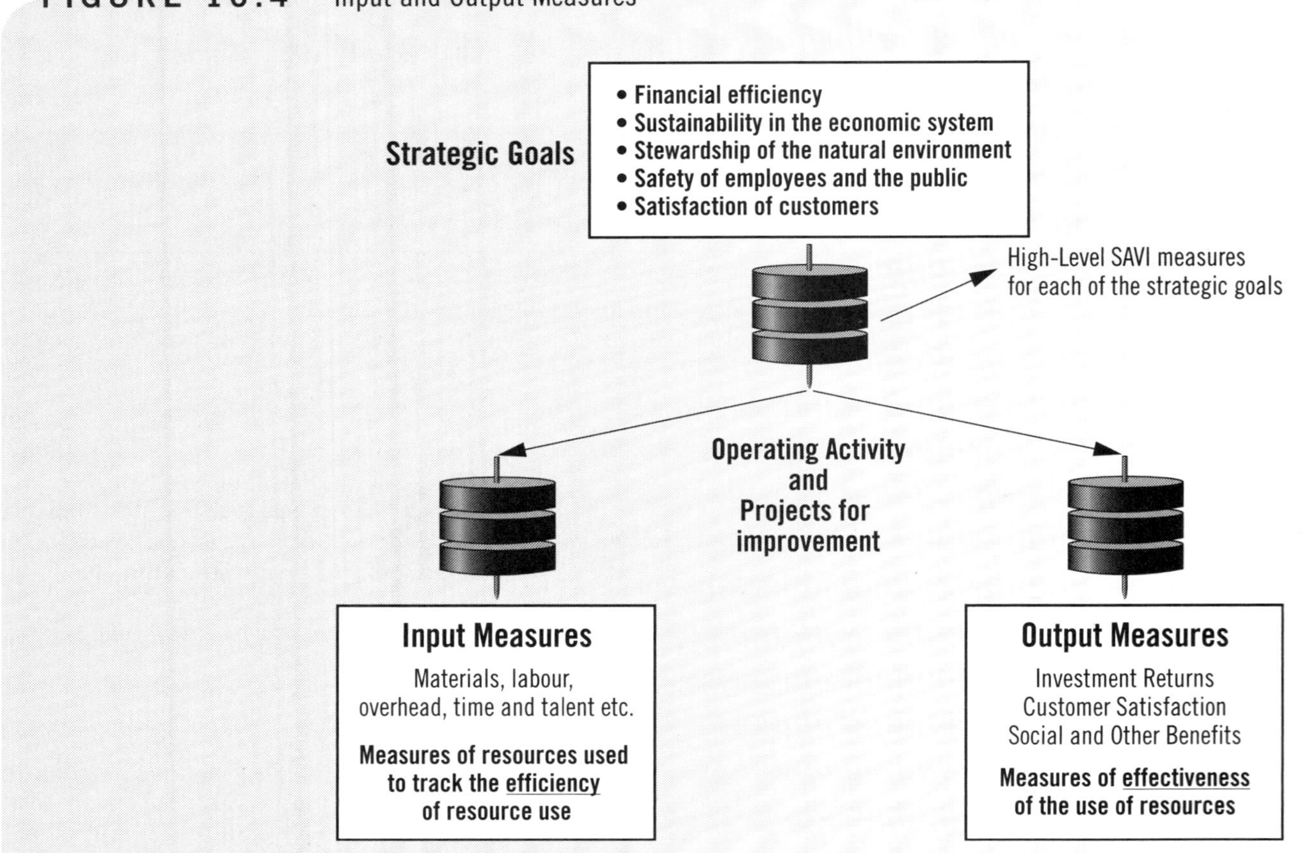

We will define the output side measures first.

On the output and results side of the formula, there are three categories of measures:

1. Investment Returns
2. Customer Satisfaction
3. Social Benefits

These are defined as follows (Figure 10.5):

FIGURE 10.5 Example Output Measures

OUTPUT MEASURES		
CATEGORY	**MEASUREMENT CONCEPT**	**MOST FREQUENTLY USED SOURCES OF INFORMATION**
Investment Returns	Financial Returns	Total profits and % rate of return on investment
	Financial Efficiency	Budget and actual cost information supplied by financial services is equated to the volume of work done using "unit measure" concepts
Customer Satisfaction	Internal customers, (intermediate results such as on scope, on time, on budget)	Data mining internal information about effectiveness at the intermediate level
	External customers (public perceptions of value, quality, function etc.)	Opinion survey of external users which captures their perception of the value of the program
Social Benefits	Non-financial social returns that are not being measured in the satisfaction category (Environmental impact, value of recreation to the health care system etc.)	Data Mining existing information within the organization and among comparable organizations from outside

The output level measures results and outcomes in the context of the needs of stakeholders. At a high level, results might be expressed using summarized or general measures, such as total return on investment or overall customer satisfaction. At the operating level, the results would be expressed using very specific measures of active and controllable performance.

ON THIS TOPIC

A Real-World Example

Molson's has the following goals and measures relating to Sustainable Shareholder Value:

- Grow operating profit by 14.5% annually
- Grow market share annually
- Grow volume by 4% to 5% annually
- Organizational renewal
- Improve quality

Molson's vision is clear: to remain one of the top performing brewers in the world, as measured by returns to shareholders.

Operating profits and sales volume are results with specific measures, market share and quality are results without measures, and organizational renewal is an activity.

Molson's would need to clarify what the expected result is from organizational renewal before it could have a measure of success attached to it.

www.molson.com/en/investors

The input measures, Financial Capital and Operating Resources, and other organizational resources, are defined as follows (Figure 10.6):

FIGURE 10.6 Example Input Measures

INPUT MEASURES		
CATEGORY	**MEASUREMENT CONCEPT**	**MOST FREQUENTLY USED SOURCES OF INFORMATION**
Financial Operating Resources	**Materials and labour**	Direct tracing of materials and labour consumed to the performance area using the financial system.
	Overhead	Allocation of overheads using an accounting allocation method that reflects the use of overheads by the performance area.
Financial Capital Resources	**Capital investment in operating assets**	The accounting system will break out the capital investments in each performance area.
Other Organizational Resources	**Non-financial resources consumed by the performance area**	Management estimates of the resources of talent and energy and other non-financial resources that have been dedicated to this performance area.

In general, input measures capture the total start-up and ongoing investment in a performance area. In most cases, a performance improvement strategy would be to reduce the amount of resources consumed while still maintaining or improving the results and outcome side of the performance area.

If an organization were to focus attention **only** on the input side of the system, *(which I have seen repeatedly in organizations that over-emphasize cost reduction)*, it might see some short-term performance gains, but in the long run, results and outcomes might be seriously hampered by excessive cost reduction. For example, when money gets tight, maintenance budgets and staff training budgets are cut. In the short run there are some savings; however, a lack of maintenance of machines or people may cause more serious problems in the future.

The same logic applies to the output or results side of the formula. Organizations that satisfy customers at all costs, or spend excessively to avoid a failure in a piece of equipment, will have short- and long-term financial inefficiencies.

The key is to know where the tradeoff between the reduction of financial inputs and the related impact on results needs to be made.

Two Kinds of Data

Notice that some of the performance data will come from observations of events where something can be counted, such as number of good products produced, dollars of financial return etc. Some measures are a reflection of opinion, such as customer satisfaction surveys and employee opinion surveys.

Measures that come from observations of events are called "Counting" measures. Measures of opinion are called "Judgment" measures.

We can achieve a high level of accuracy using counting measures if we agree on what will be counted. For example, there is little disagreement when counting dollars, assuming the counting system is counting all the dollars. We do have some difficulty measuring judgments about quality or personal satisfaction because judgments are personal. One of the important characteristics about performance measurement is that the measures report consistently. Therefore, we need to try to count "judgment."

Consider the figure skating world, in which there are two measures of performance. The **technical merit** mark measures the quality of the technical elements of a program and the **artistic impression** mark quantifies the individual judges' opinion about the skaters' "expression" of the program.

It is easy to understand how a panel of judges would rate technical merit on a six-point scale, with the results for a particular skater very close among all the judges. It is more difficult to understand how the marks come so close when artistic impression is being judged. If this judgment is indeed personal, why don't the marks range from 1 to 6?

The marks are close because judges are trained to look for certain aspects to define artistic impression. Judgment is used in determining what the aspects will be so that less judgment is needed when looking for those aspects.

We would prefer to count all performance measurement so results are reported consistently. Therefore, we try to count judgment where possible, and it's not always possible. We do this by applying numerical values to the ranking scale and then anchoring those values so that responses about personal opinion have some definition of what the range means.

For example, if I were to ask you to express your opinion about this book by asking you to put it on a five-point scale, with 5 being excellent and 1 being poor, you might have some difficulty pinpointing a score.

If I defined excellent as "Every single concept was easily understood and completely practical," and poor as "Not one page made any sense whatsoever. It was a complete waste of time," you might have an easier job placing the book on a scale.

Examples of counting measures of judgment abound. If you judge the temperature of your room as comfortable, you could count the temperature as 70° or 20°, depending on the scale you use. In practice, we will always try to find a counting measure.

DEVELOPING SAVI MEASURES

Regardless of whether you are developing input or results measures, developing high-level measures for directors or operating-level measures, there is one framework for the development of the performance measures. Knowing that we need input and output measures, the framework suggests that at every level of performance measurement we will examine four characteristics of performance to locate appropriate measures.

The bottom line of measurement is this: Everything being measured must have at least two measures, a measure of **input resources used** and a measure of **output results delivered**. In addition, you need to use the model described on the following pages to determine if there are measures from all **four categories**. It is not necessarily true that all performance areas will have one of each of the four categories of measurement, but it is true that each performance area must be examined to see if the categories apply.

The purpose behind using the model is to prompt you to do a complete search for measurement concepts. Too often we find one measurement and stop looking further. You could be missing the best performance measure yet!

The following diagram depicts the dimensions of the framework using the image of the spinning "top" (Figure 10.7).

FIGURE 10.7 Four Dimensions of Measurement

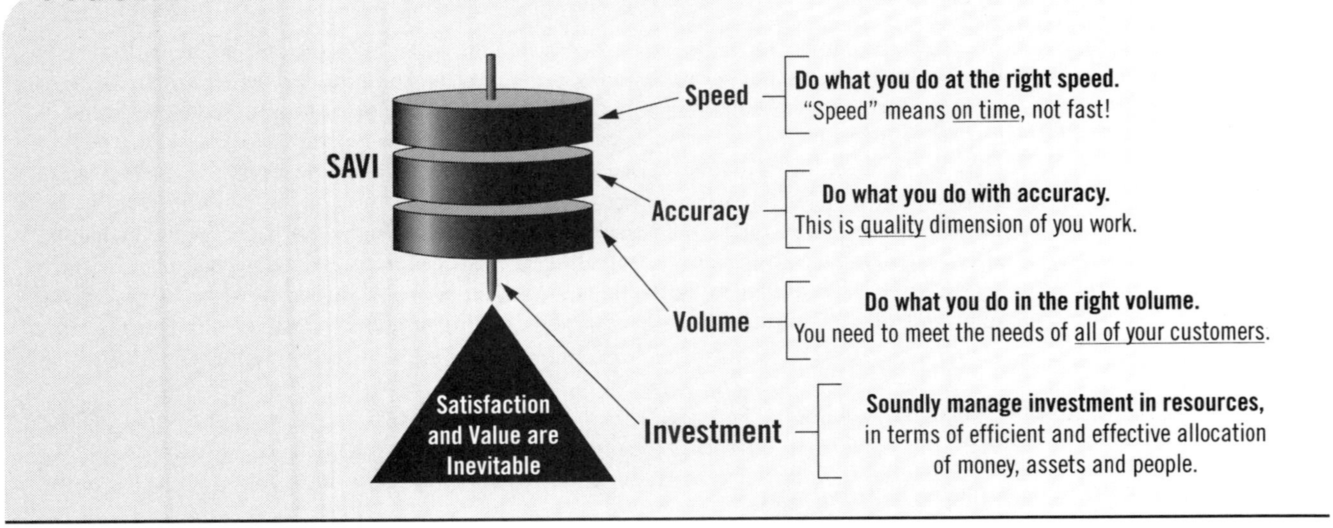

The significance of the "top" is that if the **output dimensions** (Speed, Accuracy and Volume) are maximized and in balance, and the **input dimension** (Investment), is minimized to reflect financial efficiency, the "top" will spin safely. If any dimension is managed out of proportion to the rest, the balance will be impacted and the "top" will fall, damaging satisfaction.

This performance measurement model becomes the focal point of the measurement system because we need to track performance in results, most frequently measured in the realm of "Satisfaction." We also need to track the efficiency of resource use, most frequently measured with "input side measures" of resources consumed in the delivery of results.

The definition of "Satisfaction" will be different for each stakeholder group, but in most cases, regardless of how satisfaction is defined, if we can maximize the speed, accuracy and volume of what the stakeholder wants, while minimizing the investment required to get it, we will likely improve satisfaction.

Let's be clear on the definitions of the terms used in the model:

Speed

Speed, **an output measure**, refers to the timing of the delivery of the product or service, not necessarily "how fast" it gets delivered. We want delivery matched to demand. Something is of little use to us if it is too late or too early. For example, delivering Christmas wrapping paper to retailers in February is too late and delivering in August is too early.

Accuracy

Accuracy, **an output measure**, is the quality dimension of your results. For a financial stakeholder, quality would refer to financial returns. For a customer, it refers to the durability and function of the product or service. For an environmental stakeholder, it refers to the impact of operations on the environment. Doing something accurately means that the qualitative needs of the stakeholders have been met. For example, delivering Christmas wrapping paper on time, but with a spelling error in the word Christmas will not satisfy the customer.

Volume

Volume, **an output measure**, refers to the quantity of goods and services provided. Stakeholders are groups, and each member of the group must be satisfied. There is little satisfaction for the part of the group that has not been served if only the part that was served is happy. For example, delivering high-quality Christmas wrapping, on time, to only half your customers will not satisfy the group.

Investment

Investment, **an input measure**, refers to efficiently using total organizational resources to get the job done. The output measures capture the effective use of resources.

For external stakeholders, customers and the public, the amount of investment is used to set the selling price for the products or services provided. If resources are used efficiently, the price will be fair. If resources are used inefficiently, the price will be too high. In the private sector, customers normally have alternative suppliers, so if the price is high they express their dissatisfaction by choosing someone else. In the public sector, where there are normally no alternative suppliers, customers express their dissatisfaction in the media.

For internal stakeholders, management and supervisors, the amount of investment is carefully controlled to ensure that financial and operating targets are met.

Some Simple Examples of SAVI Performance Measurement

For most organizations, the ultimate outcome sought is customer satisfaction. Experience tells us that when we measure customer satisfaction, we tend to ask the following questions:

- Did we serve you in a timely fashion?
- Did our service meet your quality requirements?
- Did we do enough to satisfy everyone?
- Was the cost or price paid for our service reasonable?

Satisfaction thus has four dimensions. If we do an effective job of managing these four dimensions, it is safe to assume that satisfaction will naturally follow. Instead of asking people to manage an intangible concept like "satisfaction," it is more meaningful to ask people to manage the tangible and measurable dimensions of whatever it is that causes satisfaction. In other words, if you can show performance improvement in the four dimensions, you will be improve overall satisfaction, which is a result or outcome of your business activities. Some brief examples follow.

The Bus Ride Riders on a bus will be happy when the bus arrives on time, **S**, it is clean and the driver is safe, **A**, everyone at the bus stop is picked up, **V**, and the fare is fair, **I**. If any one of the dimensions is out of line, satisfaction declines.

The Budget Process Internal customers and senior management will be happy when the deadline is met, **S**, the budgets are accurate, **A**, all divisions have prepared the budget, **V**, and there was a minimum investment made, **I** in preparing the budget because the process was simple.

The Restaurant Customers will be happy when the service is prompt, **S**, (fast at the drive-through, slow at the romantic restaurant), the food is good quality, **A**, the portion is the right size, **V** and the price is fair, **I**.

The Grocery Store Customers are happy when the store is open at convenient times, **S**, the goods are fresh, **A**, there is enough selection of products, **V** and prices are low, **I**.

The Car Dealership Customers are happy when the model they want is available immediately, **S**, it is clean on delivery, **A**, it is reliable for the first five years, **V**, and the price is fair, **I**.

The same four dimensions apply to each situation, although the characteristics of each dimension change.

A bus ride is a small investment with a very short duration of satisfaction, while purchasing a car is a large investment with a long duration of satisfaction. Therefore, when we judge quality, it would be meaningless to ask patrons about a bus ride they took five years ago, but not meaningless to ask a car owner about a purchase five years later.

CHAPTER SUMMARY

In order to effectively manage performance, we need to have good measures of performance. To have good measures, we need the commitment of the organization to make improving performance a high priority, and a "safe" thing to do.

Good performance measures should be:

- **Measurable**
  The data management system must be able to locate and report performance information in an accurate and timely fashion.

- **Observable**
  There is a cause and effect relationship between data reported and desired performance such that when the data show improvement, performance has actually improved.

- **Reliable**
  The goal and its measurement system should offer consistent and uniform reporting.

- **Controllable**
  The variables that cause change in a performance area must be in the manager's control.

- **Active**
  The goal must relate to an active business process that is in the realm of the manager's routine.

It is important to have each of the characteristics in a measure before we can call it a measure of performance. Measures that don't have all the characteristics are simply measures of environmental conditions that do not require management reaction. The ability to do something about it is what makes a characteristic a performance measure.

We measure the weather and react to the conditions presented to us, but we don't react by controlling the weather. Our performance will be judged on the basis of what we do in the face of the weather conditions. In this context, performance is reactive. For example, if you choose to wear your snowsuit on a hot summer day, the weather will be measured as hot, and your performance will be measured as bad.

Developing performance measures is a process of integrating all the theory discussed so far into a systematic model for developing performance measures. The systematic model will be introduced in Chapter 11.

CLOSING REMARKS

The model for performance measurement used in this book is one of several models available in the marketplace. It seems there are as many models as there are consultants. The common feature of all these models, according to the consultant, is that the model they propose will improve performance.

It's probably true that almost any model will improve performance, because models are not complicated. We know how to measure and we know how to manage performance. The problem is that most organizations are not able and willing to do it.

This chapter introduced the concepts of measurement. Chapter 11 will present performance measurement examples in detail (this should make us able to do it), and Chapter 12 will cover the human side of measuring and managing performance (this should make us willing to do it).

TERMS INTRODUCED IN THE CHAPTER

Accuracy Making sure stakeholders are getting what they want.

Activity (input measures) The measurement of the resources consumed to perform and activity (labour, materials, overhead etc).

Directors' view Board of directors, governors, stockholders representatives, the highest possible view of an organization.

Investment Making sure the cost of achieving speed, accuracy and volume is as low as it can be.

Management view Management is expected to realize gains on behalf of "directors." The management view therefore is of the whole organizational process.

Operational view The organizational process is divided into responsibility areas so that measurement can be related to those in control of the process.

Performance gaps The difference between actual performance and expected (improved) performance.

Performance management Using measures to support an organizational culture that embraces performance improvement and willingly tries to change business practices to achieve performance gains.

Performance measurement Applying scientific, counting measures to various aspects of the operation of an organization with a view to measuring progress towards achieving goals.

Project view Operational areas are divided further into individual projects for performance improvement so that measures can be applied at the most direct level.

Results and outcomes (output measures) The measurement of what has been accomplished once the activity is complete.

Speed Making sure stakeholders are served when they want to be served.

Volume Making sure all stakeholder needs are met.

QUESTIONS FOR CLASS DISCUSSION

1. Describe how performance measurement and performance management are different from each other.
2. Describe how performance measurement and performance management relate to each other.
3. Define "performance gaps" and offer en example of how a performance gap would be reported as it relates to customer service.
4. How is the directors' view of an organization different from an operational view?
5. Define "activity" and define "results." Using an example from your personal experience, show how activity and results are different.
6. Define each of Speed, Accuracy, Volume and Investment. Using an example from your personal experience, show how those four dimensions would be used to measure performance.

A CASE FOR STRATEGIC PLANNING: MALCOLM AND RUBY'S NEXT STEP

It has been three years since Malcolm said to Ruby that she could give it a try for five years, and they would see how successful her business was.

While they have had some ups and down over the first three years, things seem to be going fairly well, according to Malcolm, and absolutely stunning, according to Ruby. The bank manager is not convinced that things are going well, the production department is most displeased, but the marketing department is very happy.

Malcolm sees that at the end of the five years, there is going to be one awful fight about performance measurement. He thinks that Ruby will want to report only the glowing statistics but that he will want to see **all measures** of performance.

To save a misunderstanding in two years' time, Malcolm decides he should get an agreement about measurement now. He suggests to Ruby that they should spend some time deciding what will be measured and what the goals are associated with those measures. Ruby responded, "I don't have time for this, I am too busy running this business and you seem to be too busy trying to keep track of ridiculous things. Measurement will only slow me down. Trust me, Daddy, what you will see in two years will be so stunning it will blow you away!"

Malcolm is now very concerned about what will happen in two years and decides to press the issue by bringing in performance measurement specialists to offer some advice. Your firm, Performance Measurement Services, has been asked to make a brief presentation to Malcolm and Ruby about:

1. The reasons for a performance improvement process
2. The basic structure of a measurement system
3. Some examples of potential measures in several categories of the business

Remember, you are a consulting firm trying to get a contract with Malcolm and Ruby's to develop a full-blown measurement system.

CHAPTER ENDING CASE: A CASE ABOUT PERFORMANCE MEASUREMENT

Wilt's Florist Supply Company is a flower wholesaler that supplies about 200 flower shops and retail grocery stores in your city. Wilt has been in the business for two years and has found competing with the established flower suppliers very difficult. Those suppliers have been in the business for about 20 years and most of their customers are staying with the old suppliers simply out of habit. Wilt has found some success getting customers by lowering prices, but that only gets customers temporarily because his competition matches his price and the customers then go back to their original supplier.

Wilt wants to try something new and innovative to deal with his customers. He heard about the new SAVI performance measurement system and he thinks he could use the system to advertise how much better he is than his competition. He is thinking about making performance measurement "public" with his customers and he wants to find a way to have his customers participate in measuring his performance.

Wilt wants to create a "performance report card" that would be in his customers' hands. They would keep track of their satisfaction with Wilt's performance by ticking off some boxes on a form. Then, at the end of each month, Wilt would pay a personal visit to a few of his best, a few of his newest and a few of his worst customers. He would sit down with them and discuss the report card and use it as a means of improving his performance. He thinks he might have to offer an incentive to fill out the card, perhaps a price reduction on future orders.

REQUIRED:

1. Design the "Performance Report Card" for Wilt.
2. Role-play a meeting with Wilt where you present your idea for the report card and comment on the benefits or pitfalls you see in his performance report card idea.

CHAPTER 11

SIX STEPS OF PERFORMANCE MEASUREMENT

Our new corporate motto is READY...FIRE...AIM.

LEARNING OBJECTIVES

After reading this chapter, engaging in class discussion and doing the exercises at the end of the chapter, you will be able to:

1. Identify the benefits and pitfalls of performance measurement and performance management.
2. Apply the "six steps" of developing a performance measurement system.
3. Compare potential measures against established criteria for good measures using a performance measure checklist.
4. Demonstrate the linkage between performance measurement/management and the director, management, operations and project view of an organization.
5. Develop a set of performance measures for both public and private sector organizations.

YOUR RESPONSIBILITY

To get the most from Chapter 11, you need to become aware of the truth about performance measurement. Go to your workplace, or your school and find out what is being measured. For each measure you find, ask, "What will people do when this measure shows they are performing poorly?" (This follows from your responsibility in Chapter 10.)

Be honest and ask a few people what they would do. For example, an organization might measure the number of customer complaints by counting the answered telephone calls. Therefore, we can influence the performance report by not answering the phone!

Try to find a situation where the measurement of performance is not making performance better.

Try to find a situation where the measurement of performance is making performance better.

Feel free to imagine devious things people might do. To a large extent, that is the truth about measurement!

INTRODUCTION TO CHAPTER 11

Chapter 11 is a detailed look at measurement systems, which follows from the introduction in Chapter 10. Performance measurement, according to the management cycle (Figure 11.1) is the system that provides information to strategic planners that gains or losses are occurring, from a strategic point of view.

FIGURE 11.1 The Management Cycle

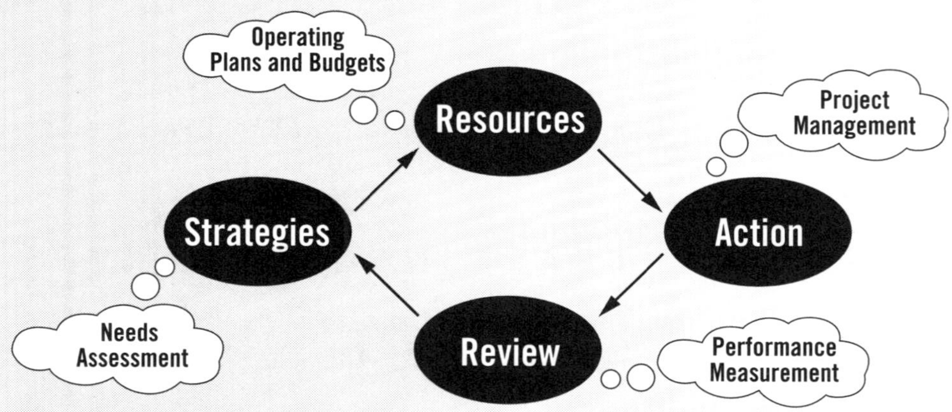

In a perfect world, this measurement system will actively promote performance improvement by measuring what matters, providing corrective feedback and positive reinforcement to enthusiastic people who enjoy being measured and who take on improvement as a challenge.

Imagine how far we could go in this perfect world.

Our world certainly isn't perfect. Sometimes we measure what doesn't matter, we use information in a negative way or unenthused people afraid of measurement take on breaking down the system as their challenge.

Chapter 11 will focus on measuring what matters and providing corrective feedback. Chapter 12 will deal with people.

ATTRIBUTES OF A GOOD MEASUREMENT SYSTEM

An effective performance measurement system should have the following attributes:

1. FOCUS ON EFFECTIVENESS

We hold two important values in the design of a results-oriented measurement system:

1. We have a need to measure better.
2. We have a need to measure less.

Presently, we collect too much data and too little information. The effectiveness of a measurement system is best when accurate, timely and relevant information is presented to a manager in a form that will be easily understood and result in appropriate management action.

Sometimes we build systems of measurement designed to control a process. The measurement system assumes that the process doesn't need to improve or change in any way, so it focuses on complying with standard practices. An effective control measure will prompt the manager to correct the process when a variance occurs.

Sometimes we build measurement systems to support change to improve a process. The measures are in place to determine if the change is positive, and to encourage and reward those involved when the change is successful. An effective change measure will prompt the manager to focus on customer driven outputs and manage the mix of inputs as well as the process.

Too much data, or irrelevant data, will cause the manager to ignore the signals from the measurement system. Managers don't have the time or inclination to separate good measures from bad ones. They tend to abandon the whole measurement system when a few bad measures are discovered.

2. FOCUS ON THE FUTURE

A major concern of business performance measurement is measuring and reporting things that will advocate and encourage superior performance into the future.

Some performance measurement systems collect data from past operations and report a historical summary of achievements, which are compared to expected results and outcomes. There are two flaws to this system:

1. Past performance does not always indicate what is desirable for the future.
2. If expected result targets are set too low, we are advocating behaviour appropriate for less than optimal performance.

Though measurement of the past does give a baseline or benchmark for performance measurement, the objective of measurement is to deal with future operations.

Business performance measurement concentrates on the set of resources, behaviours and activities that will maximize performance in the future. A performance system based on the past will recognize good behaviour from the past. A motivating performance measurement system will target opportunities into the future and motivate the team to achieve future oriented results.

There are two activities in a future-oriented system:

1) **Analysis** Collecting historical information about a process to gain an understanding of the relationships of input to output.
2) **Prediction** Using the understanding of historical relationships to predict what will happen next.

This means that we should carefully study past relationships in the development of measures, but expectations or goals should be based on assumed relationships that will exist into the future. At the risk of sounding like your parents, "Don't worry about others, just go and be the best that you can be!" We are all measured against standards that come from the past, but our goals are related to the future.

3. FOCUS ON OBJECTIVES: "KEY RESULT AREAS"

KRAs are functions or divisions of performance in which your organization must continually improve to be successful. This includes challenges and opportunities from the external environment, as well as needs and opportunities within the business itself.

The essence of strategic planning is to establish direction for the organization. KRAs provide direction by defining the areas of performance within which your organization will focus strategy and action.

KRAs are not performance indicators. They are functions or divisions for which performance indicators will be developed. The KRAs ensure that the complete set of performance indicators covers all-important facets of the organization.

Examples of "Key Result" Areas

- Customer
- Product/service
- Public/society/natural environment
- Marketing
- Human Resources
- Production
- Maintenance
- Operations
- Finance

Key result areas specify the area of concern and therefore provide constancy of focus. However, these dimensions need to be reviewed periodically in light of internal and external environmental changes, and new realities can cause these dimensions to be modified.

The list above is not complete. There are an unlimited number of key result areas that will be defined by the organization based on its current environment and its ever-changing goals and strategies. It is important to note, however, that in the list above, some key result areas are departments of divisions in an organization and others are functions or even stakeholder groups.

Good measurement systems don't just measure things that are done according to the organizational chart. Good systems measure things that are done to satisfy stakeholders.

Key Performance Indicators: "KPI's"

Let's make sure the concept of Key Performance Indicator is understood. This is the essence of measurement.

An "indicator" is a gauge or a measure that reports information.

"Performance" is the result or activity we are looking for that fits into strategic goals.

"Key" means that this measure has been pinpointed so carefully that when a reading on the indicator is bad, management knows precisely what to do. The same applies when a reading is good.

ON THIS TOPIC — *A Real-World Example*

A Story About Your Car

On the dashboard of your car is a light that says, "Service engine soon." That light is not a "key performance indicator."

The light is sending you information all the time. While you are driving and the light is off, the information you are getting is: the engine is not in need of service, so feel free to continue.

When the light comes on, the information changes to "Something about the car needs service." When this light comes on, you don't open the door and bail out at speed. You look at the gauges. If the temperature is rising, you back off the throttle, if oil pressure is zero, you turn off the engine, and if your windshield washer fluid is low, you worry about it later.

Those gauges are key performance indicators because they pinpoint one dimension of the process, management understands what is being measured and the reaction required is appropriate.

Measures are developed to capture both the input and output elements of a business system.

From the SAVI model introduced in Chapter 10, recall that there are four types of key performance indicators, Speed, Accuracy, Volume and Investment.

Regardless of what is being measured, the basic measurement system is the same, from the top corporate view all the way to measuring a specific activity on the assembly line. These four types of measures provide a framework for looking for potential measures. This does not imply that every process will have one of each of the four types of measures. At operating levels, it might be that only one dimension needs to be measured because that's all a particular person controls, say, speed of the assembly line or number of units produced.

At a higher level, it is more likely that all four dimensions will be relevant to measure because higher levels assume control of broader aspects of the business. The most important thing to remember is that measures are integrated with each other; they don't stand alone. The assembly line process can't focus on speed or volume and ignore quality and cost. Even when we pinpoint measures down to specific functions, we still need to remember that these activities are part of a larger picture.

Some examples of measures follow.

Speed Indicators

Speed indicators measure the amount of time taken to deliver a good or service. A useful approach for speed (timeliness) indicators is to state the percentage of the total output to be accomplished within a specific time period. An example is the on-time delivery statistic expressed as the number of on-time deliveries achieved within a period of time. (Your pizza place guarantees 30-minute delivery.) Some examples are:

- Response time records
- Turnaround time records
- Cycle time records
- Project completion dates
- Meeting scheduled time records

Accuracy Indicators

This is the quality aspect of providing goods and services that measures results that meet or exceed the quality standard, in contrast to the amount delivered. An example of an accuracy (quality) indicator is customer satisfaction, which is usually measured through a client survey or interview, such as the following:

- Judgment-based climate or opinion surveys
- Focus groups
- Comment cards
- Telephone surveys
- Advisory panels
- Opinions of community leaders

Another example of the quality aspect is meeting design specifications or passing an inspection point that ensures a product works.

- Reject or pass rates coming from the inspection of size, weight, colour, functionality etc. (i.e. any physical aspect of the product)
- Customer returns or warranty claims

Accuracy (quality) has these two dimensions because perception (customer opinion) and physical quality are closely related but different. If the best toaster in the world is not recognized by the customer as the best in the world, we need to manage perceptions.

Volume Indicators

Volume indicators measure the **amount** (number of) of outputs or results from a specific activity or program. The volume indicator is a reflection of whether or not **all potential customers** are being satisfied. Not enough good product is a bad thing, as is too much bad product. "Good and Bad" are being measured in the accuracy (quality) dimension. Here we are only concerned with quantity because we assume that accuracy has already been accounted for. For example:

- Number of units produced
- Number of completed transactions
- Percent of market share
- Back order statistics
- Number of failed sales due to being out of stock

Investment Indicators

Investment indicators measure the amount of resources expended on a specific program or activity, or the unit cost (cost/number of units produced ($)):

- Operating costs per unit produced
- Capital costs per unit produced
- Cost per customer as to sales and marketing expenses
- Cost per unit of after sales service and customer support

Notice that the financial measures are "per" something. It is dangerous to say that we want the absolute costs of something to decline. For example, if the organizational goal was to reduce the investment in materials in our manufacturing process, we can easily reduce the investment in materials by doing **less** manufacturing. On the other hand, if the goal was to reduce materials costs **per unit produced**, we will be motivated to increase efficiency, and if we link this with an accuracy goal, a volume goal and a speed goal, we are motivated to give customers what they want, when they want it, to everyone who wants it, at a fair price.

Developing key performance indicators from each of the four types listed above is an effective way to support a strategic plan. For example, concentrating only on delivering a service as quickly as possible with no regard for cost would not be considered sound management. A timeliness indicator, coupled with a cost indicator (for example, 10% improvement in service while maintaining the same unit $ cost/service), would be preferable.

DATA COLLECTION AND REPORTING

Every performance measure requires collecting data which are fed into the measurement system. Obtaining data is a detailed, time-consuming and costly activity. Obtaining the proper data also requires persistence, attention to detail, tact and persuasion.

Data collection, manipulation and reporting must be carefully linked to analysis requirements. There is no sense collecting and reporting data that will not have a significant impact on the process being reviewed in terms of performance improvement.

In general, the entire performance measurement system is useless unless a rigorous, systematic and accurate process of collecting and reporting data is used.

There are three essential elements in data collection:

1) Precisely defined measurement system

Whatever the measure is — a ratio, percentage or average score — the precise data elements that make up the measure must be clearly defined, understood and controllable by the manager.

2) Sources of data: Are they available? Are they reliable?

We need to determine if the data exist in present systems or if a new system of data collection is needed to trap the required information. Often, performance measurement systems provide the impetus to develop new management information systems that accrue benefits in areas other than performance measurement.

3) Frequency of data collection

The more frequently data is collected, the more timely the review will be. However, reporting also frequently escalates the cost.

In general, we should report data as frequently as management action is required. This is a function of the cost of allowing a process to continue out of control until the next data review takes place.

In the early stages of performance improvement, a frequent review might be necessary. As excellence is achieved, less frequent review is all that is needed to ensure that the process remains in control. Data collection resources should be targeted to KRAs where improvement is most essential.

ON THIS TOPIC

A Real-World Example

WestJet maintains an interactive feedback centre on their Web site. This enables the public, employees and management to express their feelings about WestJet performance on a continual basis.

The various dimensions of the measurement system are quite broad and all encompassing.

WestJet appears to have an excellent source of high-quality data to support its measurement system.

http://c0dsp.westjet.com/internet/sky/about/index.jsp

SIX STEPS IN THE DEVELOPMENT OF A MEASUREMENT SYSTEM

The development and management of performance measures is a simple, systematic process that goes through six steps:

1. Separate strategic goals into input and output dimensions.
2. Develop output and results measures for each goal.
3. Develop input measures for each goal.
4. Check with SAVI to see if the set of measures is complete.
5. Use an effective recognition system.
6. Build the culture.

Each step will be described in detail, first using an example from the private sector, and second, using an example from the public sector, which will show the development of a measurement system at the project level.

STEP 1 SEPARATE STRATEGIC GOALS INTO INPUT AND OUTPUT DIMENSIONS

Following from Vision, Mission and Values, organizations create strategic goals that identify "Key Result" areas of the organization where change and improvement are possible and desirable. Our first step in developing measures to reflect the goal is to dissect the goal into its input and output dimensions.

Imagine that an organization set a high-level strategic goal that reads as follows:

To achieve a financial return from our producing assets that is at least 5% above industry average and within 1% of the top performer in our industry by the end of fiscal 2008.

At the high level (corporate view), the organization is expecting to see improved returns from producing assets, which will be caused by a wide range of activities from a wide range of operating departments.

At the end of the day, the combined efforts of all departments will be summarized in one or two financial measures that report the level of returns coming from operating assets. Most frequently, those measures are ROI (return on investment) and ROA (return on assets).

To accomplish the strategic goal, operating departments, such as the "Toy Division" will take the goal and provide more clarity and relevance to the "Toy Division" by adding to the goal as follows:

To improve the financial returns from our producing assets in the "Toy Division" to 25% by December 31, 2002 by raising unit cost efficiency while maintaining and improving quality and meeting current and future demand, which will lower consumer prices and improve market share.

This goal has many dimensions. Financial returns is a high-level goal, while unit cost efficiency is an operating-level goal. Financial stakeholders are interested in returns, customer stakeholders are interested in quality and price and management stakeholders are interested in production efficiency and market share.

The goal can now be segregated into its input and output dimensions. Step 2 of the 6 steps will deal with output measures in detail, and step 3 will deal with input measures in detail.

In step 1, we ask for the goal to be segregated as to input and output in broad terms so we can begin some thinking that will allow a more detailed approach in the next steps.

The "Input Dimension" will be a collection of measures that capture the efficiency of the use of resources to build toys. Therefore, as Figure 11.2 illustrates, we can focus our input measures around one broad measurement concept.

FIGURE 11.2 Broad Measurement Concept of Inputs

Input dimension	**Unit cost efficiency** • How well are materials used (excessive waste)? • How well is labour used (excessive idle time)? • How well is overhead used (idle capacity)?

The input dimension is going to report on the total organizational investment made in the Toy Division.

Measurement systems will be tailored to each organization. For example, on the input dimension of a hotel, they might link efficiency measures to "customer days" and an airline might measure "passenger miles."

The output dimension is going to report on the impact that operations will have on internal and external stakeholders.

Internal results are those that are directly traceable to the organization and controlled from within, while external results are the impacts on the stakeholders that are outside of daily operations.

FIGURE 11.3 Broad Measurement Concepts of Outputs

Output Dimension	**Internal Results**	• maintaining and improving quality • lower consumer prices
	External Results	• financial returns • improving market share • meeting current and future demand

It may not always be possible to segregate internal and external results, but if you can, it adds clarity to the situation, particularly when the results of an initiative are non-financial. For example, an internal result of an environmental stewardship program could be improved employee morale, while an external result could be improved public perception, as well as the fish being saved.

Now that the goal has been expressed in both input and output terms, we can search for performance measures down both paths of measurement.

Step 2 Develop output measures for each goal

Output measures require a bit more detailed analysis. Most people, when asked, "What do you do?" describe all the activities that make up their day, e.g., "I work at the post office." When you ask, "What do you accomplish?" the answer becomes, "I deliver the mail," or "As CEO, I develop long-range policy that will maximize the efficiency and effectiveness of mail services." You get more useful information when you focus your analysis on accomplishments, rather than activities.

Outputs are accomplishments. In most organizations, accomplishments can be categorized into three groups.

1. Investment returns (what is going to the stockholder?)
2. Customer satisfaction (what is the customer's view of what we do?)
3. Social impacts (what are we doing to the social and natural environment?)

For each category there might be one or more "Measurement Concepts," which is a broad definition of where the measures will be focusing.

Figure 11.4 offers examples of potential output measures. Notice that the measures are now being refined with the introduction of performance goals. This demonstrates the link between the performance measure and the direction the measure should go to report improved performance. As indicated previously, the purpose of measurement is to promote improvement. Therefore, there is a close link between the measure itself and the goal for improvement.

FIGURE 11.4 Measures of Outputs or Results

OUTPUT MEASURES			
CATEGORY	**MEASUREMENT CONCEPT**	**PERFORMANCE MEASURE**	**PERFORMANCE GOAL (changes of specific amounts over specific time frames)**
Investment Returns	**Financial returns**	• % return on investment • % return on assets employed • Profit margin on sales	All should increase by a specific % change, to be accomplished by a specific date.
	Market share	• % market share relative to the competition • % market share relative to total market size	The proportion of the market share against the competition should increase. The proportion of the market share relative to the total market should increase at a rate that is faster than the rate of change in total market size.
Customer Satisfaction	**Product or service quality**	• Rejection rates in the production process • Sales returns	Both should decline by a specific amount in a specific timeframe.
	Deliver on time and in sufficient quantity	• Back order and delivery statistics	Back orders should decline and delivery cycle times should improve.
	Consumer prices	• Retail price by product	The retail price matched to value should decline.
Social Benefits	**Child development**	• Improvement in reading skills	Children using these toys should show a measured improvement in reading skills.
	Environmental impact	• Impact on landfills when the toy is finished	The proportion of toys presented for re-cycling should go up.

As output measures are developed, you will see the organization's sense of priority beginning to emerge. Some people in this toy company might put child development at the top of the list. Others might have financial returns as a priority. When dealing with a client, I always find it interesting to discover, this late in the strategic planning process, that his or her vision is about to be changed, because now that we are pinpointing and measuring results we are finding what is truly important to the organization.

Step 3 Develop input measures for each goal

We normally develop input measures after we have developed output measures because it is a good idea to know where you are going before you decide how to get there.

Input measures capture the amount of organizational investment used to get the job done. They are measures of the efficiency of the use of resources. Input measures can be separated into three categories.

1. Financial operating resources (how much is being consumed on an ongoing basis?)
2. Financial capital resources (how much is being invested for the long range?)
3. Other organizational resources (what else has been committed to this activity in the organization?)

Some example measures are shown in Figure 11.5. Again, note that the performance measures have been linked to performance goals.

FIGURE 11.5 Measures of Inputs or Efficiencies

INPUT MEASURES for "UNIT COST EFFICIENCY"			
CATEGORY	**MEASUREMENT CONCEPT**	**PERFORMANCE MEASURE**	**PERFORMANCE GOAL**
Financial Operating Resources	**Materials and labour**	Direct materials and direct labour per unit, expressed in both dollar and quantity terms.	Material and labour cost and/or consumption per unit should decline over a specified time period.
	Overhead	Overhead charged per unit.	Overhead consumed per unit produced should decline.
		% use of capacity.	% capacity used should increase to or remain at optimal levels.
Financial Capital Resources	**Capital investment in operating assets**	Dollars of capital investment per unit produced.	Dollars per unit of capital invested should decline over time as capital resources are used more efficiently.
Other Organizational Resources	**Non-financial resources consumed by the performance area**	Management estimates of the resources of talent and energy and other non-financial resources that have been dedicated to this performance area.	The amount consumed will increase as the project is developed and decrease after it is implemented.

ON THIS TOPIC

A Real-World Example

Subway was started by a 19-year-old man who needed money to go to college. He asked a family friend for a loan of $1,000. The family friend said he wouldn't loan money for college, but would loan money to open a small business, which would then provide two results for the young man: he would get some small business experience and he would have money for college.

The original vision was "to provide a pretty good sandwich on this street corner so I can go to college to find out what I really want to do."

In early 2003, Subway passed McDonalds in total number of restaurants.

www.subway.com

Step 4 Check with SAVI to see if the set of measures is complete

Before we can be sure that we have a complete set of measures, we need to apply the SAVI framework to categorize the measures as to Speed, Accuracy, Volume and Investment. First, let's see if we have a complete set of measures for the characteristics that define measures as to input and output, and S, A, V and I.

Figure 11.6 identifies the characteristics of each measure. For the set to be considered complete, there must be at least one from each of the input and output groups, and, it is hoped, one from each of the SAVI attributes.

FIGURE 11.6 Linking Output Measures to SAVI

OUTPUT MEASURES			
CATEGORY	**MEASUREMENT CONCEPT**	**PERFORMANCE MEASURE**	**SAVI**
Investment Returns	**Financial returns**	• % return on investment • % return on assets employed • Profit margin on sales	**Accuracy**
	Market share	• % market share relative to the competition • % market share relative to total market size	**Volume**
Customer Satisfaction	**Product or service quality**	• Rejection rates in the production process • Sales returns	**Accuracy & Volume**
	Deliver on time and in sufficient quantity	• Back order and delivery statistics	**Speed & Volume**
	Consumer prices	• Retail price per product	**Investment**

OUTPUT MEASURES			
CATEGORY	**MEASUREMENT CONCEPT**	**PERFORMANCE MEASURE**	**SAVI**
Social Benefits	**Child development**	• Improvement in reading skills	**Accuracy**
	Environmental impact	• Impact on landfills when the toy is finished	**Volume**

FIGURE 11.7 Linking Input Measures to SAVI

INPUT MEASURES for "UNIT COST EFFICIENCY"			
CATEGORY	**MEASUREMENT CONCEPT**	**PERFORMANCE MEASURE**	**SAVI**
Financial Operating Resources	**Materials and labour**	Direct materials and direct labour per unit in both dollar and quantity terms	**Investment**
	Overhead	Overhead charged per unit	**Investment**
		% use of capacity	**Volume**
Financial Capital Resources	**Capital investment in operating assets**	Dollars of capital investment per unit produced	**Investment**
Other Organizational Resources	**Non-financial resources consumed**	Management estimates of the resources of talent and energy that have been dedicated to this performance area	**Investment**

As you can see, most input measures are investment related and the output measures deal with speed, accuracy and volume.

Once we are satisfied that the set is complete, we need to subject each and every measure to a test.

The following checklist identifies the elements that must be considered for each performance measure. The shaded areas represent the correct responses. If you cannot respond yes or no as appropriate, you need to either fix that aspect of the measure, or find some other measure!

The purpose behind testing the measure is to reduce the number of measures to a few very effective, very meaningful measures that will actually have an impact on change.

FIGURE 11.8 SAVI Performance Measure Checklist (to be completed for each proposed measure)

This is a measure of:	Outputs and Results				Inputs			
The measure is reporting:	Speed		Accuracy		Volume		Investment	

If this is a "counting measure" which will collect numerical information:		
Quality of Numerical Information	**yes**	**no**
Are the measures quantifiable?		
Is the information available?		
Is the data provider reliable and accurate?		
Is information available on a timely basis?		
Is acquiring the information cost effective?		
Quality of the Measure Itself		
Is it under the performer's control?		
Do the performers agree that the data is useful in tracking performance?		
Can a performer manage the measure rather than performance?		
Can any other performer influence the measured results?		

If information is gathered using a judgment-based opinion survey:
Be sure that the proposed audience contains the demographic you are looking for to provide a valuable opinion.
If a ranking scale is used for a question, have the ends of the scale been anchored with clear terminology?
Have all the dimensions of performance been captured by the survey?
Results of Measurement
What will performers do when reported results are less than expected?
What will performers do when reported results are more than expected?

To see how the checklist works, let's use the checklist to measure the quality of one of the proposed performance measures, specifically "% return on investment."

FIGURE 11.9 Performance Measure Checklist Applied to % of Return Investment

This is a measure of:	Outputs and Results			✓	Inputs			
The measure is reporting:	**Speed**		**Accuracy**	✓	**Volume**		**Investment**	

If this is a "counting measure" which will collect numerical information:		
Quality of Numerical Information	**yes**	**no**
Are the measures quantifiable? **ROI is a widely used financial statistic**	✓	
Is the information available? **The accounting system routinely reports ROI**	✓	
Is the data provider reliable and accurate? **The accounting system is very accurate**	✓	
Is information available on a timely basis? **Financial reports are given monthly**	✓	
Is acquiring the information cost effective? **There is no added cost to get this statistic**	✓	
Quality of the Measure Itself		
Is it under the performer's control? **All the dimensions of ROI are controllable, except that operating managers have limited control over owner's investments**		✓
Do the performers agree that the data are useful in tracking performance? **The statistic is accepted**	✓	
Can a performer manage the measure rather than the performance? **The only way to improve ROI is to improve performance**		✓
Can any other performer influence the measured results? **The statistic is controlled by all performers**	✓	
If information is gathered using a judgment-based opinion survey:		
N/A		
Results of Measurement		
What will performers do when reported results are less than expected?		
Improve financial efficiency and/or improve the revenue stream		
What will performers do when reported results are more than expected?		
Use the results to feed into the planning system to do more of the same		

This measure is effective at a high level, but as a measure of operating activities, it has two shortcomings: it has no control over owners' investments and it does not focus on one single performance area. Therefore, we would keep this measure as a high-level measure and ask operating divisions to add clarity to the measure by dealing with elements that they directly control at their operating level.

Step 5 Use an Effective Recognition System

Use Measurement to Initiate Change

An effective measurement system will use the measured results as a management tool. Every result should have an automatic intervention strategy. When results are as expected we should offer congratulations and reinforcement to keep it going, when results are less than expected we should quickly isolate the cause and correct the process, and when results are more than expected we should reward, reinforce, and create a need to do more of the same (more on this topic in Chapter 12).

ON THIS TOPIC

A Real-World Example

On their Web site, Pepsi Company has a place for employees at all levels, as well as the general public, to learn about the awards Pepsi has received, awards for employment equity, civic contributions, etc. There are hundreds of awards and to demonstrate their pride, Pepsi has posted them for all to see.

Not only does this Web site reflect a very positive view of the corporation, it also demonstrates that Pepsi's commitment to excellence goes beyond traditional business practices.

http://www.pepsico.com/company/honors.shtml

Performance measures become the database for change management. When results, whether positive or negative, are not as expected, we will create new projects and initiatives that are designed to deliver performance gains. The process of measuring ongoing performance thus results in a host of performance improvement projects, which require measuring their results and outcomes.

For the Toy Division, we created measures of ongoing operations. The next example will illustrate the development of measures at the project level.

STEP 6 BUILD THE CULTURE

Good systems need good people. There is no sense examining a process unless at the same time you examine the people who govern the process. Improvement does not take place on paper. Improvement happens when people use enthusiasm, dedication, commitment, leadership and morale in their daily routine. A good system on paper is a healthy beginning, but if you want results, you need to follow up a paper system with a people system.

To build a culture, an organization must be willing to make a significant investment in changing the perceptions and attitudes of the people involved in performance. This investment usually involves two levels of training and development: technical training on the function of the model and cultural training on the use of the model.

The technical training improves the use of the model by ensuring that the measures are carefully developed to meet all the characteristics of good performance measures. The cultural training deals with removing the fears of performance measurement and teaching people to regard measurement as a constructive and positive management tool.

More important than training, though, is the need for the organization, from top to bottom, to embrace performance measurement as a positive and constructive way to manage performance improvement (more on this topic in Chapter 12).

Linking Performance Measures to Projects and Initiatives (Project SAVI)

The Toy Division example uses performance measures at the strategic and divisional levels, and those measures clearly show the link between performance in the division and the results that will be accomplished at the strategic goal level. These measures will capture the ongoing activity of the business.

The following example takes the analysis one step further by developing performance measures for a specific project that is designed to improve the results around strategic goals. The example deals with a public transit company. Note that we use the same basic steps in developing the measures, and that the process is as applicable to a private company as it is to a public company.

A detailed example of SAVI performance measurement in the public sector, focusing on "Performance Improvement Projects"

Imagine that your city has set a corporate level strategic goal as follows:

"To make SAVITOWN the most livable, and well managed city in Canada"

This strategic goal will govern the operations of all operating divisions so that ongoing activities and new projects and initiatives must show the contribution being made to the livability of the city from a public view and the efficient management of the city from an internal as well as a public view.

Now imagine that one of the strategic goal statements for the public transit service in a city reads as follows:

"To mobilize and maintain a fleet of safe, reliable and cost effective buses which will improve the use of public transit and will reduce the impact of automobile exhaust on the environment and improve the quality of life for people in the region"

STEP 1 SEPARATE THE STRATEGIC GOAL INTO INPUT AND OUTPUT DIMENSIONS

The first task is to break the core strategic goal into its input and output dimensions.

FIGURE 11.10 Inputs and Outputs for Transit Services

Input Dimension	To mobilize and maintain a fleet of safe, reliable and cost effective buses	

Output Dimension		
	Internal Results	which will improve the use of public transit and will reduce the impact of automobile exhaust on the environment
	External Results	which will improve quality of life for people in the region.

The input dimension captures the ongoing business activity of running a bus company: operating and maintenance costs, capital investment, scheduling, driver training, developing new routes, advertising and promotion etc. Performance gains in this area will be expressed as operating cost savings and new revenue streams more **efficiently**, in other words, using financial and operating resources. At the same time, it is essential to measure the **effectiveness** of the use of financial and other resources.

Effectiveness will be captured on the output side of formula. Effectiveness (results) means that inputs are delivering results to customers that are perceived as and are genuine value to customers. We separate results into two areas. Internal results are intermediate results because they can be measured by "data mining" existing information that is gathered internally. We also assume that these internal results add value to the external results. The external results are "end impacts" because they are the ultimate goal. In most cases, data regarding external results can only be collected by contacting and surveying external users.

As mentioned previously, if intermediate results are measured frequently (keeping on schedule, being safe, picking up everyone and no fare increase) then the external view of satisfaction can be measured less frequently.

We will now discuss the measurement of outputs and the measurement of inputs separately.

STEP 2 DEVELOP OUTPUT MEASURES

The ultimate output or result of the management of any system can be expressed by how satisfed the stakeholders are with the quality of results and outcomes. This is a noble objective. However, if the only important measure was stakeholder satisfaction and the stakeholder view of quality, we might build a management system that spends too much to achieve the outcome, or a system that does not respond properly when poor results are obtained, because the measure does not prompt specific management reaction.

We need to examine results and outcomes for each strategic goal using all three dimensions of external results. We don't need to actually develop measures for each dimension. In many cases, results will not have a measurable financial or social impact, but in all cases results will have some form of satisfaction impact, otherwise the project is not worth doing.

The template is a guide to prompt thinking, not an "absolute." However, don't stop the search for a results measure just because it has become difficult to find one. These result measures are extremely valuable, not only in the performance measurement process, but also in the capital and operating request process, because they define deliverables and provide excellent evidence to support expenditures. Observe the application of these concepts in the transit service example.

FIGURE 11.11 Output Measures for the Transit Company

Output Dimension	Internal Results	which will improve the use of public transit and will reduce the impact of automobile exhaust on the environment	
	External Results	which will improve the quality of life for people in the region.	
OUTPUT MEASURES			
CATEGORY	**MEASUREMENT CONCEPT**	**PERFORMANCE MEASURE**	**PERFORMANCE GOAL (changes of specific amounts over specific time frames)**
Investment Returns	**Financial returns**	Revenue flows by route from fares and new revenue streams like advertising.	Total revenue per route and new revenue sources should increase by a stated amount over a stated time frame.
	Financial efficiency	$ of subsidy per passenger and route.	$ of subsidy per passenger should go down.
Customer Satisfaction	**Product or service quality**	Opinion survey of external users which captures their perception of the value of the bus service.	Customer perception of value should increase.
	Deliver on time and in sufficient quantity	Meeting the schedule, safety records, % utilization, number of stranded passengers.	Number of times on schedule, number of kilometers accident free, % use of available seats should all go up while number of stranded passengers should go down.
Social Benefits	**Pollution**	Net change in exhaust emissions in the region.	The net change of pollution added by buses less the pollution saved by not using autos should show a reduction in environmental impact of exhaust.
	Dependence on the automobile	Number of people choosing public over private transit.	Reduced investment in road infrastructure construction and parking.

These output measures refer to the ongoing effective operation of a transit service. Because the transit service is subsidized, the profitability measures are normally expressed as reductions in the required subsidy to maintain or improve service levels.

Our social set of values places the impact on the environment and the transport of people, using a convenient and inexpensive means as very important strategic goals, even to the extent of subsidizing the financial parts of the service to achieve the social benefits. Even so, we still expect the service to be as financially efficient as possible, which is why we develop input measures as well.

STEP 3 DEVELOPING INPUT MEASURES

The next step in a performance management system is to quantify inputs in measurement terms.

FIGURE 11.12 Input Measures for the Transit Service

INPUT MEASURES to "mobilize and maintain a fleet of safe, reliable and cost effective buses"			
CATEGORY	**MEASUREMENT CONCEPT**	**PERFORMANCE MEASURE**	**PERFORMANCE GOAL**
Financial Operating Resources	**Materials and labour**	Operating costs per passenger and passenger kilometer. Operating cost per bus and per bus kilometer.	Operating costs per passenger and per bus should decline as should operating costs per km traveled. This will ensure that resources are used and not just parked.
	Overhead	As above, Overhead costs per…	As above.
Financial Capital Resources	**Capital investment in operating assets**	Capital investment per passenger kilometer.	The investment in the infrastructure should go down, or at least be an efficient tradeoff with operating costs.
Other Organizational Resources	**Senior management commitment to the operation**	Time invested in the strategic planning and performance measurement process.	In the short run, time invested will be high, gradually reducing as change takes place.

Of course, the transit service would complete the remaining three steps of the performance measurement process to ensure that the program was successful.

The purpose of this example was to demonstrate how performance measures get carried to the "Performance Improvement Project" level.

MEASURING AT THE PROJECT LEVEL (PROJECT SAVI)

Now that we have ongoing measures of performance, we can take measurement to the next step, specifically to use the same measurement concepts to determine the efficiency and effectiveness of projects and other change management initiatives. The biggest difference between a project and an ongoing activity is that the project has both an implementation element and an ongoing element that require measurement. Implementation will occur during a specific time frame and will deliver results and outcomes, and the ongoing results of a project will occur over the total project life, however long that might be.

There are corporate and divisional goals and measures at the transit service. Now, the management team will introduce steps in a work plan to take on certain aspects of operations and introduce a change to that aspect with the hope that the change will positively impact performance.

The example activity chosen from the transit company work-plan is the development of **improved maintenance practices** on the fleet of buses. This is only one of a host of work-plan initiatives. The other items might be improved scheduling, improved driver training, improved advertising etc.

The "maintenance practices activity" in the work plan refers to the portion of the strategic goal which reads "reliable and cost effective buses." The managers of the maintenance function have thus begun a review of how to improve the maintenance function, because any efficiency gains they can realize will have a direct impact on the financial costs of maintenance, and any improvement in quality they can realize will make the buses safer and more reliable.

With this in mind, the work-plan will set a goal for accomplishment for this project, which might read:

> *"We need to install a maintenance management program that will improve the efficiency of scheduling and conducting maintenance that will improve operating efficiency and reliability while reducing operating costs."*

This goal would then be used to conduct a *Total Impact* Business Case Analysis which examines alternative methods of maintaining the fleet. The analysis would look at alternative maintenance management systems, outsourcing and abandonment of the assets as alternative ways to deal with the problem.

An analysis turns into a project when a choice is made. At this point, we assume that the **"SAVI 9300 Computerized Maintenance Management System"** will make the highest contribution to reliability and efficiency at the lowest cost of all the alternatives examined in the business case process.

When the work-plan item was first designed, the sponsor would develop measures of speed, accuracy, volume and investment for the project so that deliverables could be measured and fed back into the management process. A successful project will meet or exceed expectations in each of the speed, accuracy, volume and investment accounts.

The following table illustrates how this is done.

FIGURE 11.13 Transit Company Maintenance Department — Action Plan 2000 – 2010

Core Strategy: "To mobilize and maintain a fleet of safe, reliable and cost effective buses which will improve the use of public transit, reduce the impact of automobile exhaust on the environment and improve the quality of life for people in the region."

					Team / Division / Department	Time Frame
Initiatives to Support Corporate Planning Strategy	"We need to install a maintenance management program that will improve the efficiency of scheduling and conducting maintenance that will improve operating efficiency and reliability while reducing operating costs."				**Maintenance Department**	**2000 - 2010**
	SAVI Measures					
Activities	**Speed**	**Accuracy**	**Volume**	**Investment**		
Secure a vendor and a consultant to design, install and test the "SAVI 9300 Computerized Maintenance Management System"	Was the project completed on time?	Does the design meet user needs and are the test results good?	Will the system have the capacity to deal with the entire fleet?	Were the design and installation costs on or below budget?	**Project Manager**	**January 2000-April 2000**
Integrate the "SAVI 9300 Computerized Maintenance Management System" with maintenance practices and monitor the effectiveness of the system.	Has the rate of throughput of the fleet increased?	Have there been a reduced number of breakdowns in the field?	Has the system shown that it can meet the demands of the entire fleet, now and in the future?	Are the operating costs of the computer system on budget, and has there been a decline in maintenance costs per bus or per kilometre?	**Maintenance Manager**	**April 2000-2010**

When the project is completed, the performance measures would be used to judge the efficiency and effectiveness of the project itself.

Figure 11.14 is an example of how the performance aspects of the Maintenance Management project might be tabulated to form an overall performance score that would be reported to senior management.

FIGURE 11.14 Example Scoring System

Secure a vendor and a consultant to design, install and test the "**SAVI 9300 Computerized Maintenance Management System**"		**SCORES**				
		5	**4**	**3**	**2**	**1**
Speed	Was the project completed on time?	Yes	1 week late	2 weeks late	1 month late	>1 month late
Accuracy	Does the design meet user needs and are the test results good?	Yes	10% errors	20% errors	40% errors	>40% errors
Volume	Will the system have the capacity to deal with the entire fleet?	Yes	90% of the fleet	70% of the fleet	50% of the fleet	<50% of the fleet
Investment	Were the design and installation costs on or below budget?	Yes	+10%	+25%	+50%	>+50%

The scoring system is a measurement template that puts numerical values on the four dimensions of the project as it goes through the implementation and development phases, as well as the operational phase.

The project will be judged by taking each SAVI dimension and determining where the project performance was on the scale.

For example, assume the project was two weeks late in introduction. We would score 3 on the speed dimension. As to accuracy, we score 5 because the project functions very well. In terms of volume, we found that the system can only accommodate 90% of the fleet, so we score 4, and finally, the project was more than 50% over budget, so we score 1 on investment.

On Figure 11.15, the performance results are placed on a graph, and a mathematical average of all of the scores is calculated. Our project achieved a score of 3.25 as an average of all of the dimensions being measured.

This scoring system can be used to set goals: "New project must score 4 or better in all dimensions combined." And it can be used to evaluate specific projects: "The installation was two weeks late, we got an excellent product that meets 90% of our needs, but it turned out to be very expensive!"

This particular project was fairly simple. In more complex projects, where each dimension has multiple measures, the mathematics become more complex, but the basic model remains the same.

FIGURE 11.15 Example Scoring System

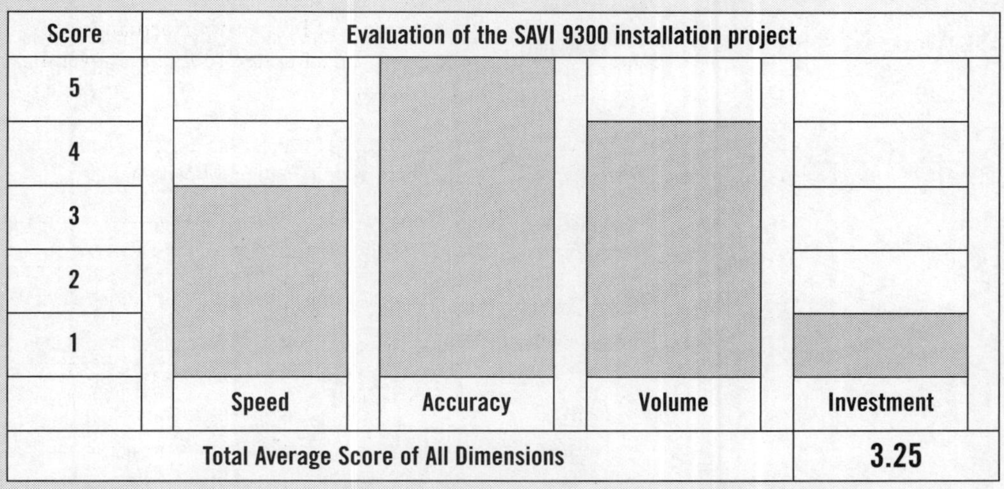

CHAPTER SUMMARY

The science of measurement is not complex. Following the steps in the procedure will enable accurate measures of performance to be developed.

Making the measures **effective** is a complex task. The complexity consists in finding the right mix of operational measures and organizational cultural elements to make measurement useful.

The purpose of the performance measurement model, specifically the six systematic steps in the development of a measurement system, is to ensure that the analysis and development of measures is sufficiently broad so that true, controllable and active performance is being measured.

CLOSING REMARKS

In the beginning of this chapter, you were challenged to find measures and see the resulting behaviour. How about the 30-minute pizza delivery guarantee? That encourages speeding, and if a delivery person has an order at 28 minutes and another at 10, which does he deliver first? And what happens if pizza delivery people are offered a cash bonus for every delivery made within 30 minutes? What does this do to pizza quality?

People are curious beings. We bring our own personal values to the job, we react differently to control systems, we are motivated by different things. A performance measurement system is a uniform set of measures that is trying to motivate a most un-uniform set of people.

The people in your organization are the performers who will make positive things happen. Therefore, making the measurement of positive results a positive experience will improve the likelihood that performance gains will happen. Chapter 12 will deal with how we need to manage people as part of the performance improvement process.

TERMS INTRODUCED IN THE CHAPTER

6 steps to performance management A systematic approach to the design of a performance management system that includes performance measurement and implementation issues.

Culture The attitude of people who are being measured as to how they will use the measurement system to improve performance.

Data collection Routinely collecting and reporting relevant performance data and feeding to those who control the process.

Data relevance Information about performance that is relevant, timely and accurate.

Input dimensions The resources used by a process including operating dollars, capital dollars and other organizational resources.

KPI Key Performance Indicator: A single measure or statistic about performance that prompts management to take the correct action.

KRA Key Result Area: any portion of an organization for which the measurement of performance would be beneficial.

Output dimensions The results of a process which can usually be categorized as financial returns, customer satisfaction and social impact.

Performance measurement check list A tool to determine the validity of a performance measure that ensures that a variety of dimensions are present in the measure.

Project performance measurement Using the performance measurement system to capture the two dimensions of a change management project, the performance during the construction of the project and the performance of the project when it is operational.

Recognition system A means of providing constructive feedback and reward to those who control a process.

Scoring system An agreed upon and systematic means of collecting quantitative date about qualitative issues.

QUESTIONS FOR CLASS DISCUSSION

1. For a small retail shoe store, identify at least three "key result areas" where performance should be measured.
2. For the same shoe store, develop at least two key performance indicators for each of the key result areas.
3. For one of the world's largest diamond mines, Identify at least three "key result areas" where performance should be measured
4. For the same diamond mine, develop at least two key performance indicators for each of the key result areas.
5. Use the four dimensions of measurement, Speed, Accuracy, Volume and Investment to design a set of performance measures for a National Hockey Team that measure performance from the customers' view.
6. Using the same model, develop a set of measures for the hockey team from an owner's view.
7. For questions 5 and 6, do any measures conflict? (Do any of the things customers want conflict with things that owners want, from a performance point of view?)
8. Identify and explain the three categories of output measures.
9. Identify and explain the three categories of input measures.
10. Explain the role that organizational culture plays in the performance management process.

A CASE FOR STRATEGIC PLANNING: MALCOLM AND RUBY'S NEXT STEP

Congratulations! Your firm, Performance Management Specialists, has been awarded the contract to develop the measurement system for Ruby and Malcolm that was discussed at the end of Chapter 10.

During the process of preparing for the presentation (end of Chapter 10) you came to a realization about your own company. Your name was "Performance Measurement Services," but in researching Ruby and Malcolm's issues, you discovered that measurement was only one dimension you could offer. Focusing on measurement was too limiting. Focusing on "Performance Management" enables you to offer the client more than just measures. You can also offer advice on how to achieve lasting performance gains.

REQUIRED:

The first step in your contract is to show Malcolm and Ruby what the finished product will look like in all aspects of the business. For each of the categories of output, (financial, customer and social), and input, (operating, capital and other), develop one measure for each category including the use of the checklists presented in the chapter. This will enable you to show Malcolm and Ruby what the system will look like.

Your second task is to make a presentation to Malcolm and Ruby that addresses the issues involved in making the measurement system become part of "performance management."

CHAPTER ENDING CASE: A CASE ABOUT PERFORMANCE MEASUREMENT/MANAGEMENT

Larry spent part of one term attending some of his business classes. He quickly realized that he knew far more than a business school could offer so he quit, sold his books and calculator and opened an automotive shop that specialized in brakes and mufflers.

He didn't do well, and couldn't understand it since he knew so much about business. He began to think about what to do, and then recalled one of the classes he had attended. To his surprise, he realized it might be useful. The class was about performance measurement and he remembered that it was a way to get employees to work harder. Larry was very excited about using this tool, so he started to measure things.

Larry measured:

1. Average time it took to do a brake job
2. Number of customers in a month
3. Number of repeat customers
4. Number of comebacks for faulty work
5. Average cost per brake and muffler job
6. Number of billed hours per mechanic

Larry couldn't think of another thing to measure, so he assumed the list was complete. He then decided to pick one measure to be the focus for his mechanics. He chose number 6.

He gathered his mechanics together and said, "Let's make this simple. You are going to be paid on the basis of the hours you bill to customers. If they go up, you get a bonus."

Three months later, Larry phones you. He says his business is bankrupt. Customers don't come back, and if they do, it is to have faulty work repaired. Costs are completely out of control, his prices are now 25% higher than industry averages and his mechanics are threatening to quit.

Larry phones you because he has heard that you went to the business classes. "Please help me," says Larry, "What have I done wrong?"

REQUIRED:

Make a presentation to Larry about how to redesign his measurement system.

CHAPTER 12

MOTIVATING PEOPLE

Companies are judged by the people they keep.

LEARNING OBJECTIVES

After reading this chapter, engaging in class discussion and doing the exercises at the end of the chapter, you will be able to:

1. Understand the importance of motivating people to do what needs to be done.
2. Understand why people either choose to support a performance improvement idea or fight the idea every step of the way.

YOUR RESPONSIBILITY

To get the most from Chapter 12, you need to refresh your memories of Chapters 1 to 11.

This chapter is about making a business work by motivating people. The truth is that none of the preceding 11 chapters will do anything for you until you understand that creating a nurturing, positive and safe environment for change is an absolutely critical element of a successful strategic plan.

INTRODUCTION TO CHAPTER 12

It is appropriate that this book ends with a study of people and how they react to performance measurement/management systems. Even the best systems will fail without people's commitment. Getting people onside with performance measurement/management is worthwhile because successful systems have a range of positive impacts on an organization. Most efforts to date have focused on processes, not people, but lasting value comes from managing people.

This chapter expands on steps 5 and 6 of the six steps to performance management, (step 5: Consider the impact on people; step 6: Build the culture)

Before we begin our study of people, let's understand why performance measurement/ management is a worthwhile investment.

THE BENEFITS AND PITFALLS OF PERFORMANCE MEASUREMENT/MANAGEMENT

At the outset, we need to recognize the benefits of designing an effective performance measurement/management system, and we need to be aware of some of the pitfalls that might limit the effectiveness of the performance measurement/management system.

There are many misconceptions about performance measurement/management — that it is dangerous, frightening and ineffective — that have formed a culture in some organizations.These misconceptions have been caused by a lack of communication about the intent and advantages of measurement, and by the design of systems that did not work the way they had been planned.

It is useful to bring these issues into our study so we know what we are dealing with.

An effective system maximizes the benefits and minimizes the pitfalls. The benefits and pitfalls of performance management can be summarized as follows:

Benefits of Performance Measurement/Management

1. **PERFORMANCE PLANNING**

   - Managers are expected to think about measurement issues in the context of the organization's strategic planning process. Integrating performance measurement/management into the realization of corporate goals is likely to make performance improvement more successful.

2. **ROUTINE PERFORMANCE MEASUREMENT/MANAGEMENT INCREASES EFFECTIVENESS OF SUPERVISION**

   - If performance expectations have been properly defined, the measurement system should largely replace the need for supervision of the business process. A supervisor's role should be to motivate and encourage!

3. **OPENS COMMUNICATION CHANNELS**

   - Horizontal thinking in business processes requires negotiating performance expectations across organizational boundaries, which enhances the manager's understanding of how component parts interact. Customers don't view the organization as a bunch of independent departments. Management should view the organization as the customer does.

4. **ENHANCES EMPOWERMENT**

   - Managers who have the authority, responsibility and control to manage performance improvement will have a tool that enables performance gains to be tracked. That puts measurement in the right hands, i.e. those most able to act.

5. **ENHANCED LEARNING FROM RECENT SUCCESS OR FAILURE**

   - Setting benchmarks for improvement in bite-sized chunks lets the user experience small successes and failures in the long-range plan. This makes it possible to correct things that are going wrong, and to celebrate things that are going right.

6. **BENCHMARKING PLOTS A PATH TO SUCCESS**

   - Managers will clearly see the relationship between achieving short-term results and long-term results.

7. **MAXIMIZE STRENGTHS AND DEAL WITH WEAKNESSES**

   - Measurement allows us to constantly examine and assess our own strengths and weaknesses. Corrective action can be taken on an ongoing basis while we compare results to expectations.

8. **GOOD FOR EMPLOYEE MORALE**

   - The measurement process will have a positive effect on morale if the system is well developed and employed equitably.

9. **IMPROVED PERFORMANCE**

   - The most important benefit of a system is the realization of change. A good system will cause the desired improvement in targeted performance areas.

Pitfalls of Performance Measurement/Management

While the benefits clearly outweigh the pitfalls of performance measurement/management, it is important to recognize the challenges to be faced. Some of the potential pitfalls and problem areas follow:

1. **ATTITUDES TO MEASUREMENT**

There are some obstacles to effective performance measurement/management. These obstacles come from management thinking that:

- some jobs can't be measured,
- measurement is too difficult to work with,
- there isn't time to measure,
- measurement is a prompt or cue for punishment.

It is important to recognize these obstacles before we begin performance measurement/management **because we need to manage perceptions before we can manage performance.**

2. **COSTS OUTWEIGH BENEFITS**

   - From a purely financial point of view, we would not want to spend more dollars administering a system of performance measurement/management than the dollars in benefits we receive.
   - From a qualitative point of view, we will use systems when the cost of the system is less than the intrinsic value we acquire from having the system in place.

3. **MEASURE TOO MUCH**

   - Often we develop measures because:
     - the data are easy to acquire,

- we think we are defending ourselves by gathering lots of evidence,
- we think that a shotgun approach will hit the target,
- we think that we have gained control over a process because we examine it in detail.

- Unfortunately, the result of this kind of logic is that we measure too much irrelevant data, which actually slows down the process we are trying to measure.

4. MEASURE TOO LITTLE

- If we allow ourselves to collect information on a few targeted indicators developed to meet the minimum reporting requirements for senior management, we run the risk of focusing effort on the indicator rather than on performance.
- An example of this syndrome might be the measurement of fuel consumed by the chairlift at a ski area. If the focus is fuel volume, the manager might never open the lifts. If the focus is efficiency of consumption, he might tune up the engine and leave it running constantly to maximize the efficiency of use. If the target is to use the budgeted amount, he might leave it running until the budget is spent, then shut it down. Someone should check to see if he had the lifts running efficiently on the days there was snow on the ground!

5. MEASURE THE WRONG THINGS

- We may be measuring the wrong data, i.e. people are targeting the measurement system rather than optimal performance. Following from the ski area manager example, though fuel consumption may be one of the indicators of efficiency, the purpose of running the lift is to maximize customer satisfaction, which in turn maximizes revenues. Fuel consumption is just an activity to achieve an end result.
- Setting indicators that are not linked to relevant key strategic goals may direct effort to processes that do not contribute to the well-being of the organization.

The bottom line is that you need two things: a working model and the willingness to make it work. The working model has been presented in the first 11 chapters. Now we can focus on creating a willingness to make it work.

ON THIS TOPIC

A Real-World Example

Let's revisit Chevron Canada and the "freedom to fail" initiative created by the new CEO, Jerry Franciscovitch (first introduced in Chapter 1). Chevron Canada had a working model for management but there was great unwillingness to use it because of a fear of failure.

Mr. Franciscovitch removed the fear of failure by making it safe to try something new.

www.chevron.ca

WHERE ARE WE AND HOW DID WE GET HERE?

Most people don't like to be measured. Those who do are already winners who use measurement to reinforce what they have accomplished and to communicate to others the success they have had.

Those who don't like to be measured have had some bad experiences with measurement in the past. They feel that the measurement doesn't truly reflect their value to the organization, that the wrong things are being measured, that the measure is punitive rather than motivating, or maybe they are jealous of the accolades given to winners.

My experience has been that there are many more bad measurement systems than good ones. Even in cases where management has tried its hardest to create a positive and motivating system, in most cases the system has failed.

ON THIS TOPIC

A Real-World Example

Employee of the Month

I went to a restaurant and over the bar was a picture of a person holding a nice plaque that said "Employee of the Month." I called the manager over and asked if this person was on duty today. The manager said no. I said I would have to come to his restaurant another day because I didn't want to be served by losers. By picking a winner, we label everyone else losers. The manager said, "All of my staff are winners." I said, "Not so. The sign says that's the only one."

A month later, I went to the same restaurant and over the bar was a picture labeled, "Employees of the Month." The manager had lined them all up, taken their picture and put it over the bar. I asked the manager why he had done that. He said, "I assumed my employees wanted the recognition of being employee of the month, so I sat them down and asked how they felt about the recognition. They said they felt foolish being recognized in that way, and in fact, they intentionally didn't do what I was looking for so that they could avoid the recognition!"

At the heart of this is the assumption that everyone wants to be a winner, i.e. if we judge and reward winners, those who are not winners (i.e. losers) will want to become winners. We assume that finding and rewarding a winner means that others will follow. Not true. If the reward for winning is not something losers want, they won't strive for the reward. But even more important is the assumption about what a winner is. The top goal scorer in a game is obviously a winner, as is the top salesperson in a real estate agency, but how about the most effective teacher, the best councillor, the most effective politician, the most visionary chief executive officer etc.?

We must be very careful to define what characteristics we are looking for and then actively promote those characteristics in all performers. If we can make all performers winners, then we will be much better off.

The essence of this anecdote is that we need to find out what our performers find positive and we need to expand the size of the winners' circle. To motivate people to want to perform better, we need a measurement and reinforcement system that is viewed by the performer as fair and motivating.

Notice that we are talking about a **measurement system** and a **reinforcement system**, two different, but highly related things. Measuring performance, then not using the measures to reinforce what you want would be a waste of resources. Similarly, trying to reinforce what you want without measures in place would be almost impossible.

What we do now to deliver reinforcement is also flawed. Sometimes we deliver reinforcement too late to be effective, deliver reinforcement to the wrong people or can't think of a way to be positive in our reinforcement, so we choose to do nothing, which, in fact, is doing something very damaging.

Finally, sometimes we attempt to get improved performance by using the "louder, longer, meaner" tactic. When we discover bad performance, we try to make it go away by yelling, getting angry, blaming and finding fault in others, none of which will create lasting good performance.

WHERE DO WE WANT TO BE, AND HOW DO WE GET THERE?

The most effective performance management system will measure specific dimensions that contribute to good performance. Those measures will be taken by motivated, enthusiastic and committed people who will use the measures to track their progress towards achieving performance excellence.

An **absolutely perfect** performance management system would have the performer collecting the measures and the motivation to improve coming from within the performer. No organizational investment to cause performance to improve would be made. Consider the speed skater training for the Olympics. Hours of lonely training with a stop watch. Only one person is responsible for performance improvement: the skater.

Wouldn't it be fantastic to have a group of salespeople as motivated and as independent as Olympic athletes? Organizations, in most cases, need to make some investment to provide the measures that will feed the system, and provide the leadership that will create the motivation to use the measures. In most organizations, a continuous investment would be made to ensure that the system of performance management remains active.

MAKING PERFORMANCE MANAGEMENT "ACTIVE"

The best performance management systems use measurement and performance reporting in a positive context. If measures are used to capture bad performers and punish them, people will be motivated to avoid punishment by doing just enough to get by. This will ensure that the minimum is done, but will not nurture and develop exceptional or even improved performance.

As a general rule, what gets measured gets done. If minimum performance is measured, minimum performance is done, but if excellent performance is measured, reported and reinforced, excellent performance will be done.

In most organizations, we can see the results of efforts from the past over and over again. A new employee joins the organization filled with enthusiasm, a willingness to take a risk, try new ideas and challenge the way things are done. Within a relatively short period of time, the enthusiasm is gone, blinders have been put in place and the new employee, like most others, is doing just enough to get by. There are some highly motivated people in the system, but in general, their motivation comes from within themselves, not from the organization. Organizations tend to make too little an investment in bringing out the best in people.

Traditionally, performance systems are designed to capture poor performance and offer incentives to people so they don't fall below the minimum. We also tend to report the negative when we want the positive to happen. We want people to come to work and be healthy, so we report sick time. We want people to be productive, so we measure the number of failures they have. We spend far too much time dealing with bad performers and not enough time dealing with the good ones. Most managers polled admit they spend 80% or more of their time trying to correct bad performance and virtually no time trying to nurture good performance.

The normal scenario for a performer is, in the early stage of employment, to voluntarily do more than is expected. Doing more than is expected is to perform above minimum expectations. After doing this, the performer waits for recognition. He or she doesn't get it because management is busy dealing with the poor performers. Now the performer has learned that there is no reward for doing more than is expected. In fact, when everyone is given a raise, the good performers learn that bad performers get the same reward they do!

This is great motivation to let performance fall until the best performers are doing just enough to get by. Similarly, if performance falls below the minimum required, the punishment is designed to bring performance back to the minimum required. It seems like we are constantly driving our organizations to mediocre performance.

Figure 12.1 indicates how people react to reinforcement over time.

FIGURE 12.1 The Evolution of Reinforcement

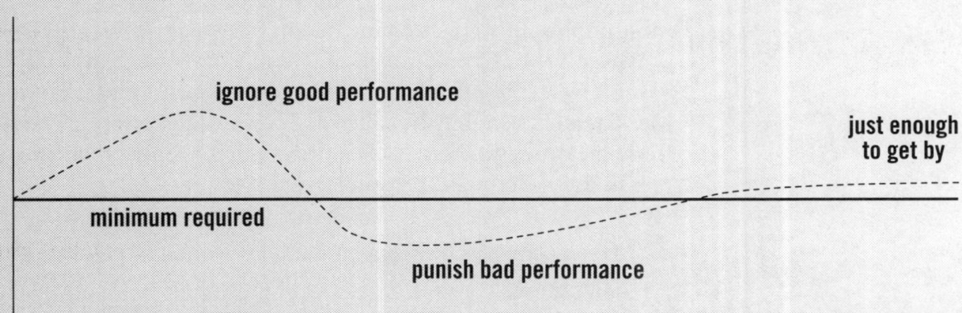

Again, the horizontal line is "minimum required." You join the company, work enthusiastically and achieve good performance, which is ignored because the system doesn't know how to be positive. You get frustrated, performance falls and the system notices when you are performing poorly, so you are punished. You quickly learn about "just enough to get by."

Ask someone how work is going. Sometimes the person says, "Staying out of trouble." That comment is so telling. That person is saying he or she found the lowest limit, and stays just above that.

If this is true, then why do we still have good performers? Why do some people play football on weekends for no pay at all, yet face the same consequence of injury as a multi-million dollar athlete? Why do some people work quietly in the wings, never asking for recognition and doing excellent work? Why do those same people stop being excellent when recognition is given?

It is because some good performers get their reinforcement from within themselves, not from the organizational system. Unfortunately, not everyone who has the potential to be a good performer knows how to get reinforcement from within, so those people wait for the system to provide reinforcement.

If, instead of ignoring good performance, we had a way of reinforcing it, we could create a culture where discretionary effort, i.e. doing more than is expected, becomes the norm. This can be accomplished by replacing "Ignoring Good Performance" with some positive reinforcement.

Figure 12.2 illustrates how "more than is expected" can be achieved by introducing positive reinforcement when people do more than the minimum.

FIGURE 12.2 The Opportunities of Positive Reinforcement

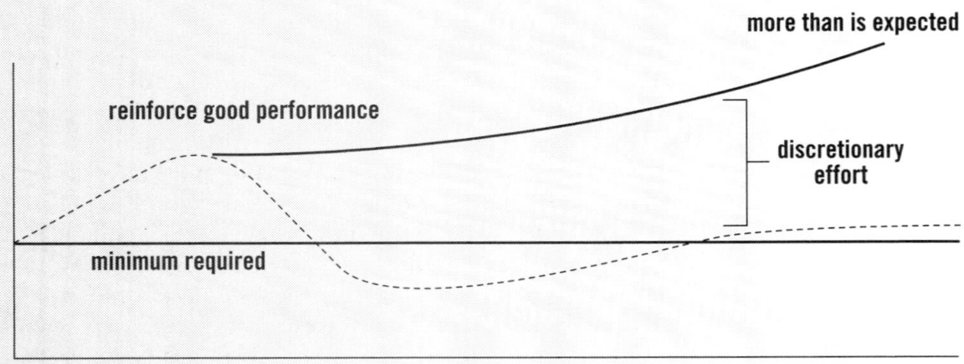

Discretionary effort, which is the effort people volunteer that is above minimum requirements, is what will make your organization excellent. There are a multitude of excellent performers who are simply **waiting for the system** to offer the reinforcement they need because they cannot find a way to get the positive reinforcement from within.

Making performance measurement/management "active" means that it becomes part of everyday life. It is referred to and reinforced constantly, it is accepted by the performers and, most importantly, it has an impact on the system.

This must be clear. Measuring and reporting frequently can be done easily by simply programming a computer to measure and report, but that is not making measurement active. Measurement can only be called active when a process for reinforcement and reward using those measures has been established, so that people become part of the process. Some principles to follow to make measurement active are:

1. Make positive reinforcement happen as often as possible, at least daily!

   Don't save up reinforcement until the annual company party. Too much time has gone by to reinforce something that happened six months ago.

2. The reward must have value to the performer.

   Be sure to know whether the trophies you give are of value to the performers involved. Unfortunately, most organizations say that the reward for good work is more work!

3. The reward should be earned.

   Don't reward people for things that happen naturally. A meaningful reward should reflect meaningful work.

4. There should be a celebration.

   A celebration is not always a huge office party or a meeting of employees. Sometimes it is simply a small gathering of team members at the end of a day or the end of a project. It is important to identify the celebration as such so that people become used to the process that is used to reinforce.

WHAT IS POSITIVE REINFORCEMENT?

Designing and administering an effective recognition system is a complex and often dangerous task. Sometimes we think we are being positive and motivating when the performer doesn't regard the reinforcement as positive. Sometimes we do more harm than good by trying to build effective reinforcement systems, then failing to recognize that the performers in the system are human.

Here is the general rule: "Positive" reinforcement can only be defined by the performer. There are many examples of situations in which supervisors took it upon themselves to decide what should be regarded as positive reinforcement by their staff, then went ahead and delivered it, with disastrous results.

Here are some brief examples:

- A manager who was an avid golfer, wanting to reward a team for being "on the ball," gave each member a sleeve of golf balls and a pass for the local golf course at the Christmas office party. One of the team members was blind. The rest of the team returned their "prize" and commented on how insensitive the manager was.
- The top salesperson at a real estate office reached a new sales record that netted the firm in excess of $750,000 in commission. The reward, given at the company gathering, was a $10 scarf. Word spread quickly that the reward for excellence was not worth the effort.
- A manager, wanting to offer some positive reinforcement to a team that had done an excellent job, went out to the office area, found a member of the team and said, "Excellent work. I am very impressed. You have brought this company to new heights. Tell that to the others, would you?" Not only was he wrong to ask one member to tell the others… he had just congratulated the worst member of the team, the one who did very little and was in a great deal of trouble with his team members.

In all of these cases, though intentions were good, the result was very negative.

A new concept, called "management by wandering around," evolved about 10 years ago. It was going to be a great idea. It involved getting management out of their offices and into the work area to wander around randomly, noticing good performance and making comments on their observations. Management was very happy with their new role and felt good when they finished their daily wandering tour. I overheard one manager say, "I can always tell when the boss is wandering around being positive. He leaves a trail of burning fires. He doesn't know how the good results were achieved, so he reinforces the wrong people, reinforces the wrong things and generally messes up my system."

It would be better if they used "management by wondering around." In this scenario, the boss would go an a wondering tour, asking how things happened, allowing performers to explain their successes, letting their reinforcement celebration happen on their own terms, making sure the boss doesn't mess up the reinforcement system that is already in place.

The distinction between legitimate positive reinforcement and reinforcement that might backfire is very subtle. That distinction is made clear if you follow a very simple rule to define what positive reinforcement is. The rule is to listen to and watch your performers. They will show you what they regard as positive and thoughtful if you observe what they choose to do in their spare time.

Rewards don't have to be expensive, they need only be of trophy value to the performer. Someone who likes old cars would appreciate an old car magazine. Someone who likes quilting might enjoy a new pattern. Someone who golfs would really enjoy time off to golf when the course isn't crowded.

Incentives and rewards are an integral part of reinforcement and money is not always available. Sometimes we are restricted as to the financial value of rewards, but we are never restricted as to the trophy value that can be given because that trophy value is defined by the performer.

PEOPLE, OUR MOST VALUABLE ASSET, AND MOST THREATENING LIABILITY

I have been using the term "performer" extensively in this chapter. I like performer instead of "employee" or "subordinate" or "he/she." A performer is anyone, at any level of any organization. You and I perform every day. Sometimes others watch and there is applause (or thrown tomatoes). Feedback is instantaneous. Sometimes we are happy with our performance. Sometimes we see flaws in ourselves and use the feedback to improve the performance.

Sometimes we choose not to perform at all. Perhaps we don't feel ready for the performance, or perhaps we don't like the feedback we get.

The strategic planning, decision-making, goal-setting process assumes that people will choose to perform what needs to be performed so that the organization can move towards achieving corporate goals. Yet, choosing to perform is a very personal, individual and misunderstood thing.

Psychologists call these performances "behaviour." Analyzing the behaviour of people is an extensive science with thousands of volumes of research. I will attempt to boil it down into a few points that are relevant to organizational performance improvement.

Every moment we are awake, we choose to perform (i.e. behave). We choose to get out of bed, brush our teeth, eat, go to work, argue with our colleagues, be disrespectful of the boss, steal from the company, sabotage something at work that causes the company to lose money, come home, be with the family, talk about good values, call it a good day and sleep.

On the other hand, you might choose to cooperate with colleagues, boss included, protect the company from loss, treat customers well and then go home. Many of your behaviours are not relevant to the job and should be left as private matters. The performances that do matter are the ones related to your contribution to the success of the organization.

Everyone chooses to perform, i.e. voluntarily. Nobody can be forced to perform against his or her will. The choices that people make regarding when and where they will perform are completely sensible to them, though not necessarily to you!

Following are some examples of bad performances we get:

1. An employee who refuses to wear a hard hat in the shop because his or her hair gets messy,
2. A drug pusher who stands on a street corner defying the law,
3. An employee who steals from the company,
4. You deciding to drink beer rather than study performance management.

All these performances are negative, all are voluntary, and all make sense to the performers. If we want these performances to stop, we can make them stop by punishing these people. Fine the employee, put the drug pusher in jail, make an example of the employee, give the student a bad grade. The problem in all these cases is that if you punish someone and leave it at that, the person will replace that performance with a worse performance!

We need to use the "No–But" rule. When something needs to stop happening, we need to say "No" to the performer, but we also need to follow that with what we want to start happening, e.g., "No, you cannot do what you have chosen to do, but you can do this instead."

What do we want instead? We want performances that add value and make the realization of goals possible.

We want:

1. The employee to wear the hard hat so that safety is taken care of in the workplace,
2. Drug pushers to choose a socially acceptable way to support themselves,
3. Employees to use the assets of the company for the benefit of the company,
4. You to study and use performance management so you can get a job and afford good beer.

So, how do we get what we want?

We begin to manage getting what we want by studying why people choose to do what they do. If we can understand why people make choices to perform in a certain way, perhaps we can influence their choice so that the performance we want is the one they choose.

People choose to perform based on their analysis of the consequences of their choice.

1. *Employees don't wear hard hats because the consequence is messy hair.*
2. *Drug dealers defy the law because the consequence is they make lots of money.*
3. *An employee steals from the company because the consequence is he or she will have what he or she wants.*
4. *You drink beer because it's fun.*

People choose to do what makes sense to ***them.***

All these performing choices were based on the performers' perception that the consequence was positive to them. If we want these choices to change to choices that, by our definition, are positive, then we need to convince the performers to think differently about their choices.

We need to make the first employee understand that a consequence of not wearing a hard hat could be a head injury. We need to convince the drug pusher that a consequence could be that he will be caught and sent to jail. We need to convince the employee who steals that a consequence could be that he could get caught, or that the company could go out of business and he will lose his job. We need to convince the student that too much fun could impact the letter grade.

It is unlikely that any of these arguments will be successful in changing anyone's mind because the arguments are very weak. What makes the arguments weak is the word "could."

1. Nice hair is a positive consequence for the employee; avoiding a head injury is a positive consequence for the employee and the employer.
2. Getting cash is a positive consequence for the drug pusher; having him change his source of income to something acceptable is a positive consequence for society as a whole.
3. Stealing is a positive consequence for the employee; not stealing has a positive consequence for the organization.
4. Drinking beer has a positive consequence for you, but so does getting good grades.

In other words, wearing a hard hat, not selling drugs, not stealing, and not going to beer parties all have negative consequences for the performers.

People are attracted to positive consequences and they avoid negative consequences. We can easily understand positive and negative consequences in our minds and in the performer's mind. We can even understand why those consequences make sense to them. What we have difficulty understanding is why performers ignore what we believe are very important, very negative consequences that they should be avoiding.

The answer is found in looking at two more dimensions of consequences relating to the word "could."

1. Having neat hair because of not wearing a hard hat occurs with certainty and right away. Suffering a head injury is a consequence that is in the future, and it is not certain it will happen.
2. Getting cash happens immediately, and with certainty. Getting caught is in the future and it is not certain to happen.
3. Stealing from the company gets you the things you want right away. Driving the company out of business probably won't happen. Anyway, it's too far in the future to worry about.
4. Parties are happening right now and grades are in the future. Besides, you aren't really sure that you won't get good grades anyway!

CONSEQUENCES: WHAT DO THEY LOOK LIKE?

Aubrey Daniels, an author of several books on performance measurement (**www.aubreydaniels.com**), uses a model called ABC, which refers to Antecedent, Behaviour, Consequences. His book, *Bringing out the Best in People* is a must read for anyone wanting to improve performance by using positive reinforcement.

In the ABC model, consequences have three dimensions, as illustrated in Figure 12.3.

FIGURE 12.3 The Dimensions of Consequences

The Performer's View of Consequences	Positive	Negative
	I get something I want.	I get something I don't want.
	Immediate	**Future**
	What I get happens immediately.	What I get happens in the future.
	Certain	**Uncertain**
	What I get happens every time I perform.	What I get may or may not happen.

The theory is that any consequence being considered before a performer makes a choice of what to do, can be classified by these dimensions.

Using the acronyms PIC and NIC and the four scenarios we have been using, we can see how consequences are perceived.

FIGURE 12.4 How Consequences are Perceived

	To the Performer	To the Organization
1. Putting on the hard hat	NIC *Hair gets messy.*	PFU *Injury could be avoided.*
2. Selling drugs	PIC *Cash in hand.*	NFU *Buyer lives could be ruined.*
3. Stealing	PIC *Goods in hand.*	NFU *Company might go bankrupt.*
4. Partying	PIC *Having fun with friends.*	NFU *Possible future career impact.*

WHICH CONSEQUENCES ARE MOST POWERFUL?

The most powerful consequences driving behaviour choices are Immediate and Certain. When something good or bad is going to happen right away, and there is no doubt about it, that consequence will have a large impact on which performance is chosen. When you depress the brake pedal on your car, the car stops, right away, every time, immediate and certain. When you see an obstacle on the road, you hit the brake as an automatic response because you believe the consequence to be true. Stopping in time to avoid an accident is a positive consequence. When you hit the brakes and nothing happens, you get immediate, certain feedback that your consequence is negative: you are going to have an accident. You now choose a new performance: you try the emergency brake, steer away, cover your eyes and scream.

If you are facing a situation where the consequence is immediate and certain and negative, you avoid a performance that triggers that consequence. You are speeding in your car and you come up behind a police car. You stop speeding because you can't afford the negative, immediate and certain speeding ticket.

The lesson learned here is that Positive, Immediate, Certain (PIC) consequences are very powerful in terms of having people choose to do something and Positive, Future, Uncertain (PFU) consequences are very weak.

Similarly, NIC consequences are very powerful in getting someone to stop doing something while NFU consequences are weak.

WHY DO WE NEED TO MANAGE PEOPLE'S PERCEPTIONS OF THEIR CONSEQUENCES?

Most of what we want in a strategic plan is change that will occur in the future, and there is some uncertainty that it will actually occur. Long-term vision and mission statements are not powerful drivers that cause people to choose their performances to meet the plan.

While long-term visionary leaders are plotting the future of an organization, performers are analyzing short-term PIC and NIC consequences and using them to make their choices of what they will actually do.

Figure 12.5 shows what we are up against:

FIGURE 12.5 Conflicting Perceptions of Consequences

Organization		Performer	
Have the largest market share within five years.	PFU	Earn a commission today by selling whatever to whomever.	PIC
Focus on customer satisfaction.	PFU		
Reduce greenhouse gas emissions to avoid ozone depletion.	NFU	Avoid paying the fine for polluting.	NIC
Focus on product quality to enhance long-term market stability.	PFU	Sacrifice quality to reduce unit manufacturing costs.	PIC

When earning a personal income, avoiding immediate cash costs or improving the short-term bottom line are up against future, uncertain strategic gains, performers will most frequently choose the short-term consequences, thus damaging the long-term consequences.

To effectively motivate people to make the right long-term choices, we need to find a way to make the consequences immediate and certain.

ON THIS TOPIC

A Real-World Example

The RCMP introduced photo radar to my city about five years ago. (The program has recently been abandoned by the new government, but that's another story.) The program was introduced because speed kills. Well-marked police cars at the roadside deter speeding, but only because people see the police car. The RCMP needed a way to make people think they were being watched all the time, so they announced their "secret" photo radar vans.

It took the community about a week to figure out that the photo radar van was a Chevrolet minivan. The secret was out. But the RCMP choice of the Chevrolet minivan was a stroke of genius.

As we drove around our city, we assumed that every Chevrolet minivan parked at the roadside was a photo radar van. We found ourselves looking under the van for the little tripod legs. There are thousands of Chevrolet minivans, all of which had been deputized by the police as speed traps because they had managed our perception of the consequence of speeding past a Chevy minivan.

The Chevrolet van is a signal. The ABC model calls it an "antecedent" signal because it is a signal that triggers the system of making a choice about behaviours. A stop sign is a signal, a poster on the shop wall that says, "Wear your hard hat" is a signal and the course outline that tells you the date of the final exam is a signal. Most important, the entire strategic plan is a signal that tells performers to begin performing because this is where the organization wants to go.

When these signals are perceived by performers to deliver PIC or NIC consequences, the performers will act on the basis of those perceptions. When they are perceived to be Future and Uncertain, they will likely choose not to perform.

When consequences are managed, performance measurement/management becomes active. When the system becomes active, performance improves, measurement shows progress, celebrations occur and the performers understand more clearly the path to excellence.

PERFORMANCE MEASUREMENT/MANAGEMENT: THE ROLE OF LEADERS

Leaders manage the framework that enables performers to excel. No significant performance improvement will take place if leaders simply tell performers to start performing. Lasting performance improvement will only come from performers voluntarily choosing to do more than just enough to get by. Given that most performers don't get their reinforcement from within and that they are waiting for the system to provide that reinforcement for them, it is now the responsibility of the leader to create and sustain an environment that is conducive to change and progress.

Senior management must pay more than lip service to performance management. They must be willing to let it succeed, fail and correct itself until the systems have been developed by the performers. This is a key point. The leaders' job is to create the framework and establish the boundaries, and then let the performers design the detailed system. Ownership of the system and commitment to the system will improve if the performers have a hand in designing it.

Leaders have four specific jobs to do. Each job is done with the full consultation of performers:

1. Define the results.

   Using the strategic plan as the reference guide, leaders define the performances they are looking for and the ones they are looking to avoid. This involves pinpointing the activities that contribute to strategic gains and pinpointing those that negatively affect progress.

2. Put boundaries on the rewards that can be used.

   Using company policy and available resources, leaders define the range of allowable rewards to use in the reinforcement system. Is money available? Can time off be used? Are there limitations to promotions? Are there appropriate or inappropriate trophies? What kinds of celebrations are allowed?

3. Monitor the scope of the distribution of rewards.

   The intent is to have a non-competitive system that expands the size of the winners' circle. Careful monitoring of rewards must take place so that the desired motivational result occurs for those who are chosen to win awards, and for those not chosen. Those not chosen must see that receiving the award is possible on a personal level.

4. Monitor the effectiveness of the performance measurement/management system.

   Ultimately, the leaders are responsible for improved performance. At the end of the day, they should be able to see evidence that the system is providing the performance gains and results that the strategic plan is calling for.

At the same time, leaders have three jobs they should not do:

1. Don't offer reinforcement that is not recognized by the system.

   "I feel a need to help this along, so I am going to wander around being positive." You will likely make some mistakes, reinforcing the wrong people or reinforcing the wrong things. Trust your system and let it function by itself.

2. Don't participate in celebrations unless you are asked.

   Celebrations are designed and managed by performers. They define what will be done and by whom. As leader, don't be offended if you are not asked to participate, and don't assume you are helping by designing and running the celebration. Celebrations are personal and they are most effective if they reflect the needs of the performers.

3. Don't abandon the system if there are glitches in the short run.

   Performance measurement/management is not easy. The system will evolve over time and in the short run there will be failures. Your job is to react to the effectiveness of the system, reinforcing its success and using its failures to correct its functioning.

CHAPTER SUMMARY

Good systems need good people. There is no sense examining a process unless at the same time you examine the people who govern the process. Improvement does not take place on paper. Improvement happens when people use enthusiasm, dedication, commitment, leadership and morale in their daily routine. A good system on paper is a healthy beginning but if you want results, you need to follow up a paper system with a people system. A good people system involves developing a culture that makes change safe and rewarding.

To build the culture, the organization must be willing to make a significant investment in changing the perceptions and attitudes of the people involved in performance. This investment usually involves two levels of training and development: technical training on the function of the model and cultural training on the use of the model.

The technical training improves the use of the model by ensuring that the measures are carefully developed to meet all the characteristics of good performance measures. The cultural training deals with removing the fears of performance measurement/management and teaching people to regard measurement as a constructive and positive management tool.

CLOSING REMARKS

Please remember three things from this book:

1. Plan for what you want.
2. Act on the plan.
3. Measure your results.

If you can and will do those three things, this text has been a success.

TERMS INTRODUCED IN THE CHAPTER

"Active" performance system	Making performance measurement part of everyday life and ensuring that measure are used constructively.
Celebration	An event that is recognized by performers as the time to celebrate success.
Consequences	Something that happens to a performer or the organization after the performance is initiated.
Discretionary effort	A voluntary choice by a performer to do more than the minimum required.
Management system	Using measurement statistics to help motivate people to achieve performance gains.
Measurement system	A systematic scientific process of collecting statistics about performance.
Performer	Any individual who is expected to do something towards achieving organizational goals.
Positive/negative Immediate/future Certain/uncertain	Characteristics that define consequences as perceived by performers.
Positive reinforcement	Delivering a consequence to a performer that will make him or her start or continue doing what you want done.
Punishment	Delivering a consequence to a performer that will make him or her stop doing what he or she is doing.
Rewards	Tangible or intangible things given to performers that provide value to them as recognition of good performance.

QUESTIONS FOR CLASS DISCUSSION

1. Distinguish between performance measurement and performance management.
2. Why is it necessary to consider the impact of a performance measurement system on people?
3. Identify the potential benefits of having an effective performance measurement/management system.
4. Identify the potential pitfalls to consider when designing an effective performance measurement/management system.
5. When people choose to do something, they tend to analyze the consequences of their choice. Offer an example from your personal life where you have chosen to do something and identify the consequence that guided your choice.
6. From question 5, identify the characteristics of your consequence using P/N, I/F and C/U.

7. Why is it necessary to understand the power of consequences when people make choices?
8. What is meant by the term "just enough to get by"?
9. What is meant by the term "discretionary effort"?
10. From your personal experience, identify a "celebration" you have had regarding something you have done that was a success.
11. What is meant by the term "trophy value" in the context of rewards?

A CASE FOR STRATEGIC PLANNING: MALCOLM AND RUBY'S NEXT STEP

As a follow-up to your contract, awarded at the end of Chapter 11, Malcolm and Ruby have asked for some specific advice.

They want you to start building a performance measurement/management system for what they see is the most critical element of their business in the short run.

Malcolm and Ruby are vitally concerned about production. They see that the sales function is moving along nicely, but they have serious problems in production. In fact, when they examined speed, accuracy, volume and investment from the last quarter, they had major shortfalls in all areas.

They think the problem lies with the production manager. Though he is a skilled technician, his people skills are dismal. He shouts, he threatens, he fires people and he seldom rewards anyone with anything positive. Meanwhile, performance is still declining.

At a recent meeting, his shortfalls were raised as an issue and he said, "I know I have dismal people skills, but I am so committed to making this thing work. It just frustrates me to see them working so poorly. All I can think of to do is get angry. I am willing to try anything, I can change my ways. Just tell me what to do."

REQUIRED:

Tell the production manager what to do.

CHAPTER ENDING CASE: A CASE ABOUT PERFORMANCE MEASUREMENT

A national retailer of home electronics has a problem in its sales force.

There are 50 locations nationwide and each location has been responsible for designing its own pay packages for its sales force. Some have gone to straight salary, some to straight commission, some to a mix of salary and commission.

Management has analyzed each of the three approaches and was expecting to see that one approach worked better than the rest. They were alarmed to see that there didn't appear to be a relationship between the pay package and the success of the sales function in a store. There were an equal number of successes and failures in each of the three pay systems.

This prompted management to look further and they discovered that successful stores had a reward and recognition system that was broader than just a pay system. Some had incentives for salespeople involving time off, some offered price discounts on their merchandise on a sliding scale related to an individual's sales and some held parties and social functions.

Management also discovered that the approaches in each successful store were very different and that the levels of success were also different.

The conclusion reached by management was that its incentive system was random and out of control. It needs to develop a national policy for performance measurement/management of the sales function that will help it achieve its goal of 35% market share by 2010.

REQUIRED:

As the newly appointed manager of performance improvement, outline the steps you would go through to see that an effective system is designed.

SUMMARY OF PART 3

Chapters 10 to 12 of this book dealt with a performance measurement/management model that reflected the strategic plan by developing measurement of results by using the SAVI acronym:

Speed Accuracy Volume Investment

The model reflected two important dimensions. First, there must be a scientifically accurate measurement system that captures relevant information about performance. Second, there must be people who are willing to use measurement as a tool to help in performance improvement.

The importance of this part of the management process can't be overstated. Planning and decision-making must be supported by evidence so that performers can see their progress, celebrate their success and use failure as an opportunity to learn and correct.

Once the loop is finished from plan to action to measurement, organizations will become familiar with success, be able to create success and be enthusiastic about challenging what they do now to maximize their success.

Index